HOMER'S
SECRET
ODYSSEY

HOMER'S
SECRET
ODYSSEY

FLORENCE &
KENNETH WOOD

First published 2011

The History Press
The Mill, Brimscombe Port
Stroud, Gloucestershire, GL5 2QG
www.thehistorypress.co.uk

British Library Cataloguing in Publication Data.
A catalogue record for this book is available from the British Library.

ISBN 978 0 7524 6041 3

Typesetting and origination by The History Press
Printed in Great Britain
Manufacturing managed by Jellyfish Print Solutions Ltd

CONTENTS

AUTHOR'S NOTE

We are indebted to Penguin Books for permission to use quotations from *The Odyssey*, by E.V. Rieu (1967 reprint; revised by D.C.H. Rieu, 1991). Quotations by other translators are occasionally introduced to illustrate that while literary styles may differ there is a consensus on content.

ILLUSTRATIONS

Illustrations include a number by Gill Garfield-Ralph which give a modern interpretation of images created by the association of mythology with stars and constellations. The caption for each of these contains the attribution 'G. G-R'.

Illustrations by Robert Flaxman (1755–1826) are from *L'Odyssee d'Homere gravee par Reveil d'apres les compositions de John Flaxman* (Paris, 1835), posted on Wikimedia, to which a contribution has been made.

HOMER'S SECRET ILIAD

Homer's Secret Iliad (1999) examined the *Iliad* as a source of considerable astronomical knowledge, including a detailed chart of stars and constellations linked to the warriors and regiments that fought at Troy, movements of the planets, an ancient concept of an earth-centred universe and observations concerning the precession of the equinoxes.

It is a superb piece of detective work … the argument is arresting. Truth has its own kind of elegance and these … authors have stumbled upon a truth that is breathtaking.

The Scotsman

It will be difficult to look at the night sky, or Homer, in the same way again.

Financial Times

A new and remarkable reading that seems to throw the *Iliad* in a completely new light.

BBC World Service

In this vast celestial board game of a book, the Woods interpret Homer's blood-stained account of the Trojan war as one huge didactic mnemonic device that enabled his audience to fix the constellations precisely in their minds. As we read, our scepticism … is increasingly undermined by flashes of open-mindedness.

The Good Book Guide

… The Woods' reading of the [*Iliad*] is highly exciting.

The Times

The poet Alice Oswald chose *Homer's Secret Iliad* as one of her books of the year in *The Guardian*, 2003.

I

ANCIENT EPICS & LONG-LOST SECRETS

Dare-devil that you are, full of guile, unwearying in deceit, can you [Odysseus] not drop your tricks and your instinctive falsehood? (*Odyssey* 13.291)

Homer is renowned as the ancient world's most famous storyteller and the finest of all the bards who, for countless generations, passed down by word of mouth the myths and legends of ancient Greece. Yet, for more than 2000 years there has been a persistent but unresolved belief that encrypted in his two magnificent epics was a wealth of secret learning. Ground-breaking research now reveals that creating and preserving the cultural heritage of the Greeks of antiquity was only part of the achievement of Homer and the storytellers known as the poet-singers. They were also the guardians of wide-ranging astronomical knowledge about the sun, moon, planets, stars and calendar-making. This learning was embedded in the stories they recited during the many centuries the Greeks did not possess a written script. *Homer's Secret Odyssey* is the extraordinary account of how the breaking of ingenious codes solves one of history's most enduring mysteries and adds a sublime new dimension to the achievements of the ancient Greeks. Sound – even breathtaking – support for these views comes from a unique analysis of the extensive numerical data that Homer deliberately and carefully inserted into the epic. A case will also be outlined for the oldest learning concealed in the *Odyssey* to have originated as early as *c.*2300 BC, and from well beyond the boundaries of Greek-speaking peoples.

Homer (*c.*745–700 BC) is a towering figure in western culture and was amongst the last of the old tradition of oral poets. He is as much a man of mystery as all of the poets who went before him and little if anything is known about his life except that he wove elements of myth from much earlier times into his two masterpieces, the *Iliad* and the *Odyssey*. The *Iliad* is the story of the last few weeks of the siege of Troy during a brutal Bronze Age war between Greeks and Trojans. The *Odyssey* tells of the strange and perilous adventures of the warrior-king Odysseus after the Greeks used the legendary wooden horse to trick their way into the stronghold of Troy. With the city reduced to smouldering ruins,

Odysseus begins his long journey home during which he encounters monsters and witches, gods and ghosts, tempests and shipwreck, and it is with an investigation of his escapades that this challenging book is largely concerned.

Odysseus & the Moon

A major advance in readings of the *Odyssey* and the *Iliad*[1] as sources of astronomical and calendrical learning was the realisation that the battlefield violence, dramas and danger-filled adventures of Odysseus' adventures are played out not only on earth but also in parallel scenarios that conjure beautiful metaphorical images of stars, constellations and the Milky Way, set against the background of the wine-dark seas of the night skies. For instance, in *Homer's Secret Odyssey*, the lands and islands visited by Odysseus on his journey home from Troy can be found amidst the glories of the heavens. In this way, and unrecognised for two millennia or more, storytelling became the vehicle for the preservation of important knowledge in a pre-literate society. If only a few short extracts of narrative had been selected to support our view it might have been considered subjective and merely a matter of opinion. The volume and consistency of the re-discovered material, however, presents exciting new aspects of Homer's genius and rolls back the history of Greek astronomy by several centuries.

Odysseus, a battle-weary hero struggling to return home after a prolonged and bloody war, is the key figure for the preservation in story of this learning. To achieve his aims Homer created for Odysseus an alter ego as a personification of the moon. So closely is Odysseus' iconic role linked to the calendar that the tempo of his adventures is governed by the rhythm of the monthly lunar cycle, from one new crescent moon to the next. Such, too, are Homer's skills that singular events that have puzzled scholars can be recognised as important components in his calendar system. A range of literary devices are employed to conceal knowledge: Odysseus' adventures contain the main body of learning but prominent characters, such as his wife Penelope, son Telemachus, the beautiful Helen of Troy, the pig-keeper Eumaeus and even his faithful hound Argus, are linked to the calculation of time.

Outside the bounds of literature, Homer's principal focus in the *Odyssey* is the construction of a calendar system in which the days and months are reckoned by the moon and the passing of the years by the sun. The serious problem of reconciling the lunar year of 354 days with the solar year of 365 days was resolved to varying degrees of accuracy in other societies by the discovery of luni-solar cycles.[2] Homer was so familiar with such cycles that the *Iliad* and the *Odyssey* are connected by the continuing thread of a 19-year cycle of the sun and moon. He knew also, at least, of the four-year Olympiad and the eight-year (*octaëteris*) luni-solar cycles, as well as cycles of the planet Venus and the Saros cycle, which makes it possible to forecast eclipses of the sun and moon, a powerful social tool in times of widespread superstitions.

There was even more evidence of Homer's genius to come, for embedded in his 19-year cycle is a detailed annual calendar that plots the lunations and passage of the sun along the ecliptic during the course of a year. So detailed is his calendar in marking the equinoxes and solstices, adjusting the lunar year with the solar year, and tracing the path of the sun through the stars of the zodiac, that it could have been used as a template for generations of calendar makers.

Calendars are much concerned with counting and numbers, and surprisingly accurate support for our projected model of a Homeric calendar system was discovered by analysis of data embedded in narrative throughout the *Odyssey*.[3] Homer records such precise information about the lunar year, the solar year, luni-solar cycles and other calendrical matters that the astronomers of the eighth century BC have to be acknowledged as being far more advanced than has previously been recognised.

Away from the world of calendars, Homer provides data which in the story of one-eyed Polyphemus points towards an exploration of π, the ratio of the diameter of a circle to its circumference – a topic so ancient that its origins are not known. Navigation is also on Homer's agenda and in two striking cases he reveals how Odysseus and his fellow sea-going Greeks could easily find the north celestial pole for navigation at night.

Homer the Astronomer

In the centuries after his death, Homer was acclaimed by certain Greek sages as a man of science, an astronomer and 'the wisest of all Greeks'.[4] The *Odyssey* and the *Iliad* were also believed to be the source of allegories that expressed learning about the natural world in the form of poetry.[5] In this work, extended metaphor is recognised as a source of knowledge about astronomy and calendars concealed behind the literal meaning of the *Iliad* and the *Odyssey*. Almost all of the data in the epic has been linked to astronomy and a calendar system and there remain only a small number of tantalising items that have yet to reveal their secrets.

Homer's Secret Odyssey does not detract from the vast body of Homeric scholarship in other fields but restores a long-forgotten element to the intellectual achievements of the pre-literate Greeks. New vistas in the history of astronomy and calendars are revealed in Homer's encyclopaedic masterpiece, as well as the crucial role played by mythology and legend in the preservation of essential knowledge. The dedication and skills of generations of classical scholars and the commentaries and translations they have created has made it possible to project a model of his astronomical and calendrical intentions. This work is only the begin-

ning of an exciting exploration of Homeric epic, and an even wider view of the
fusion of literature and science is likely to emerge in the future. We expect that
some of our conclusions, particularly in areas which are still not too clear, will be
amended, extended or improved upon in the future. The storytellers known as
the poet-singers can now also be regarded as the poet-astronomers, with Homer,
finest of them all, being indeed a 'Master of Time'.

Edna Leigh

The inspiration and ideas developed in the following chapters arose from a
study by the late Edna Leigh MSc, who, like some scholars of old, believed
there was more to Homer's epics than storytelling alone. She wrote of the *Iliad*
and the *Odyssey*:

> I read these two books over and over again, again and again. Each time I found
> the same things: an excellent narrative, superbly told; well-drawn characters;
> the world's best plots; pathos, horror, excitement, calm, philosophy, history and
> so on. Yet each time I finished reading, my reaction was the same: I felt I had
> missed the point. I read mythology, I read volumes of ancient history, I went
> to Greece, I then read criticism and comment by the world's leading scholars
> in Homeric studies. I re-read the *Iliad* and *Odyssey* several more times, but the
> same old feeling remained, that I was missing the point. Homer, so it seemed to
> me, was saying something very clearly, yet something I did not grasp. Between
> his words and my understanding was a veil. Eventually, out of all this emerged
> a few ideas. Are both epics extended metaphor? Figurative language is a poetic
> device. To sustain a metaphor for the length of two books is long. Nevertheless,
> I put everything else aside to explore the possibility for by then I had begun to
> see what might possibly be the author's purpose. What did this ancient author
> think sufficiently worthwhile to put into a book-length poem, at a time when
> writing was either unknown or, if known, an expensive process? What was the
> incentive, good literature apart, for poets and scholars to memorise both books
> even after writing was known?[6]

Above all, Edna concluded that Homer was an eminently practical man who
preserved in epic the accumulated knowledge of astronomy and calendars known
to the Greeks of his time. Edna was born in 1916 and raised on a farm in Kansas
but she lived in England for more than 40 years. A gifted scholar and teacher, the
pursuit of these ideas consumed a large part of her life until ill health curtailed
her activities and prevented her from completing her study. On her death in 1991
she left her papers to her daughter, Florence Wood. Since then Edna's research
and principles of interpretation have been extended with material from our own

investigations into the *Iliad* and *Odyssey*. It is from Edna that we adopted the phrase 'extended metaphor' rather than 'allegory'. Since *Homer's Secret Iliad* was published in 1999, work has continued on *Homer's Secret Odyssey*.

Florence and Kenneth Wood
2011

Notes

1 See Wood, Florence & Kenneth, *Homer's Secret Iliad* (London: John Murray, 1999) for a reading of the *Iliad* as a source of astronomical learning that includes a chart of 45 constellations linked to Greek and Trojan regiments, a method of comparing the magnitude of stars, movements of the planets, ancient Greek ideas on the nature and origins of the universe, and observations on the precession of the equinoxes. To avoid confusion with Odysseus' astronomical role in the *Iliad*, Homer creates for him in the *Odyssey* a new persona.

2 Hannah, Robert, *Greek and Roman Calendars* (London: Duckworth, 2005), p. 55.

3 Florence Wood is a graduate in mathematics and the history of technology.

4 Heraclitus (*c.*540–*c.*480 BC).

5 Crates of Mallus supported this theory (second century BC).

6 More details of Edna Leigh's life and research can be found in *Homer's Secret Iliad* by Florence & Kenneth Wood (London: John Murray, 1999), pp. 1–12.

2

HOMER:
A MAN FOR ALL AGES

The *Iliad* and the *Odyssey* have a compelling beauty and Homer speaks openly of powerful emotions which are as familiar today as they were in his own times in the eighth century BC. Gods and men are influenced for better and worse by love and jealousy, anger and revenge, heroism and cowardice, and are captivated by the soothing pleasures of music and storytelling. Through the ages these Homeric themes have inspired countless writers, poets, philosophers, artists and scholars who have devoted their lives to the examination of his works. Homer has been a mentor to many for brave and noble deeds. Amongst the best known of these was Alexander the Great, conqueror of many lands in the fourth century BC, who took copies of the epics on his military campaigns. Homer not only influences the high-minded but from the earliest times his spellbinding stories have had immense popular appeal and in particular have given the Greeks a pride in their heritage which continues even today. The *Iliad* and the *Odyssey* are still widely read and echoes of their epic themes are found in films and television programmes watched by countless millions. Whether Homer wrote the epics or composed them in the ancient oral tradition is a much debated question with no definitive answer. The view taken for *Homer's Secret Odyssey* is that Homer composed his epics in the oral tradition.

With so much exposure over so many centuries it is all the more remarkable that almost nothing is known about Homer as a man or of when or where he lived. Study of the oldest Homeric texts have identified elements of Greek dialects which suggest he came from the west coast of modern Turkey and lived possibly *c.*745–700 BC. It has been argued that Homer was two people, one of whom wrote the *Iliad* and the other who composed the *Odyssey*, but such is the consistency of the literary and concealed astronomical content of the two epic poems that we follow the general belief that he was one person. There was little support for the view of Samuel Butler (1834–1902) when he suggested that Homer might have been a woman. The creativity and emotions that might suggest a woman's touch in scenes of the *Odyssey* or the portrayals of love and family fidelity in the *Iliad* are overwhelmed by an aggressive male world of unrelenting warfare in the Siege of Troy and the hazardous adventures of Odysseus and his sailors and the bloodthirsty climax of the *Odyssey*.

Homer and the bards of the oral tradition had for centuries been masters of the arts of memorisation and could recite by heart the 150,000 or more words of the *Iliad*, and when they had recovered their breath might launch themselves into the 120,000 words or so of the *Odyssey*. Little wonder that Mnemosyne, the goddess of memory and universal order, was honoured as the mother of the muses. For the purposes of this study it is relevant that others of the nine muses included Urania (astronomy) and Calliope (epic poetry), whose immortal status reflects the high regard in which such skills were held in ancient Greek society. A short account of the arts of memory is given in *Homer's Secret Iliad* (pp. 46–8) and includes references to the well-regarded works of Milman Parry[1] and Frances A.Yates.[2] In presenting the complex amounts of narrative stored in their memories, the bards would have been carried along by the beat and rhythm of the music of the lyre that accompanied their recitations. As more astronomical and calendrical content was extracted from the *Iliad* and the *Odyssey* the realisation came that a vital aid to memory for the poet-astronomers was the ever-turning night sky, where the rhythms of the moon, sun, stars and constellations are unforgettably associated with events in the epics. The bards related their stories within the time frame of the 19-year cycle and linked the adventures of Odysseus after the fall of Troy with the monthly cycles of the moon during a calendar year. The minstrels may sing of heroic events, but as Phemius, resident bard in Odysseus' palace in Ithaca, says: 'I make all my lays myself, and heaven visits me with every kind of inspiration.' (22.347)

Bards & the *Odyssey*

Without the countless generations of poet-singers there could have been no *Iliad* and no *Odyssey*. So important in Homeric society were these conservators of ancient culture that much of the *Odyssey* is set against a background of storytelling by Odysseus and the roles of the mythical bards, Demodocus and Phemius, are of considerable importance. As in the real life of Homer's times, the bards of the epic recited oft-told tales of a glorious past of gods and heroes, wisdom, valour and tragedy. So elevated in society were these storytellers that Homer never records them performing before the common folk, hoi polloi, but they sing their songs in royal courts after sporting games, banquets and dancing. Homer says the bards were divinely inspired and the *Odyssey* opens with a voice seeking inspiration from the muse, a daughter of Zeus.

The greatest storytelling role of all in the *Odyssey* is reserved for Odysseus, the complex hero whose accounts of his own adventures are recalled at great length and with considerable detail. His stories not only keep the pace of literary narrative racing along but also preserve a wealth of astronomical learning. So accomplished is Odysseus' long account of his adventures to the Phaeacian court that King Alcinous says there is a style about Odysseus' language that reflects his good disposition and that he tells his stories as if he were a 'practised bard'. Odysseus' friend and slave, the pig-keeper Eumaeus, describes his master's skills as those of 'a heaven-taught minstrel … on whose lips all hearers hang entranced'. Odysseus himself, perhaps admiring his own skills, says 'there is nothing better or more delightful than when a whole people make merry together with guests sitting orderly to listen. When Odysseus visits the court of King Alcinous, the blind bard Demodocus brings tears to his eyes with songs of the fall of Troy. So overcome by emotion is Odysseus that he says Demodocus must have learned his music from Apollo and that 'there is no one in the world whom I admire more than I do you'; lavish praise from a warrior king who had fought gallantly at Troy. Demodocus had been granted the divine gift of song by the muse who had then taken away his sight, a story which has given rise to a belief that Homer was also blind. Such is the volume of learning based on astronomical observations preserved in his epics, that it is highly improbable that Homer could have been sightless.

The songs of Phemius are a continuous thread during the events before and after the slaughter of the loutish suitors who sought the hand of Penelope, the wife of the absent Odysseus. At the opening of the *Odyssey*, the 'heavenly inspired' Phemius sets the tone with a song about the return of heroes from Troy. After the clamour and mayhem of the subsequent killings there is a macabre moment when Odysseus tells Phemius to strike up a dance tune on his lyre to confuse curious citizens listening outside the walls. Homer also tells of another bard left to care for the wife of King Agamemnon when the leader of the Greek army left home for Troy. This tragic character suffered the cruellest of deaths for a minstrel whose life was built around performing before attentive and enthusiastic audiences; he was cast away on a desert island without food and water, and wasted away with no one to hear his dying song.

Decline of the Poet-Astronomers

In the centuries after Homer's death the study of astronomy and other learning in Greece underwent great changes with the rise of a new breed of intellectuals, the natural philosophers and mathematicians who challenged ancient views of natural events and sought to apply rational thought to their observations and theories. The advent of a Greek written script also contributed to the passing of the poet-astronomers as the conservators of knowledge, with their once important role gradually being forgotten. The loss of the knowledge in the *Iliad* and the *Odyssey* also suggests that the poet-astronomers were an elite sect who jealously guarded their secrets and passed them down the ages to only a select few. The scribes who later wrote down the epics were possibly not privy to such learning, but so revered was Homer that they strove to recreate his literary legacy with the utmost accuracy. In doing so, even unknowingly, the scribes also faithfully preserved the data that has now been revealed as such a treasure house of learning.

How quickly the astronomical role of Homer was forgotten is a matter for speculation, but it would seem to have been lost by the fifth century BC, when the eponymous Meton was credited with the introduction a 19-year cycle of the sun and moon into the Athenian calendar system. The cycle is of great importance for calendar makers and was so familiar to Homer that some 300 years before Meton he constructed the timescale of the *Iliad* and the *Odyssey* around it.

Voices from the Past

Homer's role as an astronomer and calendar maker is indicated in works and references by such famous Greeks as the philosopher Heraclitus (*c.*540–*c.*480 BC), Eratosthenes (*c.*276–194 BC), Crates of Mallus, who flourished in the early second century BC, and the geographer Strabo (64 BC–AD 20). Although only fragments remain of Heraclitus' work and quotations, he was greatly influential and 'continuously read, quoted, imitated and interpreted for more than seven centuries'.[3] Amongst the 100 or so surviving fragments is one which states that 'Thales practised astronomy'[4] – a brief quotation which would be accepted by both historians and classicists alike. Much more interestingly, a second fragment includes the phrase: 'Homer the astronomer, considered wisest of all Greeks.'[5] We believe that to be equally true and the extraordinary breadth and depth of Homer's learning is explored in the following chapters. The Stoic sage, Crates of Mallus, was head of one of the ancient world's most famous libraries at Pergamum, on the west coast of modern Turkey, and one of his principal works was a commentary on the Homeric epics. He was, too, a foremost supporter of a theory which maintained that Homer intended to express scientific or philosophical truths in the form of poetry.

One of Strabo's aims in life was to discover the lands, islands and cities mentioned in Homer's works and his bequest to later ages were volumes on the geography of the world. In the first book[6] he declares that both he 'and his predecessors, who included the great Hipparchus'[7] regarded Homer as the founder of the science of geography. In ancient Greece, geography and astronomy were closely allied subjects and Strabo declared that 'geography … unites terrestrial and celestial phenomena … in no sense separated from each other'. He went on to say that in the third century BC, Eratosthenes, mathematician, astronomer, geographer and keeper of the library at Alexandria in Egypt, maintained that one of the first successors to Homer was not a man of letters as might be expected, but the astronomer-geographer Anaximander, who died around 545 BC. Homer's standing as a man of wider interests than literature alone was not confined to

his homeland. Towards the end of the first century AD, Pliny the Elder wrote his
Natural History, a work which influenced western science for more than a thousand years. Although not directly mentioning astronomy, the Roman hails Homer
as 'the father and prince of all learning and learned men'; extravagant praise for a
poet but entirely in keeping for a man who used his literary powers to preserve
learning about the wonders of the night skies.

Following the collapse of Rome's western empire in the fifth century AD,
Greek learning and literature and any further clues to Homer's extended genius
were lost to Europe for many centuries. Then, as western intellect flourished at
the time of the Renaissance and scholars rediscovered the literary and philosophical treasures of ancient Greece, so too were revived memories of Homer
being much more than a poet alone. Early in the eighteenth century, Alexander
Pope translated both the *Iliad* and the *Odyssey*, and in the 1715 introduction to the
former he says of the long-forgotten achievements of Homer: 'If we reflect upon
those innumerable Knowledges, those Secrets of Nature and Physical Philosophy
which *Homer* is generally suppos'd to have wrapt up in his *Allegories*, what a new
and ample Scene of Wonder may this Consideration afford us?'[8]

Others in later times have pursued Pope's tantalising idea with its echoes of
Crates' notion of Homeric allegory. In 1907 the distinguished scholar Gilbert
Murray,[9] Regius Professor of Greek at Oxford University (1908–36) drew attention to 'myth of a pronounced and curious kind. The point has not yet been
noticed and needs a fairly full statement. It is a matter of the solar and lunar
calendar,' he wrote:

> Time has been generally measured by the '*eniautoi*' or repeated circuits of the
> moon and the sun, i.e. by the month and the year. The object of a scientific
> calendar has always been to find a period in which the two circuits should cor-
> respond; the New Moon[10] should coincide with a winter solstice, and the Sun
> and Moon begin their life together.

Declaring Meton's 19-year cycle to be 'the greatest effort of ancient calendar
making', Murray drew attention to Odysseus' arrival home after 19 years away:

> Now when *did Odysseus* return to Penelope? The date is given with a precision
> most unusual in epic poetry. He returned to Ithaca 'just at the rising of that
> brightest star which heralds the light of the Daughter of Dawn' (13.93). He
> rejoined his wife 'on the twentieth' year; i.e. he came as soon as the twentieth
> year came, as soon as the nineteenth was complete. He came at the new moon,
> on the day which the Athenians called 'Old-and-New', 'when one month is
> waning and the next rising up'. This new moon was also the day of the Apollo
> Feast, or Solstice festival of the sun, and the time was winter.[11]

Murray's remarks on the *Odyssey* and the 19-year cycle were perceptive, but as far as we know he never pursued the matter further or conceived of the epic as a wide-ranging discourse on time and calendars. In less than two pages in an essay on 'The historical content of the *Iliad*', Murray also refers to the '*solar* characteristics that seem to cling' to Odysseus rather than his role in this work as a lunar icon, a projection that holds the key to the discovery of the epic's calendrical material. It is also interesting to note that in drawing attention to the climax of the *Odyssey* occurring at the end of a 19-year cycle with a new crescent moon at a winter solstice, he would have known that such a cycle would have begun at a new crescent moon at a winter solstice. Murray makes no mention of this nor suggests where can be found in the *Iliad-Odyssey* cycle a metaphorical image of Odysseus' departure for war at a midwinter with a new crescent moon in the sky (see Chapter 12). Edna Leigh's only reference to Murray is included in a note in which she wrote:

> I worked through an hypothesis in which I assumed a purpose of Homeric epic to be time reckoning. I devised calendars of five or six types to incorporate an *Iliad-Odyssey* combined time to equal the 6939–6940 days of the Metonic cycle or something similar. (*Murray remarked once, we have made too little of this*).

Later chapters will reveal how Odysseus' lunar role enables Homer to embed in epic the long-forgotten arts of ancient Greek calendar making. Whilst most, if not quite all of the knowledge is contained within the pages of the *Odyssey*, its companion epic, the *Iliad*, plays an important part in calculating the 19 years that Odysseus is away from home. Before exploring these new fields the following summaries of the epics may be useful.

The Siege of Troy: Fact or Fiction?

Even when considered only as literature there are a number of unanswered questions concerning the veracity of Homer's stories. For many centuries after his death, the epics aroused passionate belief in Troy as a real place and the Trojan War as an historic event. Such views were expressed not only by ancient scholars such as Herodotus, Thucydides and Eratosthenes, but also by the great rulers Xerxes of Persia and Alexander the Great. That notion gradually fell out of favour, but in the latter part of the nineteenth century Frank Calvert and Heinrich Schliemann had independently become convinced that a city named Troy had existed at a place known as Hisarlik, on the east coast of Turkey. Calvert's hopes of excavating were thwarted by lack of financial support and the honour of discovering Troy went to Schliemann, a rich German entrepreneur with a burning fascination of Homeric epic. In his mid-thirties, Schliemann retired from the world of business and in the 1870s became a founding father of modern archaeology when his excavations uncovered the many-layered ruins of the ancient city. He extended his work to the Peloponnese, where his greatest achievement was the excavation of the city of Mycenae, said by Homer to have been the home of Agamemnon, commander in chief of the Greek forces at the Siege of Troy. Magnificent as Schliemann's discoveries were, his reputation has been marred by destructive excavation techniques and over-enthusiasm about some of his discoveries. Even though he had no supporting evidence, he declared that precious items found at Troy were the jewels of Helen of Troy and that a gold mask discovered at Mycenae was that of Agamemnon; both ideas were later proven wrong. Schliemann's views on the site of Troy were rapidly taken up by others and archaeology with its origins in Homeric epic became a flourishing discipline that continues unabated. The discoveries of Schliemann and other archaeologists have given substance to many of the places listed in the *Iliad* and the *Odyssey*, and show that Homer had good knowledge of the geography of the Greek mainland, Asia Minor, Crete and the islands of the Ionian and Aegean seas.

The site of Troy is now generally accepted, but whether Homer's Siege of Troy ever occurred is another matter. Excavations have revealed no artefacts to support a view that there ever was a war between Greeks and Trojans such as that described so graphically by Homer. Nor is there any evidence that such great heroes as Hector and Achilles, Agamemnon and Odysseus, ever existed except in traditional myths. Archaeologists say the site of Troy dates back to *c.*2500 BC and nine levels of continuous human habitation, one on top of the other, have been uncovered. Certainly Troy would have been a city famous throughout the region in antiquity for it occupied a prime strategic position from which to control and tax shipping passing through the Dardanelles. According to Herodotus, Troy was destroyed in the twelfth–thirteenth century BC, but a lack of archaeological findings suggests this could have been caused not by war but by an earthquake, to which the region is prone. It is not unreasonable to suggest that stories and folk memories of such a catastrophe were used by Homer as a central theme in his epics. In transposing the city's destruction by a natural occurrence to a mythical event in epic, Homer created a vehicle for the preservation of the astronomical and calendrical knowledge accumulated by the pre-literate Greeks.

The *Iliad* & the Siege of Troy

Homer's *Iliad* covers mainly just a few weeks of conflict during the final months of the Siege of Troy, whose seeds were first sown when the beautiful Helen left her husband, King Menelaus of Lacedaemon (Sparta), and ran off with the Trojan prince, Paris, leaving behind her 'darling daughter', Hermione. Menelaus was distraught and humiliated and urged his brother, King Agamemnon of Mycenae, to form a mighty army which would sail for Troy and restore Helen to her rightful place as his wife. Helen's was the face renowned for launching an invasion fleet of a thousand ships, or more accurately, the 1186 Greek vessels that Homer lists in the *Iliad*.

Distraught though Menelaus was, he brooded for nine years before the fleet was assembled and it was almost a further ten years before Troy was destroyed and Helen returned to him. Helen, now 19 years older than when she was abducted, seems not to have mourned Prince Paris very much and jumped back into bed with Menelaus and they lived happily ever after. The passing of so many years before Menelaus regained his wife raises questions of credibility but we will show that recording the passing of long periods of time has a central purpose in Homer's grand design.

Homer picks up the story of the war in the ninth year after the siege of Troy began and the *Iliad* opens with a bitter dispute between Agamemnon and Achilles, the most powerful warrior in the Greek army. As the tide of battle surges to and fro over the following weeks, Homer devotes much narrative in describing bloody combat, with gory details of men being struck down by sword, spear and arrow in every part of the body. One prominent feature of the bloodshed is that Homer gives a number of heroic soldiers, such as Agamemnon, Menelaus and Odysseus, a day of glory when he describes in detail their feats on the battlefield. Priam, King of the Trojans, is too old to join the fighting and his army is led by his eldest son, Hector, a man of courage and honour who knows that his days – and those of Troy – are numbered. In the climax of the fighting Hector kills Patroclus, the close companion of Achilles, who in turn kills Hector in single combat on a midsummer's day. As the epic draws to a close the Greeks hold a series of sporting games in honour of the dead Patroclus, before the Trojans honour the death of Hector with a great banquet.

Our reading of the *Iliad* as the source of considerable but quite different astronomical knowledge from that of the *Odyssey* can be found in *Homer's Secret Iliad* (John Murray, 1999). In creating a chart of the night skies, Homer transposes the battlefield of Troy into the night sky and identifies Greek and Trojan regiments with constellations, and many hundreds of stars with individual warriors. Other topics covered are a link with the fall of Troy and an ancient concept of the precession of the equinoxes, the magnitude of stars according to a military hierarchy, the roles of the gods and astronomy as a tool for navigation.

The *Odyssey*: Complex Story of Time & Place

Time and place in the *Odyssey* are complicated matters and the plot is as complex as the character of its hero. During the final days of the epic there are extensive flashbacks during which Odysseus recalls parting from his wife, Penelope – the events that led to the sacking of Troy and his adventures as he struggled for years on his homeward journey to Ithaca. To make matters more difficult, Odysseus doesn't always tell the truth when entrancing his listeners with his yarns.

The *Odyssey* opens with the gods debating whether to allow Odysseus to return to Ithaca after years of wandering. At the same time his son, Telemachus, is in difficulty in the family palace, where more than 100 suitors, hoping that Odysseus is dead, are seeking to marry Penelope. She keeps the suitors at bay by promising to choose one of them when she has finished weaving a shroud for her father-in-law, Laertes. For almost four years she weaves during the day and unpicks her work at night so never finishing the shroud and never having to make a choice. As the *Odyssey* opens Telemachus has not quite come of age at the end of his nineteenth year and lacks the authority to banish the suitors who treat him with contempt. With the help of the goddess Athene, however, he sets off on a journey to seek news of his father from King Nestor of Pylos and King Menelaus, two veterans of the Trojan War.

Homesick and shedding tears of self-pity, Odysseus makes his delayed entrance after the gods agree to let him leave the enchanted island of the witch Calypso, where he had been held captive for close to eight years. He builds a raft but is shipwrecked when Poseidon, the sea god and father of Polyphemus whom Odysseus had blinded, whips up a storm. He drifts for two days before being washed up on Scherie, the island where live the Phaeacians, kind and mysterious seafarers whose ships 'glide along like thought, or as a bird in the air' (Butler 7.39). Odysseus is welcomed to the palace, where he holds King Alcinous and his courtiers spellbound as he recalls his adventures and the progressive loss of his ships and men after leaving the ruins of Troy.

In the first of his escapades, Odysseus sacks Ismarus but is then outfought by the Cicones and driven from their land with heavy casualties. Beset by a storm, he seeks refuge on an unmarked land before continuing his voyage down the Aegean Sea, where he is blown off course into a fantasy world of monsters, witches and other perils. After the land of the Lotus Eaters, Odysseus sails to the homeland of Polyphemus, the one-eyed Cyclops, from whom he escapes by trickery. Encounters follow with Aeolus, King of the Winds, the giant Laestrygonians and the enchantress Circe, with whom he spends a year. Odysseus then journeys to Hades where he meets the seer Teiresias and ghosts of the dead, including his mother and heroes such as Agamemnon, Achilles and Great Aias. Returning to the upper world, he proceeds to Circe's island to give an uncommonly splendid funeral for a humble sailor and then goes on to escape the alluring songs of the Sirens, the perilous Wandering Rocks, the six-headed monster Scylla and the deadly whirlpool of Charybdis. Eventually he reaches the island of Thrinacia, where his starving crew defy warnings that there will be dire consequences if they eat the cattle of the sun god Helios. The revenge of Zeus is brutal and with a thunderbolt he destroys Odysseus' remaining ship. Odysseus is the only survivor and drifts to the island of Ogygia, where he is held captive by lovelorn Calypso until the gods let him begin the last leg of his journey. After leaving Calypso, Odysseus is shipwrecked but declines an offer to stay with the Phaeacians. Loaded with gifts, he sails on one of their magical ships to his island home of Ithaca where he is left sleeping on the shore. The *Odyssey* is now approaching its climax, but Odysseus does not immediately storm off to the palace to be reunited with Penelope but is cunningly disguised as a beggar by Athene and stays for three nights with Eumaeus, a pig-keeper to whom he tells a lying tale about his past. Meanwhile, Telemachus has been away seeking news of his father from Menelaus and Nestor. The suitors, eager to see one of their own marry Penelope and become King of Ithaca, have no wish to see Telemachus return but their plan to ambush and kill him comes to nothing when he sails home during a moonless night and lookouts fail to spot him. Athene again intervenes later and in a moment of magic Odysseus is briefly revealed to Telemachus and together they plan to confront the suitors.

Odysseus, still in disguise, finally makes his way to the palace and even though he tells Penelope a long rambling tale, she does not recognise him. Penelope fears that Odysseus is dead and when her trick with the shroud is exposed she promises to marry the suitor who can string the great bow which Odysseus left behind when he went to fight at Troy. None of them are able to do so, but when the 'beggar' steps up he strings the bow and fires an arrow through 12 axe heads. Odysseus then throws off his rags and reveals his true self. In a brutal act of revenge and with the help of Telemachus, the pig-keeper Eumaeus and faithful herdsman Philoetius, the suitors are slaughtered and shortly afterwards 12 house maids who had consorted with them are hanged. Odysseus and Penelope are reunited and go to bed on the longest night of the year, when Athene 'held back the dawn'. The following day after visiting his aged father, Laertes, Odysseus is accosted by relatives of the suitors he killed, but after a short skirmish all ends well when Athene steps in and restores harmony to both sides. How astronomical and calendrical knowledge is preserved in these adventures and situations is revealed in following chapters.

Odysseus: Hero or Lying Cheat?

Illustrious Odysseus, flower of Achaean chivalry

Iliad, 10.535

Any one who met you, even a god, would have to be a consummate trickster to surpass you in subterfuge. You were always an obstinate, cunning and irrepressible intriguer. So you don't propose, even in your own country to drop your tricks and lying tales you love so much.

Athene speaking to Odysseus, *Od.* 13.291, Rieu

Odysseus, the sacker of cities, is one of the most intriguing characters in the long history of western literature and in each of Homer's epics there are striking contrasts of his character in both literary and astronomical terms.[12] In the *Iliad* he is the gallant leader of the Cephallonian contingent of the Greek forces and one of a group of heroic warriors who dominate the story of the Siege of Troy. A man of 'nimble wits' and a 'master of intrigue and stratagem', Odysseus is trusted to undertake personal tasks for Agamemnon and his words carry great weight in the counsels of the Greeks. Even so, he is sensitive enough to take umbrage when accused of being less than eager to join the fray, but once in combat he excels in bravery. Risking his own life, he beats off Trojan warriors who had brought Menelaus to his knees and does great slaughter before being badly injured. Even then he stands his ground and spears an attacker in the back as blood pours from his own wound. 'Like an antlered stag beset by jackals', Odysseus kept his attackers at bay until he too was rescued.

Amongst other deeds, Odysseus volunteers to accompany Diomedes when, in *Iliad* Book 10, the Greek leaders send two men on a foray into the enemy lines to steal horses and they 'set out like a pair of lions through the black night'. Encountering a Trojan on his way to spy on the Greeks, they interrogate him before brutally beheading him. On go the Greek pair to the Thracian camp where they kill many soldiers, including the King of Thracia, before returning to the Greek lines with stolen horses. Athene is Odysseus' guardian god and when at the end of the *Iliad* funeral games are held to honour Patroclus, she ensures that her protégé wins a race by tripping up Great Aias, who had been in the lead.

Odysseus' role in the *Odyssey* changes so dramatically that at one point the heroic warrior of the *Iliad* is even called a lying cheat by Athene. In the yarns he spins he claims credit for the idea of building the wooden horse used to infiltrate Troy and in which he accompanied the Greek soldiers hiding inside. When the gullible Trojans hauled the horse into the walled city, the Greeks waited until night before creeping out and opening the city gates to let in the Greek army. With Troy in ashes, Odysseus and his fleet of 12 ships begin their homeward voyage, during which all of his men are either taken captive, eaten by a cannibal or drowned. Eleven of his ships are pelted with rocks and sunk by a race of giants and the remaining one is later destroyed by a thunderbolt. Only Odysseus returns to the island kingdom of Ithaca.

Odysseus recalls his adventures when addressing the court of Alcinous, King of the Phaeacians, in Books 9–12, and gives a brief summary to Penelope at 23.310. His adventures are as follows:

Battle with the Cicones.
A terrible hurricane.
Cape Malea and the land of the Lotus Eaters.
Goat Island and Polyphemus.

Aeolus, King of the Winds.
Return to Aeolia and encounter with the Laestrygonians.
Killing of a giant stag and the witch Circe.
Circe's warnings and the death of Elpenor.
Hades and ghosts of the dead.
Return to Circe's island and funeral of Elpenor.
The Sirens, the Wandering Rocks, and Scylla.
Thrinacia and eating of the cattle of Helios, the sun god.
Zeus sinks Odysseus' remaining ship, Charybdis.
Safe arrival on Calypso's island.

With Odysseus' captivity on Calypso's island in its eighth year, the last 40 days of the *Odyssey* begin. In recounting his past adventures, Odysseus proves himself to be a man of many devious parts, from the cunning courage displayed when he outwits the Cyclops to the tears he sheds when held captive by Calypso, and the lies he tells when recounting his adventures. Just as his literary adventures drive the pace of the *Odyssey*, so do those same escapades drive the preservation of calendrical knowledge.

Puzzles of the *Odyssey*

Sometimes even the noble Homer nods, said Horace, the Roman poet of the first century BC, when he commented on what appear to be moments of inconsistency in the epics. While minor contradictions do not affect the telling or the overall content of the stories, there are more serious questions to be asked about other matters in the *Odyssey*, which, it will be shown later, can be resolved in terms of calendars and cycles of the sun and moon.

For instance, when Odysseus lands on the shores of Ithaca after 19 years away, it would be reasonable to expect that he would instantly dash in anger to his palace to clear out the suitors and be reunited with his wife. Not so. He is transformed by Athene into a tattered and torn beggar and for some days goes into hiding and is not recognised by foes, friends or family. His later magical transformation into a heroic warrior is stunningly dramatic. Odysseus is also disguised as a beggar when he makes a reconnaissance inside Troy, and at other times he removes himself from the story while he sleeps or is concealed in a cave. These instances of when-you-see him, when-you-don't are quite strange – unless they have a purpose that concerns phases of the moon. On Odysseus' voyage from Troy to Ithaca he enters the realms of supernatural lands, one-eyed monsters, cannibal giants, witches, the sirens and other deadly perils. Scholars and intrepid sailors through the ages have tried to chart Odysseus' course but there is no common agreement on where – on earth – Odysseus might have travelled. With astronomy in mind, we asked whether Odysseus' geography, like his fantastic creatures, was without substance in the world about us. If so, just where did he sail on the wine-dark seas and why is Homer so specific about his hero sailing for 'six days and on the seventh' or for 'nine days and on the tenth' or for 'seventeen days and on the eighteenth'?

Homer directly names only a handful of stars and constellations but it is quality that is important and not the quantity. From those named can be deduced such an awareness of the heavens that Homer was able to instruct Odysseus how to use the stars at night for navigation. Another curiosity occurs when Odysseus arranges a funeral fit for a king for a young sailor whose only claim to fame comes when he dies after falling from the roof of a building after a night of heavy drinking. Might there be other matters concealed in his story?

The many numbers, both individual and in groups, which are scattered throughout the *Odyssey* are an area of Homeric study that does not seem to have attracted much attention. For Homer these numbers were practical and not mystical and proved a decisive factor in the unlocking of the many secrets encoded in the epic. Odysseus' journey home is hardly underway when six men are taken from each of his 12 ships and, as the story continues, more crewmen are taken by Polyphemus, Antiphates and Scylla, or lost in storms until all are gone. There is a careful counting of the number of suitors pursuing Penelope; the goats killed on a lush island are precisely listed, as are the trees and vines in an orchard and the boars, sows and pens on the farm of Eumaeus. Elsewhere there is no end to the flow and Odysseus performs the highly unlikely feat of shooting an arrow through 12 axe heads before 12 maids are hanged in a heinous act of revenge.

Penelope, we learn, dreams of a flock of 20 geese being devoured by a single eagle, the sun god is proud of his 350 cattle and 350 sheep, a jar of wine is diluted at a ratio of 20:1 and what is so special about 22 four-wheeled wagons? These are just a few of the puzzles and curiosities which are resolved in an astronomical reading of the epic. In considering the *Odyssey* in this manner it is important that only those matters which Homer includes specifically in his epics are considered, and that elements of myths from other times and other sources are excluded.

Radical as it may appear to propose Homer as a calendar maker, he was not the only poet of his times to have a practical knowledge of such skills. Hesiod, who also lived in the eighth century BC, created *Works and Days*, a homespun guide for farmers in which observations of stars are reminders to begin various seasonal tasks. Homer's calendar system is of a much higher and more complex order, and incorporates cycles of the sun and moon that occur over long periods of time. Another major difference between the two is that Hesiod's calendar was openly available to all those who worked the land, while the data and structure of Homer's system was so carefully concealed in epic that it has been lost for many centuries. This suggests that the knowledge concealed in Homer's works was confined to an influential group of people who recognised that such learning was a source of powerful social influence.

Notes

1 Parry, Adam (ed.), *The Making of Homeric Verse: The Collected Papers of Milman Parry* (Oxford: Clarendon Press, 1970).

2 Yates, Frances A., *The Art of Memory* (London: Routledge & Kegan Paul, 1966), p. 29.

3 Kahn, Charles H., *The Art and Thought of Heraclitus: An Edition of the Fragments with Translation and Commentary* (Cambridge: Cambridge University Press, 1981), p. 39.

4 Thales of Miletus, *c.*625–547 BC, is commonly known as the 'Father of Greek Astronomy', but none of his original work survives.

5 Kahn, Charles H., 'The Art and Thought of Heraclitus', in 'Hippolytus: Comment on Fragment 13', ix 9.10. The quotation attributed by Hippolytus to Heraclitus is: 'Men deceive themselves in their knowledge of the obvious, even Homer the astronomer, considered wisest of all Greeks. For he was fooled by boys killing lice who said: what we see and catch we leave behind; and what we neither see nor catch we carry away.'

6 Strabo, *The Geography of Strabo*, trans. Horace Leonard Jones, Loeb Classical Library (Cambridge MA: Harvard University Press, 1917–32), 1:2:3.

7 Neugebauer, Otto, wrote in his *Notes on Hipparchus*: 'Even the most casual discussion of ancient astronomy will not fail to call Hipparchus of Nicaea in Bithynia the greatest astronomer of antiquity.' Weinberg, Saul S. (ed.), *The Aegean and the Near East. Studies Presented to Hetty Goldman* (Locust Valley: J.J. Augustin, 1956), pp. 292–6.

8 Pope, Alexander, *The Iliad of Homer*, 1715–20 (London: Grant Richards, 1902), p. xi.

9 Murray, Gilbert, *The Rise of the Greek Epic* (Oxford: Oxford University Press, 1907; 4th edn 1934; reprinted 1961), pp. 211–2.

10 In modern astronomy the term 'New Moon' is used when the moon is in conjunction with the sun and cannot be seen. In historic times the lunar month began with the sighting of the new crescent.

11 Murray, Gilbert, *The Rise of the Greek Epic* (Oxford: Oxford University Press, 1907; 4th edn 1934; reprinted 1961), p. 211.

12 See *Homer's Secret Iliad*.

3

ODYSSEUS & THE MOON

At the heart of our calendrical model of Homer's *Odyssey* is the amply supported proposition that Odysseus' alter ego is that of a personification of the moon. As will be seen, his experiences both before and after the fall

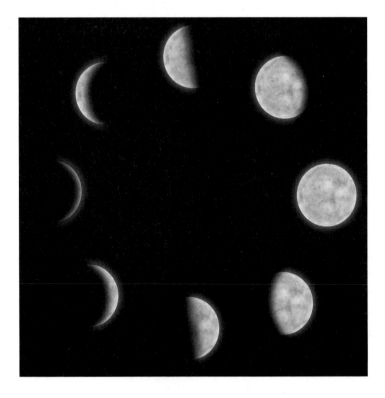

3.1 Odysseus' adventures are linked to phases of the moon from the sighting of the new crescent (centre left), quarter moon (bottom centre), full moon (centre right), third quarter (top centre) and then waning into the dark period. (Marleen Smits/Fotolia)

of Troy are generally driven by the rhythm of the lunar month, the counting of lunations and cycles of the sun and moon; from this proposition all of the astronomical and calendrical matters discovered in the epic fall into place. The initial source of Odysseus' lunar role was discovered in Edna Leigh's papers on a single foolscap sheet of now yellowing paper with notes written in pencil. The layout appeared to be a lunar calendar of sorts and it became clear that this sheet, on which were plotted phases of the moon during the last 40 days of the *Odyssey*, was of fundamental significance. Edna Leigh noted that those 40 days were the only occasion during the entire epic that events occurred in the present tense, an opinion which agreed with that of her contemporary, the eminent scholar W.B. Stanford, in his *Commentary on the Odyssey*, published in 1959.[1] In our study we use the term 'real-time' days to cover the 40 days from the opening lines of the *Odyssey*, when Odysseus is still a captive on Calypso's island, to the last day of the epic after his triumphal return to Ithaca. It is during this period that Odysseus and others recall in historic terms events of the previous 19 years. Selecting a 40-day period for those days was no more a random choice for Homer than any other numerical data in the epic and it defines the parameters of a unit of time known also to Hesiod and the Hebrews. Some 800 years after Homer, Julius Caesar was honoured for his military successes during a 40-day period.

Table 1. Storyline of the *Odyssey* during the 40 'real-time' days

The *Odyssey* opens, the gods meet and Telemachus goes in search of news of his father, Odysseus.	6 days
The god Hermes tells Calypso to allow Odysseus return home to Ithaca. That night Odysseus sleeps with the goddess.	1 day
Odysseus builds a raft for 4 days and …	4 days
… sets off on the fifth and sails without mishap for 17 days.	17 days
Odysseus' raft is destroyed in a storm sent by Poseidon and he clings to a piece of timber.	1 day
Odysseus drifts at sea. Lands on the island of Scherie 20 days after leaving Calypso.	2 days
Odysseus meets Nausicaa, daughter of the King of the Phaeacians.	1 day
Odysseus on Scherie with the Phaeacians.	2 days
Odysseus lands on Ithaca, goes to the hut of Eumaeus disguised as a beggar.	1 day
After three days with Eumaeus, Odysseus goes to his palace.	3 days
Climax of the *Odyssey*. Still in disguise, Odysseus strings his great bow and fires an arrow through 12 axe heads. He casts off his beggar's clothes and kills the suitors. Reunited with Penelope. It is the winter solstice.	1 day
Odysseus visits his father, Laertes, and the *Odyssey* ends.	1 day
Total number of 'real-time' days.	40 days

Forty days is intriguing in terms of astronomical observations and concerns the time each year when a star or stars on or adjacent to the ecliptic are not visible during the hours of darkness. A 40-day heliacal period would begin with the brief sighting at dusk of a star or small group of stars, such as the Pleiades on the western horizon, before setting just after the sun; this is called the heliacal setting. Those stars will not be seen again until their heliacal rising 40 days later, when they will be briefly visible on the eastern horizon at dawn just before being obscured by the light of the rising sun. Another interesting point about the 40-day period is that it is very close to being one-ninth of a solar year: 9 x 40 = 360 days.

The 40-day period was a useful time-keeping device and extended the marking of time by lunar days and months to a longer stellar period. It is also a good example of how astronomical observations have influenced ancient texts. In *Works and Days* Hesiod advised: 'When the Pleiades ... are rising begin your harvest, and your ploughing when they are going to set. *Forty nights and days they are hidden and appear again as the year moves round*, when first you sharpen your sickle' (383).[2]

The Old and New Testaments of the Bible have many references to this period, including the 40 days and nights of rain when Noah was in the Ark (Genesis 7.12); 40 days after sighting the tops of the mountains, Noah sent out a raven and a dove (Genesis 8.6); Moses spent 40 days on the Mount (Exodus 24.18); the embalming of Joseph's father took 40 days (Genesis 50.3); the Philistine Goliath challenged David every morning and evening for 40 days (1 Samuel 17.16); Jonah threatened the people of Ninevah with destruction in 40 days (Jonah 3.4); the temptation of Jesus lasted 40 days (Matthew 4.2); and there were 40 days between His crucifixion and His ascension into heaven (Acts 1.3). The 40 days of Lent are also observed before Easter in the Christian Church.

In Rome, a noted civil achievement of Julius Caesar was his reorganisation in 45 BC of the calendar, which became the foundation of the modern calendar. So skilled was Caesar in such matters that according to Plutarch he consulted the best scholars and mathematicians before forming a method of his own which was more accurate than any other. To celebrate Caesar's military conquests in Gaul, Egypt, Syria, Africa and Spain, a series of five spectacular triumphs were held over 40 days. Casius Dio records (43.14.3): 'sacrifices should be offered for [Caesar's] victory during forty days, and ... permission [for him] to ride ... in a chariot drawn by white horses.'

A Calendar in Reverse

The final days of the *Odyssey* may not have excited much interest in numerical terms in the past but, coupled with the progressive phases of the moon, it led Edna Leigh down a path in which she created the single most important page of all her papers and from which came great things. There is no argument about the phase of the moon when Odysseus arrives home in Ithaca for he says that he will return 'between the waning and the waxing moon', in other words during the dark period of the lunar cycle. Stanford remarks that Odysseus' homecoming is 'a definite reference to dating by moon and months' but does not pursue the matter further.

Edna Leigh's unusual approach to the 'real-time' days was that she plotted in reverse order the daily events from Homer's narrative from Day 40 to Day 1. The Feast of Apollo occurs on the penultimate day of the epic and marks the day of the appearance of the new crescent moon. Using the new crescent as her endpoint, this enabled her to link each of the preceding days of narrative to specific days in the lunar month. In the first column of her table (below) was inserted the day of the lunar month and the phase of the moon; the second column named the constellation in which she believed the sun to be on that day; the third column was the day of the *Odyssey* in the 40-day sequence; the fourth column had a brief summary of events on that day; and the fifth column gave a surprising date on which those events could have occurred. How such a date could be assigned to the origins of the oldest knowledge in the epic is explored in Chapter 4.

The 29.53 days in a lunar month do not fit easily into a calendar system and to make calculations of the passage of time easier the Greeks used a system of 'full' and 'hollow' months; a full month had 30 days and a hollow month 29 days, giving an average of 29.5 days. Before a calendar could be created in reverse and the days of the month aligned to events in the narrative, the question of whether the last lunation of the epic was a hollow month of 29 days or a full month of 30 days had to be resolved. By extrapolating backwards Edna Leigh showed that the epic begins during the moon's third quarter, on the 22nd day of a hollow month and then passes through a full month of 30 days.

Forty Days & Phases of the Moon

From Edna Leigh's calendar it can be seen that the *Odyssey* opens when the moon is in its third quarter and waning, and her calendar records the passing of the 40 days in terms of phases of the moon rather than weeks. There are two waning moons, two periods of dark moon and two new crescents, but only one full moon during the 40 days. We entered into the spirit of her research and arranged the 40 'real-time' days, not in terms of action or books or days, but in terms of phases of the moon divided into quarters.

Table 2. Edna Leigh's lunar calendar of the 40 'real-time' days of the *Odyssey*

Phase of moon Day of month	Position of the sun	'Real-time' day of *Odyssey*	The 40 'real-time' days	Date 2296 BC
21	Sagittarii			1 Dec
22 Third Quarter	Sagittarius	1	1 The 40 'real-time' days of the *Odyssey* begin. The gods convene to discuss Odysseus' future.	2
23		2	2 Telemachus seeks news of his father, Odysseus.	3
24		3	3 Telemachus arrives in Pylos and meets king Nestor.	4
25		4	4 Nestor sacrifices to Athene. Telemachus leaves.	5
26 Waning moon ☾		5	5 Telemachus arrives in Lacedaemon to see King Menelaus.	6
27 Dark moon ●		6	6 Telemachus with Menelaus. Penelope dreams.	7
28 Dark moon ●		7	7 Odysseus weeps on the seashore before sleeping with Calypso.	8
29 Dark moon ●		8	1 Odysseus begins to build a raft which takes four days.	9
1 New Crescent ☽	235th lunation begins	9	2 Raft building.	10
2		10	3 Raft building.	11
3		11	4 Raft building.	12
4		12	5 (1) Odysseus sails for ten days and seven without mishap.	13
5	Capricornus	13	2 Sailing.	14
6		14	3 Sailing.	15
7 First Quarter		15	4 Sailing.	16
8		16	5 Sailing.	17
9		17	6 Sailing.	18
10		18	7 Sailing.	19
11		19	8 Sailing.	20
12		20	9 Sailing.	21
13		21	10 Sailing.	22
14 Full moon ○		22	1 Sailing.	23
15		23	2 Sailing.	24
16		24	3 Sailing.	25
17		25	4 Sailing.	26
18		26	5 Sailing.	27

Phase of moon Day of month	Position of the sun	'Real-time' day of *Odyssey*	The 40 'real-time' days	Date 2296 BC
19		27	6 Sailing.	28 Dec
20		28	7 Sailing.	29
21 Third Quarter		29	(18) Poseidon stirs up a storm and wrecks Odysseus' raft. Odysseus drifts at sea.	30
22		30	(19) 1 Odysseus drifts at sea.	31
23	Capricornus	31	(20) 2 Odysseus lands on the Phaeacian island of Scherie in the evening.	2295 BC 1 Jan
24		32	1 Odysseus awakens after midday, startles Nausicaa, and in the evening arrives at the Phaeacian palace.	2
25		33	2 Odysseus takes part in the Phaeacian games during the day. In the evening he recounts his adventures.	3
26		34	3 Phaeacians prepare for Odysseus' departure and he sails overnight.	4
27 Waning moon ☾	Venus	35	1 Before dawn Odysseus lands on Ithaca. Athene transforms him into a beggar. He goes to Eumaeus' hut but is not recognised.	5
28 Dark moon ●		36	2 Odysseus shelters unrecognised in Eumaeus' hut all day and night.	6
29 Dark moon ●		37	3 Odysseus briefly meets Telemachus in Eumaeus' hut.	7
30 Dark moon ●		38	4 Late in the afternoon Odysseus, still in disguise, goes to his palace. His old nurse Eurycleia recognises a scar on his leg.	8
235th lunation ends 1 New Crescent ☽ New month begins	Aquarius Winter solstice	39	5 Odysseus strings his great bow and fires an arrow through a row of axe heads, throws off his disguise, kills the suitors and is reunited with Penelope.	9
2		40	6 Odysseus visits his father, Laertes. Harmony is restored. Odysseus is now fated to pick up an oar and set off once more on his travels.	10

It can be seen from the general rhythm of Odysseus' experiences that during the period between the moon's first and third quarters, when one might expect most activity, nothing untoward happens. We were puzzled why 17 days out of the 40 'real-time' days were dismissed in a single line: 'Days seven and ten did he sail over the sea' (5.277). We then began to look more closely at possible links between phases of the moon and Odysseus' changing fortunes and came to the following conclusions:

Moon's third quarter: The *Odyssey* opens with a period of discord. The gods debate whether to allow Odysseus to leave Calypso's island and return home; the suitors hold sway in unruly Ithaca and much-troubled Telemachus goes to Pylos and Lacedaemon in search of news of his father. When the suitors learn that he has left Ithaca they plan to ambush and kill him on his return. Meanwhile, Penelope, wife of Odysseus, sleeps fitfully and has strange dreams.

Dark period: Hermes tells Calypso that the gods have said she must allow Odysseus to go free. Odysseus enters the story bemoaning his fate and goes to bed with the goddess, hidden deep in a cave on a moonless night.

New crescent: Odysseus builds a raft and embarks with a happy heart after Calypso gives him advice on how to use the Pleiades, Boötes, the Bear and Orion to navigate his craft.

The moon waxes to full and then wanes: All goes smoothly for Odysseus as he sails for 'seven days and ten' across the seas, a period which covers the days when the moon is at its most prominent from first quarter to third quarter.

Third quarter: As the moon wanes tension increases and disaster strikes. On his eighteenth day at sea Odysseus' raft breaks up in a storm created by Poseidon. He loses everything, including his clothing, and drifts for two days before scrambling ashore on the island of Scherie in the evening. He sleeps until well after midday and then meets Nausicaa, daughter of Alcinous, King of the Phaeacians. The same evening Odysseus arrives at the king's palace and weeps at Demodocus' songs of Troy. The following day Odysseus takes part in the Phaeacian games and later recounts his terrible adventures to the Phaeacians, who the next day take him on an overnight voyage to Ithaca.

Last sighting of the waning crescent: Only the last thin crescent of the waning moon can be seen when Odysseus lands on Ithaca before dawn. The crescent disappears in the morning sunlight as the moon goes into conjunction with the sun and Athene disguises Odysseus as a beggar so that he, like the moon, is hidden from view.

Dark period: Odysseus hides away for three dark nights in the hut of the pig-keeper Eumaeus, who fails to recognise his long-lost friend and master. Telemachus returns safely from Lacedaemon after sailing unseen through a dark night, and when Athene magically and briefly reveals Odysseus to his son they plot the downfall of the suitors.

New crescent imminent: Odysseus, still in disguise, travels to his palace to be reunited with his wife after 19 years away. The new moon is not yet risen, but when the nurse Eurycleia washes his feet she recognises a scar on his leg made by the curved white tusk of a wild boar; both scar and tusk are metaphors for the impending new crescent.

Appearance of the new crescent: Next day Odysseus strings his mighty curved bow and to mark the coming together of the sun and moon he fires an arrow (the sun) through a line of 12 axe-heads, representing the months of a lunar year. As the new crescent moon appears in the evening sky it marks the coming together of the sun and moon after 19 years. Odysseus casts off his disguise and like the moon is dressed anew as the suitors who had been seeking to marry his wife are killed.

The cycle continues: On the second day of the new lunation – the final day of the *Odyssey* – Odysseus meets his father, Laertes, and Athene restores peace between Odysseus and relatives of the slain suitors; in other words the lunar and solar calendars are at that moment in harmony at the beginning of both a new calendar year and a new 19-year cycle of the sun and moon.

Establishing the time of year for the climax of the *Odyssey* is neither difficult nor contentious, and Homer's narrative affirms that Odysseus – and the new crescent moon – are revealed in all their glory on the Feast of Apollo at a winter solstice. In conversations between Odysseus and Eumaeus they say the nights are long and the weather is so cold that Odysseus is in need of warm clothing. In recalling that the homeland of Eumaeus lies in the direction of the 'turning point of the sun', Homer gives another hint of the winter solstice. On a more romantic level, Odysseus is eager to spend the night with his wife Penelope, whom he has not seen for 19 years and to ensure they linger over their time in bed together Athene holds back the dawn on the longest night. In the following table, references are given to the phases of moon, the season of year, and the winter solstice:

Table 3. Phases of the moon on Odysseus' return to Ithaca

Phase of moon Day of month	Narrative	*Odyssey* reference
27 waning crescent ☾	Venus, the Morning Star, shines as Odysseus returns to Ithaca between the waning and the waxing moon. The moon could have been seen at dawn but is in its dark phase as Odysseus and Eumaeus talk far into the night. Eumaeus gave Odysseus a cloak to keep out the cold – a hint of midwinter – and put his sword about his shoulders.	13.92, 14.162, 14.456, 14.520
28 no moon ●	The nights are long. Eumaeus says his homestead is Syrie, lying in the direction of the turning point of the sun – the winter solstice.	15.393, 15.404
29 no moon ●	Odysseus remains hidden, known only to Athene and Telemachus.	16.172
30 no moon ●	Eumaeus confirms that the 'beggar' had stayed with him for three nights as he speaks to Penelope.	17.515
1 new crescent ☽ Winter solstice	Climax of the *Odyssey* on the Feast of Apollo held to celebrate the arrival of a new crescent moon and a new lunar month. Odysseus throws off his disguise and kills the suitors. Athene holds back the dawn on the longest night.	20.278, 21.408, 22.1, 23.243
2	Odysseus goes to visit Laertes, his father. Athene restores peace between Odysseus' party and relatives of the suitors, who are then, like the lunar and solar calendars, once more in harmony.	24.205, 24.545

Beliefs have persisted throughout history that phases of the moon have benign or malign influences on the affairs of mankind. It might be claimed there is positive evidence for such ideas but in modern times fluctuating moods and experiences during the lunar month may largely be considered circumstantial. However, strong support for Edna Leigh's linking of the rhythm of Odysseus' adventures to phases of the moon is found in the contemporary works of Hesiod. Both poets project a view that some days of the lunar month were more auspicious than others. In *Works and Days*, Hesiod's concern is for the moon's daily influence on farming and family matters. The synopsis of the 40-day real-time calendar reveals Homer's vision of the fortunes of Odysseus and other characters. There are similarities in both works and each considers the arrival of the new crescent as a 'lucky' or holy day. Hesiod says the fourth day of the month is a good day to construct a narrow boat from timbers already gathered, and Odysseus in his turn completes building a raft on the fourth day. As the moon waxes to mid-month, times are good but as it wanes to the dark of the moon times can be 'fickle, bland and bring no luck'.[3] Hesiod states:

Again few know, the twenty-first is best,
At dawn, and worsens toward the evening time.[4]

During Homer's 40 'real-time' days, the twenty-first day of the lunation begins well, but Poseidon later brings calamity to Odysseus and capsizes his raft. There are differences between Homer and Hesiod; for instance, Hesiod says the first night of the moon's dark period is 'lucky', whereas for Odysseus it is generally a time of misfortune.

With her intrinsically beautiful and intriguing short calendar complete, Edna Leigh's written conclusions came to an abrupt halt. So far as we knew then – and now – her work stood alone and was unique amongst scholars. There was sufficient detail in the calendar to reveal her conviction that generations of oral poets, culminating in Homer, had a far greater purpose than entertainment alone. For these authors it was a revelation that brought a major problem for we had no idea what Edna's wider vision of Homer's *Odyssey* might have been. An exciting breakthrough came in a moment of inspiration when we noticed for the first time a similarity between the fortunes of Odysseus during the last six days of the *Odyssey* and a story told by Helen of Troy about Odysseus' role in the fall of the city. Helen tells Telemachus (4.242) that when his father was on reconnaissance outside the walls of Troy he first beat himself about the shoulders, then disguised himself as a beggar and went into the city unseen, where she eventually recognised him and gave him a bath and new clothes. Dressed anew, Odysseus drew his long sword and killed many Trojans.

Table 4. Odysseus' reconnaissance of Troy

Phase of moon, Day of month	Narrative
21 Third Qtr	Odysseus beat himself most appallingly and threw a cloak of dirty rags over his shoulders as if he were a slave.
22	Dressed in beggar's rags, Odysseus did not look like a warrior as he entered the broad streets of Troy.
23	Completely unrecognised, he explored the city. The Trojans did not know anything was amiss for they did not cry out.
24	Odysseus was able to go about Troy collecting valuable information.
25	Despite the disguise, Helen suspected it was Odysseus and questioned him.
26 ☾	Odysseus avoided Helen's questions …
28 Dark ●	Odysseus avoided Helen's questions …
29 Dark ●	Odysseus avoided Helen's questions as he went about Troy.
30 Dark ●	Helen bathed Odysseus and gave him a new set of clothes. He told her of his plans and made her promise not to betray him until he had returned to the Greek ships.
1 New Crescent ☽	With his long sword he killed many Trojans and returned safely to the Greek camp with his information about Troy. Despite the lamentations of the Trojan women, Helen was glad for she thought longingly of home, her husband, Menelaus, and her daughter, Hermione.

The similarities in rhythm and mood between his reconnaissance of Troy and those of the final six days of the *Odyssey* were exhilarating: each tale begins with Odysseus suffering – in Troy he beats himself and on his final voyage to Ithaca Poseidon wrecks his raft (Table 2); in both Troy and Ithaca Odysseus is in disguise and cannot be recognised for a few days; in both Troy and Ithaca Odysseus sheds his disguise and at the new crescent moon is dressed anew as a powerful and vengeful warrior; in Troy Odysseus uses a long sword to kill Trojans, and in Ithaca uses a 'curved bow' to slaughter the suitors, both weapons suggesting similes for the new crescent moon.

From the comparison of events in Troy and Ithaca came the notion that both incidents could occur at the same time of the lunar month – from the third quarter of the waning moon, through the dark period and to a successful conclusion with the sighting of the new crescent moon. If two such episodes could be linked to phases of the moon, why not others? Did the rhythm of other of Odysseus' adventures follow the same pattern as those of Troy and Ithaca? Would Odysseus begin the lunar month in good heart until encountering difficulties as the moon waned, be taken out of play for two or three days during the dark period, and be given a fresh start with the appearance of the new crescent moon? And if it were so, what was the wider purpose?

From the 40-day calendar it can be seen that Poseidon destroyed Odysseus' raft at the waning moon which led us to make a list of other storms he had endured: a fierce gale after his clash with the Cicones forced his fleet to take shelter on an unknown land; winds and currents sent his fleet off course past Cythera; Aeolus' bag of winds caused turmoil; a storm drove Odysseus on to Helios' island; and finally during a tempest a thunderbolt sank his remaining ship.

Add these storms to the one which broke up Odysseus' raft after he sailed from Calypso's island and there are six incidents which follow a similar pattern in narrative: he is battered by unfavourable winds, forced to flee until he reaches safety, shelters for two or three days and finally continues his journey. During these storms there are similar images of peril when sails are torn to shreds, the stays are broken or a mast is tossed into the sea during the diminishing crescent of the waning moon.

In searching for other repetitive events we noted several concerning Odysseus' sword and later were able to link them to phases of the moon: at the appearance of the new crescent his sword was drawn from the hip or thigh, but when he drew his sword and then sheathed it, as in episodes with Polyphemus (9.300), Circe (10.322) and Eurylochus (10.440), it was the dark of the moon. Similarly we found that Telemachus, Menelaus and Eumaeus carry their swords on their shoulders – but only at the time of the waning crescent.

So began our long haul to find evidence for the belief that each of Odysseus' adventures takes place during one lunar month. To put substance to the idea that the rhythm of the moon's phases could be directly related to the rhythm of his escapades sometimes seemed as arduous as that of Odysseus' journey home. We followed false trails, came up against stone walls and struggled with the calendrical content of difficult narrative. But with ever-increasing confidence in Homer's metaphors we applied a similar approach to all of the adventures with which Odysseus enthralled the Phaeacians. The results were stimulating and, with Odysseus foremost as an icon for the moon, it has been possible to create a model of a calendar in which a lunar year runs in harmony alongside a solar year and which is contained within the parameters of a 19-year luni-solar cycle.

The calculation of time in lunations, synchronisation of cycles of the sun and moon, and much supportive data that was essential to calendar makers, is at the heart of this study and is examined in detail in Chapters 7–11, Odysseus' adventures. Edna Leigh's 40-day compilation on that single sheet of foolscap was the catalyst that enabled us to eventually uncover many of the secrets embedded in the *Odyssey* and to rediscover learning that had been lost for more than two millennia. Many of the exciting discoveries in Homer's epics were so challenging that they severely tested the limits of our imagination and understanding. So unexpected was the quality and breadth of learning about astronomy and calendars that eventually spilled from the narrative that it was at first difficult to come to terms with the notion that such knowledge could have been preserved in ancient literature.

Notes

1   Butcher, S.H. & Lang, A. (trans), *The Odyssey of Homer* (London: Macmillan & Co., 1879) pp. xvii–xxiv: here real-time days were counted as 42.

2   Hesiod, *Works and Days*, trans by Evelyn-White, Hugh G. (1914), line 383.

3   Wender, Dorothea (trans), *Hesiod and Theoginis* (Hamondsworth: Penguin Classics, 1973), line 818.

4   Ibid., line 816.

4

ELEMENTS OF TIME
& A 19-YEAR ODYSSEY

There is unchallenged literary genius in Homer's stirring stories, but brilliance of a quite distinctive order is revealed in the manner in which he uses an elaborate structure to preserve – and conceal – a wealth of calendrical knowledge. In this chapter an exploration of narrative and data opens new perceptions about the organisation of time in the *Iliad* and the *Odyssey*. The concept introduced in Chapter 3 that the 40 'real-time' days of the *Odyssey* could be aligned to the phases of the moon provided the initial idea that other episodes in the narrative may follow a similar pattern and each of Odysseus' adventures might form part of a luni-solar calendar. Eventually we had accumulated sufficient material for our notion to become a hypothesis, but before that could be developed we explored alternative aspects to some of the conventions surrounding the *Odyssey*.

4.1 After 19 years away, Odysseus returns to the rocky shores of Ithaca. (Argonautis/Fotolia)

At the heart of Homer's calendrical system is a 19-year cycle which begins when Odysseus leaves home for Troy and ends when he is reunited with his wife, Penelope. After leaving Troy for the second time, he sails down the Aegean Sea, round treacherous Cape Malea at the foot of the Peloponnese, and into the realms of myths and monsters. Since the Golden Age of Greece there has been much speculation about Odysseus' homeward journey and over the centuries scholars and adventurers have tried to connect these mysterious lands and islands with places in and around the Mediterranean. We propose that Odysseus' metaphorical adventures occurred amongst the stars and constellations. Also, when attempts have been made to plot Odysseus' voyages on the seas of earth it has been acknowledged that the days he spends sailing along do not make much navigational sense. A solution to the mystery is found by matching his days at sea with the number of days between phases of the moon.

The fall of Troy is a central event in Homer's epics, but if such an event ever occurred in reality, convention suggests the city fell at about 1200 BC. There are, however, several levels to the city, one of which was flourishing *c.*2300 BC, and a case will be made for the oldest astronomical learning in the *Odyssey* dating back to that time.

The topics introduced above are expanded in the following pages and provide support for a reading of Odysseus' adventures in the form of a hypothetical annual calendar of the sun and moon, which is ingeniously embedded within the parameters of a 19-year luni-solar cycle. The final item in this chapter is a panel 'Calendars and the *Odyssey*', which lists discoveries concerning Homer's calendar system which will be introduced in the course of later chapters.

Returning Home in the 'Twentieth Year'

The ancient Greek method of counting the passing of the years can cause misunderstanding in modern times. Today the luni-solar cycle that spans the *Iliad* and the *Odyssey* is expressed as a period of 19 solar years, but this was not the case in Homer's Greece. The poet-astronomer says more than once that Odysseus will return home 'in the twentieth year', and the apparent contradiction of how arriving home 'in the twentieth year' can be recognised as the end of 19 solar years caused confusion in ancient times as well as our own. Other examples noted by Gilbert Murray include the 'double year', known as the *trietèris*, and the four-year period that regulated the Olympian and Pythian festivals as the *pentetèris* (five years).[1] In *Cretan Cults and Festivals*, R.F. Willetts further explains the confusion surrounding the counting of the passing years:

> There is clear evidence from literary, mythological and archaeological sources
> of a close connection between the octennium [period of eight years] and the

kingship. The most important and the most familiar of these allusions occurs in that passage of the *Odyssey* where Minos is described by Homer as a nine-year king, familiar of Zeus (Od. 9.179). Literally interpreted the word *enneoros* in this passage means 'for nine years', not 'for eight years.' But since, in reckoning intervals of time numerically, *the Greeks included both the terms separated by the interval (whereas we include only one)*, *enneoros* must mean 'intervals of eight years'. Similarly, the *ennaetèris*, though meaning literally 'a period of nine years', was a term defining the octennium or eight-year cycle. This passage was, however, variously interpreted, even in antiquity. But Plato, followed by Strabo and by most moderns, understood that Minos consulted with Zeus 'every ninth year'; that is to say, at each octennium.[2]

To add further confusion, this method of counting was not applied in every instance and the luni-solar cycle known as an *octaëteris* (eight years) was regarded as an eight-year period. Willetts quotes Sir James Frazer,[3] who said 'the existence of the term octaëteris is an example of the inconsistency of the Greeks in this matter, which caused ambiguity in antiquity, as it does for us'.

With all of this in mind, the time structure of the *Odyssey* is not at all straightforward and although the question of the 19-year cycle is resolved there are differing interpretations of other periods of time concerning the activities of Odysseus. These include the period from when Odysseus firsts leaves home to the fall of Troy, the period after the fall of Troy and the period that he spends with the witch Calypso. In this study we have used a conventional method of counting that includes setting the parameters of the *octaëteris* as an eight-year period.

It is no mean task to arrange the events of the *Odyssey* into chronological order, as Homer darts in and out of current time into blocks of historic times. Indeed the *Odyssey* is more than two-thirds done before Homer even describes the day that Odysseus first left home to join his comrades at the Siege of Troy. There are long periods, such as the years from when he left Ithaca to the opening of the *Iliad*, when little if anything is recorded about his activities. Similarly, accounts of Odysseus' life during the year he spends with Circe and the years he is held prisoner by Calypso are conspicuous by their absence.

These longer units of time are elements that enable Homer to construct a sophisticated 19-year luni-solar cycle that incorporates a detailed annual calendar which could have been used as a matrix for ancient calendar makers. Also built into the 19-year cycle are the four-year cycle known as an Olympiad (*pentetèris*) and an eight-year luni-solar cycle (*octaëteris*) which, in his exposition, also includes an eight-year cycle of the planet Venus. In addition he also defines the number of lunations in the Saros eclipse cycle. An outline of how in terms of plot and narrative the *Iliad* and the *Odyssey* were constructed around these complex cycles is seen in Fig. 2 and in greater detail in Chapters 6–14. Detail of luni-solar cycles and how Homer embeds in the *Odyssey* accurate data concerning them are discussed in Chapter 5.

Much of the information concerning the 19-year cycle and other periods of time is found within the pages of the *Odyssey* but important supportive detail can be gleaned from the *Iliad*. By combining these two sources it can be determined in chronological order when major events occurred during the 19-year cycle:

- It is 19 years from when, at a winter solstice, Odysseus first leaves home for Troy to his eventual return.
- Hector dies at the summer solstice in the ninth year of that cycle (after eight and a half years).
- Odysseus sails away from Troy at the end of the ninth year.
- Odysseus is on Circe's island of Aeaea for one year.
- Odysseus stays almost eight years on Calypso's island of Ogygia.
- In the final 40 'real-time' days, the *Odyssey* culminates at a winter solstice.

The calculation in years is:

Hector dies at midsummer 8.5 years after the siege begins	8.5 years
Troy falls six months later at midwinter	0.5 year
Odysseus spends a year on Circe's island	1.0 year
Odysseus is with Calypso almost eight years, which together with the days leading to the climax of the epic gives 8 full years – an *octaëteris*	8.0 years
Total	18.0 years

With 18 of the cycle's 19 years accounted for, this leaves one year during which all of Odysseus' other adventures after the fall of Troy had to take place. With Odysseus' alter ego as a personification of the moon in mind, we began to investigate the notion that each of his post-Troy adventures was linked to one of the lunations during a solar year. In other words, Homer was familiar with a system in which a solar calendar and a lunar calendar ran side by side.

This primary observation raised several questions, the most important being that of discovering a technique to reveal how Homer might have recorded in literary narrative the annual passage of the sun along the ecliptic, while at the same time incorporating a lunar calendar in the form of Odysseus' metaphorical adventures. The question of how Homer adjusted the 11-day shortfall of the 354-day lunar year with the 365 days of the solar year also needed to be resolved. After reading and re-reading the *Odyssey* an outline plan was formulated and eventually a model annual calendar based on narrative and numerical data was created. Analysis revealed that the hypothetical annual calendar was divided into two parts:

The first part: begins with the appearance of the first new crescent moon after a winter solstice when Troy has fallen. Six months later, and after a number of stirring exploits which occur during separate lunations, Odysseus arrives on

Circe's island at midsummer. Homer then puts the annual calendar on hold for a year while the 19-year cycle continues to tick on.

The second part: continues from when Odysseus leaves Circe's island and the annual calendar ends on his arrival on Calypso's island.

Odysseus' stay with Calypso introduces the eight-year luni-solar cycle, which is second only to the 19-year cycle in its importance in his epics. If the pursuit of accuracy in calendar making was a progressive matter then the *octaëteris* would appear to have been an earlier discovery. Although not so accurate as the 19-year cycle, it was a considerable advance on the older method of intercalation, the periodic insertion of an extra month into the lunar year to keep it in step with the solar year. The eight-year cycle also had the additional advantage of being allied to a cycle of the planet Venus, the third brightest object in the skies (see Chapter 5).

Translators at *Od.* 7.260 have expressed the time Odysseus spends with Calypso as seven years, plus such additional information as:

> … when the eighth came wheeling round (Robert Fagles)
> … when the eighth came round in its course (E.V. Rieu)
> … when the eighth year came in circling course (A.T. Murray)
> … when in the turning of time the eighth year had befallen me (Richmond Lattimore)
> … then came the eighth year on the wheel of heaven (Robert Fitzgerald)
> … when the eighth year came round in its course (S.H. Butcher & Andrew Lang)

These expressions of time have great literary merit but also a certain ambiguity. If Homer meant that Odysseus left Calypso precisely after seven years then why introduce in rather vague terms the 'coming round in its course' of the eighth year? With calendars in mind we suggest Odysseus did in fact leave *during* the eighth year.

If this were so then the time Odysseus spends with Calypso would be seven full years and most of the eighth, which, with the addition of the 40 'real-time' days leading to the climax of the *Odyssey*, would become the eight-year cycle. The images created by such phrases as the eighth year 'came in its circling course', the 'wheel of heaven', the eighth year 'came wheeling round' and 'the turning of time', very aptly and fortuitously describe the recurring nature of luni-solar cycles. This extended view of Odysseus' time with Calypso makes it possible to construct a credible timetable for the *Iliad–Odyssey* period, its inclusive annual calendar and *octaëteris*.

Elements of time

Homer's Cycle	Odysseus leaves home, Hector is killed, Troy falls.	◄— 9 years
	Annual calendar-1 Clash with Cicones, fleet hit by storms, Lotus Eaters Polyphemus, Aeolus Laestrygonians and Circe	◄— 6 months
	Odysseus spends one year with Circe	◄— 1 year
19 solar years and 235 lunations	**Annual calendar -2** Circe, Hades, Sirens, the Wandering Rocks, Scylla Cattle of the Sun, Charybdis	◄— 6 months
	Odysseus is with Calypso into the eighth year **Final 40 days** Gods agree to let Odysseus return home. He builds a raft, is wrecked in a storm, visits Phaeacia and returns to Ithaca. At cycle's end he is reunited with Penelope at the new crescent moon.	Odysseus with Calypso + days to climax of Odyssey = an 8-year cycle of the sun, moon & Venus

4.2 This chart shows how Homer's epics are arranged into units of time which incorporate a 19-year cycle of the sun and moon and an eight-year cycle of the sun, moon and Venus.

Adventures & Destinations in the Heavens

From antiquity to the present day, one persistent question about Odysseus' adventures on his journey home to Ithaca has been just where did each of them occur? After apparently sailing down the Aegean and rounding Cape Malea, Odysseus visits many places which have never been positively identified on charts of the seas and the lands of Greece and the wider Mediterranean. Strabo the geographer of the first century AD was amongst those who sought in vain to plot his course, and he quoted the famed astronomer Eratosthenes as saying,

'You will find the scene of the wanderings of Odysseus when you find the cobbler who sewed up the bag of the winds.'[4] Despite many centuries of conjecture and exploration, definite locations on earth have proved elusive for the homelands of such people as the Lotus Eaters, the Cyclopes and the witches Circe and Calypso.

An astronomical solution emerged from an observation that Odysseus' adventures largely occur after he has arrived on the shores of various lands or 'islands'. Rarely are these the safe havens that Odysseus hopes will provide food and water for his crews, and more often than not he has to overcome disaster or seek freedom from seduction and captivity before he can continue his journey home. These islands include Goat Island, Aeolia (the island home of the King of the Winds), Aeaea (the island of Circe), Thrinacia (the island of the sun god's cattle), Ogygia (the island of Calypso) and even Odysseus' own kingdom on the island of Ithaca. It was an exciting time when we concluded that the islands and lands of Odysseus' adventures were not on earth, but that each took place in the constellations of the starry heavens.

From these beginnings and Edna Leigh's assertion that Troy fell when the sun was in Aquarius, evolved the idea that each of Odysseus' adventures takes place during one of the lunations that occur while the sun is making its annual journey along the ecliptic; Homer was indeed constructing a luni-solar calendar and ingeniously keeps the 354 days of the lunar year in step with the 365 days of the solar year. The following table links Odysseus' lunar adventures to the solar year:

Table 1. Path of the sun and Odysseus' lunar adventures

(Winter Solstice)	
Aquarius–Pisces	Troy falls, clash with the Cicones
Pisces	Fleet hit by hurricane
Aries and Cetus	Cape Malea and the Lotus Eaters
(Spring Equinox)	
Auriga	Goat Island
Taurus	Polyphemus
Gemini	Aeolus, King of the Winds
Cancer	Laestrygonians sink 11 ships
(Summer Solstice)	
Leo – 1	Giant stag and Circe
Annual calendar on hold for one year as Odysseus stays with Circe	
(Summer Solstice)	
Leo – 2	Circe's warning and death of Elpenor
Virgo	Hades and ghosts of the dead
Libra	The Sirens
(Autumn Equinox)	
Scorpius	Wandering Rocks, Scylla, Charybdis
Ophiuchus–Sagittarius	Helios' island of Thrinacia

Sagittarius–Capricornus	At sea, no land in view
Aquarius	Return to Charybdis, Calypso's island
Annual calendar ends as Odysseus begins his stay with Calypso for almost eight years	
40 'real-time' days	
Sagittarius–Capricornus	Gods allow Odysseus to return home
Capricornus	Odysseus leaves Calypso, raft wrecked, the Phaeacians, departs for Ithaca
Capricornus–Aquarius	Dark of moon: Odysseus disguised as a beggar
Aquarius	New crescent moon: Odysseus revealed and reunited with Penelope at the winter solstice

Stations of the Sun: Days of the Month & Months of the Year

The discovery that Odysseus' travels are not on earth but amongst the stars and constellations of the zodiac raised the question of how Homer could create a calendar system in which time was calculated according to both the sun and the moon. A solution was found as follows:

> **Lunar year:** The passing of lunar months through the phases from new crescent moon to the dark period is linked to the rhythm of Odysseus' adventures. At the appearance of each crescent a new adventure begins with Odysseus generally coming to no harm during the days up to full moon and beyond but as the moon wanes towards the dark period his fortunes take a turn for the worse.
> **Solar year:** To link solar time with lunar time, the scenarios for each of Odysseus' adventures are set amongst the stars through which the sun passes during the course of a lunation. Homer's fulsome images of the lands and islands on which Odysseus finds himself are proposed as brilliant metaphorical descriptions of constellations, largely on or close to the ecliptic. For instance, star charts reveal that the lavish portrayal of Goat Island as a bucolic paradise is a fine metaphor for the beautiful star-studded constellation of Auriga, through which runs the Milky Way. On the other hand, when Odysseus encounters the giant Laestrygonians the sun is passing through the relatively dark-sky constellation of Cancer and their land is described as a bleak and rocky stronghold. In the lunation that takes place during Odysseus' encounter with one-eyed Polyphemus, Homer invokes metaphorical images of Taurus, the Pleiades, the Hyades and the bright red star Aldebaran, α Tauri. In brief:

- Days of the month are marked by phases of the moon.
- The months of the year are each linked to Odysseus' lunar adventures.
- The sun's journey along the ecliptic from winter solstice to winter solstice records the passing of the years.

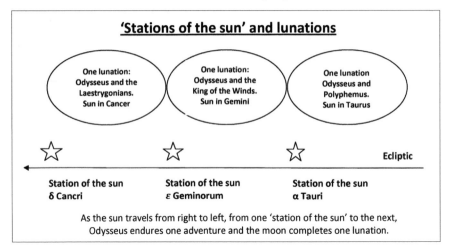

4.3 An example of 'Stations of the Sun' and lunations.

In support of this premise, a study of constellations in and about the zodiacal band reveals a series of relatively prominent stars on or close to the ecliptic, each of which is about 30° apart and it takes the sun some 29–30 days to travel between them. In our calendrical model, a new lunar month (adventure of Odysseus) begins when the sun reaches one of these prominent stars which we refer to as a 'station of the sun'. Fig. 4.3 shows the progress of the sun as it passes through three stations, in Taurus, Gemini and Cancer. At the same time there are three lunations and the scenarios for Odysseus' three adventures are with Polyphemus, Aeolus, King of the Winds, and the Laestrygonians. In this way the low point of each of Odysseus' adventures takes place towards the end of a lunation while the sun is travelling some 29–30 days along the ecliptic from one station of the sun to the next.

Summary: calendars of the moon and sun running together

As the moon, represented by Odysseus, proceeds through one lunation from new crescent to dark period, the sun travels some 30° along the ecliptic. The scenarios for Odysseus' adventures are Homer's extended metaphorical descriptions of the constellations in which the sun lies during a particular lunation. By the end of a year the rhythm of Odysseus' exploits will have recorded a lunar calendar and Homer's sequential descriptions of the constellations of the zodiac will have marked the annual passage of the sun along the ecliptic. See Fig. 4.3 and the Ship's Log (Appendix 1).

While the stars that Homer might have used to plot the path of the sun are not named, our choices have been made on the reasonable grounds of their position and magnitude. Homer would not have perceived the zodiac in the modern manner, in which the zodiacal band is conveniently divided into twelve 30° sections. Star patterns do not lend themselves to fitting neatly into a 30° box and current star charts show how a number of constellations overlap and may include stars from constellations not regarded as belonging in the zodiac. A prime example of this is found in the division named after the constellation of Scorpius; only about one-third of the stars of Scorpius are on or near to the ecliptic and a large part of that division contains stars from Ophiuchus. In this work the zodiac is seen as a continuous band of sky, with the result that the sun can apparently travel through the stars of more than one constellation during one month.

The table below lists the stars designated as 'stations of the sun' and their links to the adventures of Odysseus. It will be seen in later chapters how Homer adjusts the 354 days of the lunar year with the 365 days of the solar year so that both the lunar year and solar year end on the same day.

Table 2: 'Stations of the Sun' and Lunations

	Station of the sun	Lunar adventure of Odysseus
Winter Solstice	β/α Aquarii	Troy falls
	γ Piscium	Raids the Cicones
	η Piscium	Fleet hit by a hurricane
	α Piscium	Rounds Cape Malea
	Aries/Cetus	Arrives at the Lotus Eaters
Spring Equinox	η Tauri	
	α Aurigae	Hunts for goats
	α Tauri	Polyphemus eats six men but is blinded
	ε Geminorum	Aeolus, King of the Winds
	δ Cancri	11 ships sunk by Laestrygonian giants
Summer Solstice	α Leonis	
	ρ Leonis	Meets the witch Circe
Narrative break for a year		
Summer Solstice	α Leonis, δ Leonis	Elpenor dies in a fall, Leaves Circe
	β Virginis	Visit to Hades begins
	α Virginis	Visit to Hades ends
	α and β Librae	Lured by the Sirens
Autumn Equinox	β Scorpii	Sails between the Wandering Rocks.
	Milky Way	Sights Charybdis
	α Scorpii	Scylla eats 6 men
	Milky Way	Marooned on Helios' island
	σ Sagittarii	Men kill the cattle of the sun god
	θ Capricorni	Zeus destroys Odysseus' remaining ship
Narrative break for almost eight years		Odysseus stays with Calypso
	δ Capricorni	Entertains the Phaeacians
Winter Solstice	β/ α Aquarii	And finally, Odysseus fires an arrow through a row of 12 axe-handle heads

Days at Sea & the Lunar Month

Earth-bound researchers have long been puzzled by the number of days Odysseus spends at sea voyaging between various islands and lands in the Aegean and Mediterranean. Homer does not measure time by weeks but he does specify numbers of days: 'We sailed for six days and on the seventh'; 'I drifted for nine days and on the tenth'; 'I sailed for seven days and ten and on the eighteenth'. In earthly terms, Homer sometimes lists too many or too few sailing days for voyages between Mediterranean lands and islands.

On one occasion so many days are noted that it has been said that Odysseus sailed through the Pillars of Hercules and on to the island of Madeira. Tim Severin, who undertook a modern voyage of Homeric exploration, said, 'even if [Odysseus'] adventures were imaginary did Homer think that they took place somewhere real? Or was his geography, like his fantastic creatures, without any footing in this world?' He goes on to say Odysseus' 'vessel jumps up and down the length of the Mediterranean like the knight on a chessboard. It skips over inconvenient land masses, skids around capes, travels at speeds that would do credit to a modern cruise liner in its attempts to link up sites that appear to be suitable.'[5]

By releasing Odysseus from the shackles of the earth and propelling him into the skies, these 'sailing days' become parts of the lunar month and, from time to time, progress Odysseus through a lunation.

Phases within the lunar month can be divided in the following manner:

Old crescent to first quarter	=	9 days
New crescent to first quarter	=	6 days
New crescent to full	=	13/14 days
First quarter to third quarter	=	16/17 days
Third quarter to dark moon	=	6 days
Third quarter to new crescent	=	9 days
Moon absent (dark moon)	=	2/3 days
Old crescent to new crescent	=	4/5 days

Therefore, when Odysseus sails for 'seven days and ten' the lunar month is advanced from the first quarter to the third quarter. Having discovered that 'sailing days' could be linked to periods of the lunar month, it became apparent that the days Odysseus spends resting or in disguise were also linked to the moon; such phrases as 'We rested for two days and on the third' represent the dark period of two to three days that the moon cannot be seen during each lunation. Equally, when Odysseus, our lunar icon, arrives in Ithaca at the beginning of a dark period he is disguised as a beggar and cannot even be 'seen' by his wife or close friends until the arrival of the new crescent. The following table gives references to the times Homer mentions intervals of days which can be deduced as particular parts of a lunar month:

Table 3: Days in narrative as part of a lunar month

Passing of one day	Odysseus sleeps, rests or hides for 2-3 days	'6 days and on 7th'	'9 days and on 10th'	'17 days and on 18th'	'for a month'
Lotus Eaters: 9.90	Drifts at sea: 5.388	Laestrygonians: 10.80	Alcinous: 7.253	Odysseus: 5.278	Aeolus' islamd: 10.14
Laestrygonians: 10.105	Hurricane: 9.74	Feast on cattle: 12. 399	Aeolus: 10.28	Achilles' funeral: 24.63	Helios' island: 12.325
Scylla: 12.245	Polyphemus: 9.250	Lying tale: 14.250	Cape Malea: 9.82		
Charybdis: 12.430	Circe's island: 10.142	Eumaeus: 15.475	Ship's keel: 12.447		
	Eumaeus' hut: 17.515	*Iliad*[6]	Threspotians: 14.314		

Apart from when Homer specifies a particular period of days during a lunation, he generally lets the phases of the moon and the rhythm of Odysseus' exploits take care of the passing of time. With the appearance of the new crescent moon and the beginning of a new adventure and lunar month, together with such phrases as 'and presently we reached the island of Aeolia' (10.1), his audiences would have known the time of month from the visible phases of the moon and the time of year from the story linked to a particular constellation. In the case of Aeolia, the constellation is Gemini and in our model calendar is the fourth month of the year.

Sighting of the Moon

On a number of occasions Homer is so precise in introducing Odysseus, the lunar icon, into narrative that it is possible to establish the phase of moon and to determine the time of day or night when certain events occur (see Table 4 below). For instance, when Odysseus' fleet is driven on to the shores of the island of Thrinacia, Homer says that the night 'is two-thirds gone' (12.312). This signals that on Odysseus' arrival on Thrinacia the moon is in its third quarter and appears in the latter part of the night. Another instance of pinpointing the time of night occurs when he tells a lying tale to the pig-keeper Eumaeus (14.483). Earlier, on his arrival in Ithaca, he is transformed into a beggar as the moon enters its dark period. The most dramatic lunar event of all happens just a few days later as the dark period ends the new crescent moon becomes visible in the late evening sky. At that moment Odysseus casts off his disguise during the violent climatic scene of the slaughter of the suitors and is revealed as his true self. Such information is valuable in confirming the progress of a lunar calendar.

4.4 The astro-myths of Homer's *Odyssey* are woven around the fall of the ancient citadel of Troy..

Table 4. Phases of the moon

Phase of moon	Location of the rising moon	When the moon can be seen
Third quarter	Southern skies at sunrise	Third part of the night until noon
Old crescent	Eastern sky	Early morning before sunrise
Dark moon	Unseen	Unseen
New crescent	Western sky	Early evening, for a short time at sunset
First quarter	Southern skies at sunset	Midday and first half of night
Full moon	Eastern horizon at sunset	All during the night from evening to morning

2300 BC: Origins of the Oldest Astronomy in Homer's Epics

Edna Leigh's papers state her belief that the oldest calendrical material in the *Odyssey* reflected astronomical events that could only have occurred at around 2300 BC, some 1500 years before Homer's own times. Her work began long before the advent of computer programmes that quickly show the day-by-day positions of stars and constellations as they were seen from Greece and the eastern Mediterranean thousands of years ago. She had to calculate her dates with pencil and paper.

There is no compelling evidence from the excavated ruins that Troy was ever attacked by a Greek army led by a king named Agamemnon, but there is a consensus that it was severely damaged, possibly by earthquake, in the decades around 1200 BC. This is usually taken as the era of the Trojan War but evidence that the city was flourishing many centuries earlier can be linked to the pioneer archaeologist Heinrich Schliemann. Amongst his discoveries was a hoard which he erroneously claimed to be the treasure of King Priam and included jewellery that had once belonged to Helen of Troy. The jewels were found just outside the city but whether they were discovered as a single cache or whether Schliemann added finds from other excavations to give more substance to his romantic claims is a matter for conjecture. However, the British archaeologist Frank Calvert, a contemporary of Schliemann's, compared pottery from Ur to that found at Troy and concluded that Troy II, the level at which the jewels were found, could be dated to *c.*2200 BC. That date is some 1000 years before the assumed time of 'Homeric Troy'.[7] Michael Wood notes that when American archaeologists re-excavated the same level in the 1930s they 'found scattered gold in almost every room, as if the inhabitants of Troy II had fled in panic before an onslaught which engulfed their city: so Troy II remains a possibility for the site of the so-called 'Jewels of Helen'. Schliemann's find showed that towards the end of the third millennium there was a prosperous city guarding the entrance to the Bosphorous during an era when the sun rose on midsummer's day, with Regulus, α Leonis, and when the Pleiades in Taurus marked the spring equinox.

While the story of the sacking of Troy was historically important to Homer as a narrative theme, his knowledge of astronomy and calendars points to a connection with much older civilisations of Mesopotamia. Edna Leigh was not alone in her view that the skills and enduring stories of the poet-astronomers made it possible for collective wisdom to be orally transmitted from then to the time of Homer. The origin of the oldest constellations known to the Greeks has been a much debated topic but archaeological evidence shows that such peoples as the Sumerians had considerable knowledge of astronomy in the third millennium. In 270 BC the poet Aratus wrote a 730-line poem in honour of Eudoxus of Cnidos, the mathematician and astronomer who lived *c.*409–356 BC. In his *Phaenomena*, Aratus put into verse an astronomical treatise by Eudoxus and named 45 constellations and a number of stars.[8] The source of Eudoxus' information was said to be an ancient celestial globe which originated either in Babylon or was 'brought back from Egypt'. The globe, if it ever existed, has long been lost.

In his paper on 'The origins of the constellations', Michael Ovenden[9] of Glasgow University indicated that the skies described by Aratus could have been seen between 3000 BC and 1800 BC at a latitude between 34°N and 37°N, a band that includes Babylon and Crete. The constellations, he said, were an ordered mapping of the skies that could have been used for an agricultural calendar and navigation, and could have been devised *c.*2800 BC, when the pole star was Thuban, α Draconis. He put forward a claim for the seafaring Minoans, a people who lived at the right time and the right latitude, as the creators of the patterns of stars we know as constellations. When Ovenden addressed the question of how learning could have survived from early Minoan times to the fourth century BC, he said: 'the tradition of the constellations must have been handed down by word of mouth for two millennia.' Archie E. Roy, also of the University of Glasgow, has said that 'Phaenomena' leaves little doubt that it refers to a celestial sphere of about 2000 BC, with an uncertainty of 200 years each way.[10]

Other sources give credit to the Sumerians:

> who invented the cuneiform writing system shortly before 3000 BC and thereby laid the foundation of what is characteristic of Mesopotamian civilisation, [and] were plainly the first to give names to the constellations, names still familiar to us in some cases as the Bull (Taurus), the Lion (Leo) and the Scorpion (Scorpio).[11]

Of the constellations in the zodiac, Robert Hannah says: 'The names of these zodiacal figures as they have come down to us (Aries, Taurus, Gemini etc) are simply Latin translations of earlier Greek names (Krios, Tauros, Didymoi etc) which in their turn are translations of the Babylonian names for these groups of stars.'[12] So far as calendars are concerned, R.F. Willetts indicates a link between the Minoans and later Greek learning:

> In Greek antiquity the year was divided into 12 [lunar] months alternating between 29 and 30 days, the deficit of eleven days being made good by intercalating a thirteenth month in three years out of every eight. There is also much evidence in support of the view that this luni-solar calendar based on an octennial [eight-year] cycle, goes back into the Minoan period.[13]

While it is possible — or even likely — that the Minoans of Crete were the conduit along which the astronomy of Mesopotamia was passed down to the Greeks, it is a notion not without difficulties. The Minoans, a cultured and prosperous people, left behind impressive archaeological evidence but their origins are still a mystery

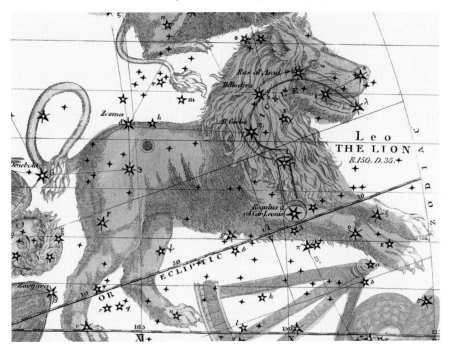

4.5 The constellation of Leo, from Elijah H. Burritt's *Atlas of the Heavens*, 1835.

and their language, inscribed on Linear A tablets, has never been deciphered. Their civilisation went into decline *c.*1600 BC after a disastrous volcanic eruption on the nearby island of Thera (Santorini) and they slipped from the pages of history when the Greek-speaking Mycenaeans of mainland Greece became dominant.

Of the suggestion that the astronomy and calendars preserved in the *Odyssey* had at least some of its origins *c.*2300 BC, Anna Jenson, an expert on the languages and astronomy of ancient Mediterranean countries, said:

> You are proposing a dating saturated with implications: that Homer's *Odyssey* is a product of an era when the powerful mercantile cities of Byblos, Ebla, Mari, Hamazi, Akkad, Kish and many more, controlled Syro-Turkey and Iraq. This was an era of literacy and organised archiving of administrative records, poetic literature, gazetteers, and scientific manuals.

An important clue to the era of Homer's astronomy lies in Edna Leigh's original calendar of the 40 'real-time' days. One column carries the heading 'Position of the Sun' and reveals that at the end of the *Odyssey*, when Odysseus kills the suitors at a winter solstice, the sun had just moved into the constellation of Aquarius. Armed with a specific event, we began a computer search to more accurately fix the time of the foundations of the astronomy of the *Odyssey*. With the winter solstice defined, the equinoxes and summer solstice soon fell into place and it required only a little patience and the tapping of a computer keyboard to come to the conclusion that the basic structure of Homer's calendars could have arisen within a couple of centuries on either side of 2300 BC when:

> The winter solstice lay in Aquarius.
> The spring equinox lay in the Pleiades in Taurus.
> The summer solstice lay at Regulus, α Leonis.
> The autumn equinox lay in Scorpius.

Further investigation revealed that the equinoxes and solstices were crucial markers for Homer's calendar year and that he reserved memorable tales for all them:

> Winter solstice – the taking of Troy.
> Spring equinox – the blinding of Polyphemus.
> Summer solstice – the killing of a giant stag and Circe outwitted.
> Autumn equinox – monstrous Scylla devours six men.

Edna Leigh concluded that the latter part of the third millennium was the time of the oldest material in the *Odyssey*, when she associated events in narrative with constellations in which the sun lay at the equinoxes and solstices in that era. From the annual calendar beginning at a winter solstice, when the sun was in Aquarius, each of Odysseus' subsequent adventures can be closely identified with Homer's metaphorical descriptions of the individual constellations through which the sun would pass in the course of a year. It is worth noting that in *Homer's Secret Iliad* these authors independently concluded that metaphorical astronomical events in that epic could only have happened at that time.[14]

Important Events in the Heavens

The likelihood that part of the astronomy of the *Odyssey* was a thousand years older than the presumed date of the Trojan War raises the question of whether there were noteworthy astronomical events *c.*2300 BC that might have inspired ancient people to preserve them as part of an oral treatise. A computer programme revealed three observations that would have been recognised by watchers of the skies studying the heavens not only for practical astronomical purposes but also for signs on which to conjure the prognostications on which they based astrological forecasts.

The first significant observation concerns the constellation of Leo and its most prominent star, Regulus, α Leonis. It would have been a memorable event for ancient watchers of the sky when the sun on the day of the summer solstice rose with Regulus, the star which outshines every other on the ecliptic and was in

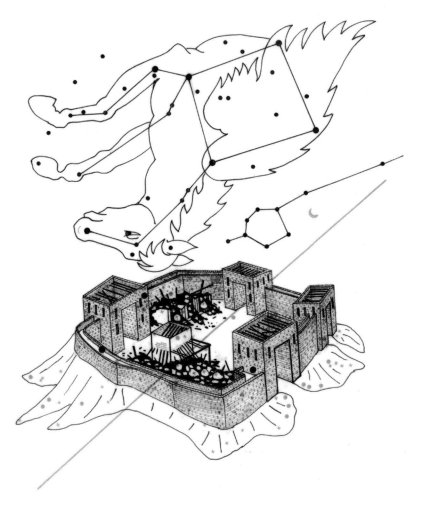

4.6 The constellation of Pegasus is poised threateningly above Aquarius (Homer's Troy). Was Pegasus the inspiration for the wooden horse of Troy? The line running diagonally through Troy is the ecliptic, the path of the sun. (By GG-R)

ancient cultures linked to kingship and believed to rule the affairs of the heavens.[15] Regulus gained its prominence in human and celestial affairs from around 2600 BC to 2000 BC and, more precisely, *c.*2300 BC, when the sun and Regulus rose together on midsummer's day. With Regulus pointing the summer solstice in 2300 BC, markers for the spring and autumn equinoxes fell into place but no prominent star marked the winter solstice which lay between β and α Aquarii. There was, though, a stunning surprise, for poised threateningly above Aquarius, Homer's place in the heavens for the citadel of Troy, stand the stars of Pegasus, the magical horse that might even have been the inspiration for the wooden horse of Troy. The second observation that could have been made by astronomers of old concerns the

4.7 Minoans and the cult of the bull, from a wall painting at the palace of Knossos, Crete.

precession of the equinoxes and which over time had possibly caused great alarm and brought fears of impending doom and disaster in those superstitious times. For more than 1500 years the sun at the vernal equinox, the first day of spring, had been amongst the stars of Taurus, the magnificent constellation which even then was linked to mythology. Indeed at *c.*3200 BC, Aldebaran, the red eye of the bull and the brightest star in Taurus, would have risen with the sun at the spring equinox, and like the sun rising with Regulus in midsummer, would no doubt have been regarded as an omen of great consequence. As the centuries passed, observers would have become increasingly aware that at the spring equinox the sun was slowly moving away from Aldebaran and by 2300 BC it had moved into the Pleiades, an asterism well away from the main body of Taurus. Because of precession of the equinoxes the sun appears to move over many centuries in a clockwise direction against a background of stars and this eventually leads to changes in the constellations in which the sun lies at the solstices and equinoxes. It would have been apparent in ancient times that at some time in the future the spring equinox would move out of Taurus entirely and into the relatively insignificant stars of Aries. From ancient times in the near east, the influence of Taurus and bull worship was a common feature and in the Sumerian *Epic of Gilgamesh* (*c.*2600 BC), the Bull of Heaven killed by the eponymous hero and his friend is believed to be a direct reference to the constellation. The Minoans of Crete acknowledged their veneration of the heavenly beast in the mythology of the bull of Minos, artefacts of horned bulls found at Knossos and a glorious wall painting of traditional Cretan 'bull dancers' who performed dangerous acrobatics over the horns of these symbolic animals. The spring equinox in Taurus also influences Homer's telling of the wonderful story of the one-eyed Polyphemus, which contains a wealth of astronomical metaphor.

The third observation concerns precession of the equinoxes which not only leads to a shift in the constellations in which the equinoxes and solstices lie, but also to a change of the star which acts as a pointer to the North Pole. The pole star *c.*2300 BC was Thuban, α Draconis; today it is Polaris, α Ursae Minoris. In the context of the *Odyssey*, Calypso in her navigation instructions to Odysseus mentions two constellations, Boötes and the Wain (Ursa Major), whose stars can be used to easily locate Thuban, as we will later show. Homer's story of Elpenor, the drunken young sailor who falls to his death from the roof of a house, also conceals another pointer to Thuban. At the time of Homer the North Pole lay in an area of sky lacking prominent stars. It may seen curious why narrative should identify a pole star that was at its most accurate more than 1000 years earlier, but even in much later centuries it would have drawn the eye towards celestial north. The discovery of precession is attributed to Hipparchus, the Greek astronomer of the second century, but narrative in the *Iliad* suggests that even if Homer did not know the cause of precession he was aware of its visible effects.[16]

Astronomers of ancient times had an ingenious way of determining the position of the sun against a background of stars even during the day when sunlight blocked stars from sight. Their method used the heliacal settings and risings of constellations on the path of the sun and was further refined by selecting a particular star within a zodiacal constellation which lay on or near the path of the sun. For instance, when Regulus makes its heliacal setting it can be seen briefly after sunset on the western horizon before disappearing below the horizon. Some 40 days later Regulus makes its heliacal rising when it can be seen briefly on the eastern horizon, just before its stars are hidden by the light of the rising sun. By using their observational skills, astronomers of ancient times had little difficulty in determining when the sun rose with Regulus or any other star in the zodiac.

In the following chapters it will be noticed that days and months of the year given for the solstices and equinoxes are not the same as those of today. Because of an effect known as the 'obliquity of the earth's axis', the days of the year on which the equinoxes and solstices occur change over long periods of time. Today the earth's axis is inclined at 23° 26', but *c.*2300 BC, it was approximately 23° 57'. Today, the winter and summer solstices occur on or about 22 December and 21 June, while the spring and autumn equinoxes fall on or about 21 March and 22 September. At *c.*2300 BC, and reckoning by the Gregorian calendar, the winter solstice fell on 9 January, the summer solstice on 14 July, the spring equinox on 10 April and the autumn equinox on 11 October. These are the dates used in the Ship's Log (see Appendix 1) to plot the path of the sun. The Gregorian calendar adjusted to compensate for precession of the equinoxes is used throughout our study and data is derived from 'The Sky' computer programme by Software Bisque.

Table 5. Solstices and equinoxes 2300 BC to AD 2009

	*c.*2300 BC[17] Origins of the astro-myths of the *Odyssey*	*c.*1250 BC	*c.*725 BC (Homer's era)	AD 2010
Winter solstice	Aquarius, α/β Aquarii	Aquarius→Capricornus	Capricornus	Sagittarius →Scorpius
Spring equinox	Taurus, Pleiades	Taurus→Aries	Aries	Pisces→Aquarius
Summer solstice	Leo, α Leonis	Leo→Cancer	Cancer	Gemini→Taurus
Autumn equinox	Scorpius	Virgo→Libra	Libra	Virgo→Leo

Searching for a Model 19-year Cycle

With the origins of Homer's astronomy attributed to the third millennium, there remained the challenge of discovering a more precise time for a 19-year luni-solar cycle, which began and ended at a winter solstice and a new crescent moon. With the help of computer-generated charts we began a search over the two centuries on either side of 2300 BC and discovered that during those 400 years there were perhaps 20 such cycles that would have met requirements. The search was narrowed by including Venus in the criteria for when Odysseus returns to Ithaca the Morning Star is visible in the sky. A further search eventually revealed a 19-year cycle that began in 2314 BC and ended in 2295 BC, when Venus appeared as a 'morning star', followed a few days later by a new crescent moon at a winter solstice. Whether the 19-year cycle we discovered is the particular cycle embedded in Homer's astro-myths, or whether he was influenced by a similar cycle at a different time, or even whether he and his predecessors created a theoretical cycle, is not known and never likely to be. Nevertheless, the selected 19-year cycle between 2314 and 2295 BC can be linked with surprising accuracy to the metaphorical activities of Odysseus.

Calendars & the *Odyssey*: a Summary of Discoveries

In this chapter we have outlined the organisation of time in the *Iliad-Odyssey* cycle and introduced some of the important themes that support a projection of the *Odyssey* as a great work of literature into which is woven wide-ranging detail of an ancient luni-solar calendar system. The limits of the astronomical and calendrical knowledge concealed in the epic are still open and it is our belief that more remains to be found.

    The story of progress so far is told in following chapters.

Calendars and the Odyssey: Summary of Discoveries

Long-lost knowledge discovered in the *Odyssey* includes:

- The importance of encoded numerical data.
- Odysseus' iconic role in a 19-year cycle of the sun and moon.
- An annual luni-solar calendar.
- Defining the number of days in lunar and solar years.
- Synchronisation of the lunar year (354 days) with the solar year (365 days).
- 'Full' lunar months and 'hollow' lunar months.
- The rhythm of Odysseus' adventures linked to phases of the moon.
- Eight-year cycles of the sun, moon and Venus, and the four-year Olympiad.
- Projection of a 96-year cycle of the sun, moon and Venus.
- Lunations in the Saros eclipse cycle.
  2300 BC and the origins of the oldest astronomy of the *Odyssey*.
- How Odysseus the sailor used the stars to find celestial north.
- π in the sky and one-eyed Polyphemus.

Homer's Secret Odyssey provides answers to other puzzles about the epic:

- Where does Odysseus sail on his long journey home from Troy?
- Where are the lands and islands on which his adventures take place?
- What is significant about the diminishing number of Odysseus' men and the destruction of his ships?
- Why is Odysseus disguised as a beggar when he arrives home in Ithaca?
- Why did Homer describe an impossible feat of archery?
- Why does Penelope, the wife of Odysseus, wait patiently for his return?
- How old is Helen of Troy as the *Odyssey* draws to a close?

Notes

1 Murray, Gilbert, *The Rise of the Greek Epic* (Oxford: Oxford University Press, 1907; 4th edn 1934; reprinted 1961), pp. 211–2.

2 Willetts, R.F., *Cretan Cults and Festivals* (London: Routledge & Kegan Paul, 1962), pp. 92–3.

3 Frazer, Sir James G., *The Golden Bough* (New York: Macmillan, 1922) pp. 58–92.

4 Strabo, *The Geography of Strabo*, trans Horace Leonard Jones, Loeb Classical Library (Cambridge MA: Harvard University Press, 1917–32), 1.2.15. This quotation is a reference to the bag of winds given to Odysseus by Aeoleus. See Chapter 9.

5 Severin, Tim, *The Ulysses Voyage: Sea Search for the Odyssey* (New York: E.P. Dutton, 1987), p. 22.

6 The phrases 'for six days and on the seventh' and 'for nine days and on the tenth' are also found in the *Iliad* on six occasions.

7 Trail, David, *Schliemann of Troy* (London: John Murray, 1995), pp. 102–24, 304–5 & 307. Also, Wood, Michael, *In Search of the Trojan War* (London: BBC Books, 1985), pp. 14–6 & 55–61.

8 *Homer's Secret Iliad*, the 45 Greek and Trojan regiments which fought at Troy are linked to 45 constellations, 'Warriors as Constellations', pp. 123–55.

9 Ovenden, Michael, 'The Origin of the Constellations', in *The Philosophical Journal*, Vol. 3, No 1 (1965), pp. 1–18.

10 Roy, Archie E., 'The Origin of the Constellations', in *Vistas in Astronomy*, Vol. 27 (1984), pp. 171–97.

11 Britton, J. & Walker, C., 'Astronomy and Astrology in Mesopotamia', edited by C. Walker, *Astronomy before the Telescope* (British Museum Press, 1996), p. 42. Additional sources reveal that the constellation now known as Taurus was, to the Sumerians, GU.ANNA (the Bull of Heaven); Leo = UR.GULA (the Lion); Scorpius = GIR.TAB (clawer, cutter); and Aquarius the water carrier = GU-LA (Lord of the Waters).

12 Hannah, Robert, *Greek and Roman Calendars* (London: Gerald Duckworth, 2005), p. 9.

13 Willetts, R.F., *The Civilization of Ancient Crete*, (London: Phoenix, 2004), p. 127.

14 *Homer's Secret Iliad*, Chapter 7, p. 190ff.

15 Allen, R.H., *Star Names, their Lore and Meaning* (New York: Dover, 1963 reprint), p. 255ff.

16 *Homer's Secret Iliad*, pp. 63–8.

17 Schultz, J., *Movement and Rhythms of the Stars* (Edinburgh: Floris, 1986), p. 30. (Data for 'Table 1: Solstices and Equinoxes 2300 BC to AD 2007'.)

5

HOMER'S WIZARDRY WITH NUMBERS

On his homeward journey Odysseus endures many trials and torments, more than once comes close to a terrible death and even when he reaches Ithaca there is still much to overcome. Carried along by a stirring flow of narrative, the reader may not linger over the many numbers scattered throughout epic. Homer includes, for instance, a precise count of goats killed in a hunt, a roll call of suitors idling in Odysseus' palace, and an inventory of trees and vines on a country farm. Over the centuries these and much other data have attracted only modest consideration. It is important to note, however, that while translations of the *Odyssey* reflect the literary styles of the times in which they were made, the data they contain remain consistent. An example of this can be seen from the numbers 3, 12, 9 and 10 contained in translations of the same event by scholars of the sixteenth and twentieth centuries:

5.1 The Minoan builders of the palace at Knossos in Crete would have required arithmetical skills as demanding as those needed to create calendar data. (Loshkaryov Sergey/Fotolia)

To our fleet we flew
Our crooked bows took, long-piled darts, and drew
Ourselves in *three parts* out; when, by the grace
that God vouchsafed, we made a gainful chace.
Twelve ships we had, and every ship had *nine*
fat goats allotted [it], *ten only mine.* (Od 9.233)
From the translation of the Odyssey *by George Chapman (1559?–1634)*

At once we went and took from the ships curved bows and javelins with long
sockets, and arranging ourselves in *three divisions*
cast about, and the god granted us the game we longed for.
Now there were *twelve ships* that went with me, and for each one *nine goats*
Were portioned out, but *I alone had ten* for my portion.
From the Odyssey *(9.156) translated by Richmond Lattimore, 1965*

Homer's Secret Odyssey makes a sound claim that numerical data was deliberately embedded and encoded in the *Odyssey* to preserve accurate observations of cycles of the sun, moon and Venus. In turn, this data gives technical support to a metaphorical reading of the experiences of Odysseus as a discourse on calendars. In this chapter a sampling is given of instances where Homer cleverly, cunningly and successfully conceals the secrets of the *Odyssey*.

Calendars are dependant upon accurate counting and a mastery of numbers, and the rediscovery of the purpose of Homer's data confirms his arithmetical brilliance and genius as a calendar maker. That ancient peoples were capable of sophisticated methods of calculation is reflected in their achievements in fields outside astronomy. The magnificent palaces of Knossos and Phaistos in Crete and fortresses such as those at Mycenae and Tiryns on the mainland were built during the second millennium BC and would not have been constructed by guesswork. The skilled craftsmen who built and designed them would have required at least some of the expertise which is practised today by civil engineers, surveyors, architects, estimators of quantities and suppliers of labour and materials – services which demand considerable arithmetical agility. The shipbuilders who constructed the multi-oared craft of Homer's times would, too, have required a firm grasp of design and mensuration.

Numbers & Objects

Impressive support for our model is found in the listings and detailed counting of sailors, ships, suitors, princes, sheep, cattle, goats, boars, sows, dogs, trees, vines, gifts, weapons and clothing. Whilst the objects linked to the numbers are valuable as *aides memoire* and categorisation, it is the numbers themselves which are the key to preserving essential information. For instance, in the following examination of a hunt for goats, Homer lists three parties of men and 12 ships, with nine goats awarded to each ship, plus 10 more for Odysseus. In this case, Goat Island will be linked in memory to the structure of the lunar year and an important link to the solar year. The incident, like others throughout the epic, is memorable and unique which makes it easier to recall without confusion, data associated with specific calendrical matters. When this observation is applied to other passages from the *Odyssey* the breadth of the accumulated knowledge of calendars and astronomy known to Homer and the Greeks of the eighth century BC becomes apparent.

To complicate matters, calendrical data is not found in a logical sequence and is embedded throughout the epic. For instance, when Odysseus arrives on Goat Island the annual calendar is in its third month but only then does that data provides basic detail of the seasons, months and days of the lunar year. Similarly, it is only in the last pages of the *Odyssey*, when Odysseus visits the farm of his father, Laertes, that Homer discloses vital information about the number of lunations in luni-solar cycles. In other words, before the poet-astronomers could combine data with the flow of narrative they would have had to be as familiar with the epic's calendrical structure as they were with its literary content. Whether this was a deliberate technique to increase the level of encryption or whether epic as a vehicle for the preservation of knowledge had developed in this manner over the centuries is an open question.

The storytellers of pre-literate Greece would have been familiar with methods of memorisation that enabled them to recite at will large amounts of narrative. Evidence of one technique of memory in post-Homeric times is found in the work of the poet Simonides of Ceos (*c.*556–468 BC) who believed that memory could be assisted by assigning striking images to the data to be remembered and then placing them in the rooms of an imaginary house. By letting the mind wander through these 'rooms', the images and knowledge associated with them could be recalled.[1] Homer's association of data to a wide range of objects possibly served a similar purpose.

Homer's selection of numbers, both single and within groups, was critical and enabled the poet-astronomers to make calculations concerning calendars and complex cycles that are indeed sublime. Each number was selected with such precision that even if one number in each group was different by only one digit Homer's task of preserving calendar data would have failed. In this chapter we briefly examine the question of probability, which indicates that any notion Homer might have plucked his data out of thin air can be rejected by the truly astronomical odds involved. Homer does not use fractions in his calculations but rounds up to the nearest whole number. Nor did he have the decimal system which we have used in the following pages to compare his data with modern calendrical calculations.

5.2 Goat Island – source of data about the lunar year. (Oleg Zabielin/Fotolia)

Odysseus & the Goat Hunt: Days, Months & Seasons of the Year

Our decoding of calendrical data begins with an examination of three passages from narrative and all connected by the number 118. The first quotation concerns the arrival of Odysseus' fleet on an idyllic uninhabited and unnamed island which we refer to as Goat Island:

> we fetched our *curved bows* and our long spears from the ships, separated into *three parties*, and began shooting at the goats … when it was shared out, *nine goats* were allotted to each of the *twelve ships* under my command, but to me [Odysseus] alone they made *an allotment of ten*. (9.156 Rieu)

The curved bows of the hunters are splendid metaphors for a new crescent moon and give a hint of calendrical matters to come. On going ashore to forage for food the sailors are delighted to find such an abundance of wild goats that many are slaughtered and awarded equally to each ship, with the exception of Odysseus who is given an additional 10 for himself:

Goats killed:		
12 ships x 9 goats	=	108
Odysseus' share	=	10
Total number of goats	=	118

Narrative has now provided this basic data:

12 ships
3 parties of men
118 goats

As metaphor the episode is interpreted as:

12 ships = 12 lunar months = a lunar year
3 parties of men = three lunar 'seasons'
118 goats (108 + 10) = 118 days (in each lunar season)
3 'seasons' x 118 days = 354 = days in a lunar year.

Homer has now defined the days, months and seasons of the lunar year and in addition provides an important link with the solar year:

Odysseus + the 10 goats he is given = 11

Eleven is the number of days difference between the 354-day lunar year and the 365-day solar year, a problem that bedevilled calendar makers for many centuries and was eventually resolved by the discovery of luni-solar cycles. More about those later.

Homer's use of metaphorical clues to conceal calendrical matters have for more than 2000 years provided a highly successful level of encryption. His security is further extended by a system which we refer to as 'add-ons'. These apply when a smaller number (the 10 goats given to Odysseus) is added to a larger collective number (the 108 goats awarded to his ships). The technique of 'add-ons' to further encrypt data is also found in a list of suitors seeking the hand of Penelope, in the trees and vines on the farm of Laertes and in Homer's description of Eumaeus' herd of pigs. This technique is a simple tool but its recognition was essential to the decipherment of the calendrical knowledge of the *Odyssey*.

Years of three seasons were well known in the ancient Mediterranean world and Robert Graves said that 'Hephaestus' three-legged workshop tables ... are apparently representing the number of three-season years for which a "son of Hephaestus" was permitted to reign in the island of Lemnos'.[2] At around the beginning of the third millennium, an Egyptian lunar calendar was also divided into three seasons; it began in midsummer with the heliacal rising of Sirius, α Canis Majoris, which occurred at about the time of the annual flooding of the river Nile. The first of the Egyptian seasons was 'Inundation' when floods deposited rich silt on the Nile banks; the second, 'Going Forth', was when the flood receded and farmers planted crops; and the third was 'Low Water'. In Assyria and Babylon too, a three-season year was recognised.

The calendrical implications of the goat hunt were discovered in a paper written by Edna Leigh in which she discussed patterns of numbers and 'simple beginnings to arithmetic'. Initially we thought that example of numerical data was a singular event, until, almost by accident, we examined more closely the list of suitors besieging Penelope. That, in turn, led to an exciting and productive investigation of all the data in the *Odyssey*.

The Suitors Pursuing Penelope: Full & Hollow Months

From Dulichium there are *fifty-two*, the pick of its young men with *six serving men*. From Same there are *twenty-four*, and from Zacynthus *twenty noblemen*; from Ithaca itself a *dozen of its best*, and with them *Medon* the herald, and an inspired *minstrel*, besides *two servants*, expert carvers. (16.246 Rieu)

Our second example of calendrical data in narrative comes from the list of suitors who Odysseus must overcome if he is to win back his wife, Penelope. After Odysseus arrives on Ithaca he meets his son, Telemachus, who gives an implausible tally of the suitors who descended upon the royal home in the hope of seizing the throne and lands of the long-absent warrior-king by marrying Penelope. That Penelope should, in the first place, be pursued by more than 100 lusty young men has been described as 'absurd' and classical scholars have criticised Telemachus'

5.3 Penelope's suitors discover her trick of weaving a shroud for Laertes by day and unpicking her work at night. (John Flaxman, 1755–1826)

counting of the suitors. It has been said to be unlikely that so many well-born suitors could have come from three small islands and an area, Dulichium, that has never been identified. In addition, such a large group could hardly have squeezed into the *megaron*, the main room of a house in the Homeric period, for their later fight to the death with Odysseus and his companions. One idea suggests that Homer began with 108 suitors but later reduced the number so that he could dramatically describe the individual deaths of 15 of them.[3] Nevertheless, the initial list of suitors and their servants do have calendrical importance and it was their story which later led to the discovery of a second lunar season of 118 days.

With the incongruity of so many suitors and their servants crowding into one place arousing such conjecture amongst classicists, perhaps Homer was hinting there is more to this scene than first meets the eye. A solution to the confusion is found when Homer defines a second season of 118 days. The basic data is of 108 suitors with the add-ons of six servants, plus Medon, a minstrel and two carvers:

Suitors from Dulichium	=	52	
Plus 6 Servants	=	6	
Suitors from Same	=	24	
Suitors from Zacynthus	=	20	
Suitors from Ithaca	=	12	
Plus Medon, a minstrel, and two carvers	=	4	
Total		118	= days in four lunar months

This, however, is not the whole story and examination of the carefully selected numbers reveals how the ancient Greeks divided the lunar calendar into 'full months' and 'hollow months'.

As seen in Chapter 3, the lunar month of 29.53 days does not fit easily into a calendar marked in whole days, but a solution was found in ancient Greece and Babylon by alternating a full month of 30 days with a hollow month of 29 days, to give an average of 29.5 days. A 'season' of four months would have two full months of 30 days and two hollow months of 29 days, making a total of 118 days. Thus the 52 suitors plus their six servants from Dulichium equal the 58 days in two hollow months. All of the other suitors, plus the add-ons of Medon, the minstrel and the two carvers add up to 60, which is the number of days in two full months. It also follows that in one full month and a consecutive hollow month there are 59 days, which is such an important number in Homer's calendar system that he invokes it on many other occasions. Such is the complexity in Homer's listing of the suitors that these authors feel there is yet more knowledge to be extracted from this episode.

Having now found two pieces of narrative concealing the number 118, it seemed reasonable that elsewhere in the *Odyssey* would be a third, as suggested by the three parties sent out to hunt for goats, which gave: 3 x 118 = 354 days in a lunar year.

This proved to be so and the final part of the equation was eventually discovered when the *Odyssey* draws to a close and Odysseus goes to visit his father on the final day of the epic.

The Remarkable Farm of Laertes: Cycles of the Moon, Sun & Venus

After the bloody slaughter of the suitors and Odysseus' reunion with his beloved wife, the *Odyssey* moves on to a strangely low-key ending when Odysseus, Telemachus, and comrades-in-arms Eumaeus and Philoetius, travel into the countryside for a touching reunion with Laertes, the hero's aged father. To identify himself after his lengthy absence, Odysseus reveals a scar on his thigh and gives a tally of the fruit trees and rows of vines given to him by Laertes in times long past: 'You gave me *thirteen* pear-trees, *ten* apple-trees, and *forty* fig-trees, and at the same time you pointed out the *fifty* rows of vines that were to be mine' (24.339 Rieu).

That short extract of narrative gives the calculation:

Pear trees	=	13		
Apple trees	=	10		
Fig trees	=	40		
Rows of vines	=	50		
Plus: Odysseus, Telemachus, Eumaeus, Philoetius & Laertes	=	5		
Total	=	118	=	the days in four lunar months

Detail of Odysseus' orchard and vineyard is the last of three scenarios linked by the number 118 and another example of Homer completing his calculations of lunar days by 'adding on' the smaller number of five humans to the larger collective number of 113 trees and vines. In the first example of Goat Island he added the ten goats given to Odysseus to a larger number and in the listing of suitors the addition of six servants and four others served a similar purpose. Although the listing of fruit trees and vines was the most troublesome of the 118 passages to take to a deeper level, the eventual rewards were staggering.

As with Goat Island and the suitors, we felt that the list of fruit trees and vines given to Odysseus by his father contained more calendrical data than first met the eye. The major problem was that we had no idea at first of what we were looking for or that, when we did eventually discover Homer's well-hidden secrets, we would enter a realm of sophisticated cycles of the sun, moon and planet Venus. Eventually our belief was upheld in a manner which could never have been imagined and it took our admiration of Homer's calendrical achievements to

5.4 An orchard of apple, pear and fig trees together with a vineyard contains a wealth of knowledge about cycles of the sun, moon and Venus. (Vibe Images/Fotolia)

a new and higher level. It was a sublime moment when, during the long hours of a winter's night, Florence cracked the code and revealed that in the scene on Laertes' farm Homer accurately preserved the number of lunations in four-year, eight-year and 19-year luni-solar cycles, as well as cycles of Venus and the Saros eclipse cycle.

Decoding the scene on Laertes' farm was the major breakthrough which revealed that lunations were indeed the key to understanding Homer's calendar system. This success led us to believe, and to later confirm, that all other numerical data in the *Odyssey* must be connected to calendars and it encouraged us to greatly widen our investigations.

Calendars & Cycles of the Sun, Moon & Venus

Observations of the 'coming together' of independent cycles of the sun and moon were essential to improving the accuracy of calendars and keeping the lunar calendar in step with the solar calendar. When or where luni-solar cycles were first discovered is not known, but Homer was so familiar with cycles of eight years and 19 years that they became critical components in the structure of the *Odyssey*. Homer begins both cycles at a winter solstice, when there was a new crescent moon in the sky. After eight years – almost – there would, at the winter solstice (the same day of the solar year), be a new crescent moon visible against the same background of stars as when the cycle began. For the wider population the 'coming together' of the sun and moon in this manner would probably have been an event of great excitement. For practical astronomers, however, it meant that the lunar calendar and solar calendar were once again in harmony. The 19-year cycle, which would have provided a similar visual spectacle, was considerably more accurate. Both cycles reflect the skill with which ancient astronomers were able to use observations over long periods and they also recognise their arithmetical abilities. Our calculations concerning luni-solar cycles in this and later chapters are based on data from *The Movement and Rhythms of the Stars* by J. Schultz.[4]

The *octaëteris* was the first cycle to be teased from data embedded in the story of the farm of Laertes, and Homer records that in eight solar years there are 99 lunations. At the end of this cycle the moon is very nearly in the same position in the sky as when the cycle began, but reaches the same phase a little later. With the solar year calculated at 365.24 days and the lunar month at 29.53 days, the discrepancy between eight solar years and 99 lunations is just over 1.55 days. Over a single cycle of eight years that discrepancy may not appear particularly important, but in the longer term the error is much magnified and this may have been the impetus that drove astronomers to seek a more accurate cycle, which was eventually found in a period of 19 years.

The eight-year cycle begins in the *Odyssey* when Odysseus arrives on Calypso's island and ends, together with the 19-year cycle, on the day he kills the suitors. There was another stunning surprise concerning the eight-year cycle awaiting in narrative that describes his return to Ithaca on a morning when Venus, the 'bright star that heralds the approach of dawn' (13.93), is in the sky.[5] In this way Homer enhances the scope of the eight-year cycle by introducing two observations concerning the rhythms of Venus. The first observation is a cycle that begins, for instance, when Venus appears before dawn in the eastern sky after a period of absence and it will be 584 days before the planet's cycle runs its course and begins again. The second observation is an extension of the first and consisted of five cycles of 584 days, which was close to the number of days in 99 lunations and eight solar years.[6] The idea that Homer had combined the three brightest objects in the sky in his eight-year cycle was overwhelming. It would also have been the record of a rare event when the planet made a reappearance at the beginning of the luni-solar cycle on a winter solstice and a new crescent moon. Five Venus cycles fall short of 99 lunations by 3.87, or four, days and this again reveals Homer's calendrical accuracy, for when the planet appears on the morning of Odysseus' return it is still almost four days to the climax of the *Odyssey* and the end of the eight-year luni-solar cycle.[7] Venus has arrived on time.

Lunations & Cycles in the Orchard of Laertes

12 lunations	=	a lunar year
49/50 lunations	=	an olympiad
99 lunations	=	8 solar years (approx.)
99 lunations	=	a Venus period (approx.)
235 lunations	=	19-year solar years
223 lunations	=	Saros eclipse cycle

The Rhythms of Venus

Venus cycle:	approx. 584 days
Venus period:	approx. 5 x 584 = 2920 days
	approx. 8 years and
	approx. 99 lunations

Odysseus' stay with Calypso and the run-up to the climax of the *Odyssey* is not the only occasion on which Homer refers to eight-year units of time: Menelaus of Lacedaemon returned home from the wars 'in the eighth year' (4.82) and that day attended a funeral feast in honour of Agamemnon, who had been murdered by Aegisthus and who in turn had been killed in the eighth year of his reign by Orestes (3.305).[8] In a lying tale, Odysseus tells the pig-keeper Eumaeus that he stayed in Egypt 'going on for eight years' until a cunning Phoenician persuaded him to leave (14.287).

Fifty Rows of Vines: Counting in Lunations

The breakthrough of identifying the number of lunations in the eight-year cycle was a curious matter and arose from Florence's recognition of the way in which Homer separates fruit trees and vines into two distinct groups. Odysseus counts the pear, apple and fig trees on his father's farm as individual items but the vines are numbered in rows. A visual image of a vineyard planted in 50 rows, separated by wide aisles or intervals to allow for growth and harvesting of grapes, suggested that Homer conceals an additional number in this extract of narrative. Indeed, the translator Samuel Butler's[9] observation that 'there was corn planted between each row' (24.340) was the clue that led to the following calculation:

5.5 In ancient times, as in modern, vines were planted in rows with wide spaces between. (Herbert Rubens/Fotolia)

50 rows of vines + 49 'intervals' or 'rows of corn' = 99

99 is the number of lunations in the eight-year luni-solar cycle and the eight-year Venus period

While Butler may have been alone in introducing 'spaces' between the rows his image of a crop of corn being grown between the vines on rocky Ithaca and harvested before the grapes matured would have been familiar in Ancient Greece and of particular value where good land was scarce. A paper published by the University of Florida says: 'The use of cover crops dates back some 2,500 years. Several ancient Greek and Roman sources suggested the growing of crops to produce manure for vineyards and other crops'.[10] Indeed, even if the spaces between the rows of vines had lain fallow as in the picture above, there would still be 49 prominent intervals between the 50 rows, to give a total of 99.

Olympiads & 8-year Cycles

The 50 rows of vines and 49 intervals had a further purpose, concerning the Greeks and the world's most famous sporting events. In the early decades of the eighth century BC Greece was so beset by plague, famine and wars between the city-states that King Iphitos of Elis went to Delphi to seek advice from the Oracle on how to bring the troubles to an end. Told to restore an ancient festival in honour of Zeus that may have begun as early as *c.*1354 BC, he declared in 776 BC that a grand sporting event would take place every four years at Olympia. These sports, known as the Olympic Games, were such an important part of ancient Greek life that they continued for more than 1200 years, until AD 395. If Homer did live during the years *c.*745–700 BC it is more than likely that he would have heard the beating of the drums of the heralds, the *spondophoroi*, who wandered the land before each Olympic Games to declare a truce between warring clans. These messengers would also declare when the full moon would appear to mark the period of the Games. It may seem strange in modern times that the populace would need to be told such information but, as Judith Swaddling writes, 'the central day of the Olympic festival always coincided with the second or third full moon after the summer solstice'.[11] Bearing in mind each lunar year falls 11 days behind the preceding one, it is not easy to determine when the second or third full moon after the solstice arrives and the *spondophoroi* were indeed required to act as timekeepers.

The four-year period between each set of Games was a measure of time so familiar to Homer that his expression of the eight-year cycle as 99 rows of vines and the intervals between them was not merely literary ingenuity, but also divides the cycle neatly into units of 50 and 49 lunations, or Olympiads. It is not known when these periods of some four years were first embedded in Greek culture but they may have been used in calendrical terms long before ever being connected to athletics. The question of why Homer went to such trouble to conceal the number 49 in the rows of vines can be answered by the connecting thread of the scenes concerning the killing of goats, the listing of the suitors by Telemachus, and Odysseus' description of the fruit trees and vines given to him by Laertes. All are linked by the number 118, but if Homer had openly added the number 49 into this scene it would have given a total of 167 and broken the relationship between the three narrative passages which make up the 354 days in a lunar year.

Epic & Homer's 19-year Luni-solar Cycle

With the vineyard having revealed its secrets, Florence's exploration of the numbers of individual trees in Odysseus' orchard advanced our regard for Homer even further. It is not known when or where some unknown watcher of the skies discovered a 19-year cycle of the sun and moon that has influenced the accuracy of calendars down to the present time. It was, however, a momentous discovery. During 19 solar years there are 235 lunations and at the end of the cycle the moon is at the same phase and at the same position against a background of stars on the same day of the solar year – as it had been at the beginning of the cycle. The visual spectacle of lunar and solar events at the beginning of the cycle being repeated at its end is dramatically described at the climax of the *Odyssey* and is examined in Chapters 12 & 13.

The form in which the cycle was known in Greece long after Homer has been attributed to the eponymous Meton, *c*.432 BC. As the *Odyssey* reveals, however, some three centuries before that time the cycle was so familiar to Homer that he made it the period from when Odysseus first left Penelope to fight at Troy to the day exactly 19 years later when he was reunited with his wife. The cycle was also known in Babylon and China and, as its origins are uncertain, it is not attributed in our work to either Homer or Meton, and is referred to as the '19-year cycle'. In modern times the cycle is the basis of the Jewish calendar and is used to establish the time of Easter in the Christian calendar.

The structure of the cycle is rather more complicated than merely stating there are 235 lunations in 19 solar years, for in 19 lunar years (12 x 19) there are only 228 lunations. To keep the solar and lunar calendars in harmony seven extra lunar months have to be inserted (intercalated) into the cycle. In the Metonic cycle months were intercalated in years 3, 6, 8, 11, 14, 17 and 19. Distribution of 'full' and 'hollow' months also had to be taken into consideration and in Meton's cycle the 235 lunations were divided into 125 full months of 30 days and 110 hollow months of 29 days. With these calculations complete, the luni-solar cycle was then accurate to a little over two hours in 19 years. In Chapter 10 it will be shown how Homer uses intercalation to create a 13-month year and a model projection is made of the years in which months might have been intercalated.

Homer records the 235 lunations of the 19-year cycle by manipulating the numbers of individual fruit trees together with the five men who provide the element of add-ons:

10 apple trees + 5 men	=	**15**
15 x 13 pear trees	=	195
Plus 40 fig trees	=	40
Total	=	235

235 = lunations in a 19-year luni-solar cycle

In Chapter 12, Figs 4 & 6, we give a visual demonstration of the phenomenon of how the moon, after 19 years, will have returned to the same phase against the same background of stars. Despite the introduction of the 19-year cycle into Greek calendar making, Homer's recognition of the older and less accurate cycles of four and eight years suggests that in his times they were still in use in the shorter term calculation of time.

The following calculation uses the decimal system to show how cycles of 19 solar years and 235 lunations give calendar makers a marker accurate to within 0.086 of a day, or two hours four minutes.[12]

19 solar years x 365.24 days	=	6939.688 days
235 lunations x 29.53 days	=	6939.602 days
Difference	=	0.086 days

The 18-year Saros Cycle

The last surprise to be teased from the account of Odysseus' fruit trees was an eclipse cycle of 18 years and 11 days, during which there are 223 lunations, following which the sun, moon and earth return to almost the same alignment and the cycle of lunar and solar eclipses begins to repeat itself. Known as the Saros cycle, it not only makes it possible to predict eclipses but was also of importance in the history of calendar-reckoning.[13] Full and partial eclipses occur during daytime, when the moon moves across the face of the sun; at night eclipses occur when the moon moves into the shadow of the earth. Eclipse cycles are today a major study in themselves,[14] but they have fascinated observers from the earliest of times and the configuration of Stonehenge has even been suggested as a means of predicting eclipses.[15] Eclipses have no physical effect on humans, but 'have always been capable of producing profound psychological effects. For millennia, solar eclipses have been interpreted as portents of doom by virtually every known civilisation. These have stimulated responses that run the gamut from human sacrifices to feelings of awe and bewilderment.'[16] It is little wonder that the ability to predict eclipses by using the Saros cycle was a powerful social tool. At 6585.32 days, the length of the Saros is marginally shorter than 18 years and 11 days, and during each cycle there are some 43 solar and 28 lunar eclipses.[17]

Homer records the 223 lunations of a Saros by again manipulating the five men and individual fruit trees on the farm of Laertes:

5 men x 40 fig trees	=	200		
13 pears trees + 10 apple trees	=	23		
Total	=	223	=	lunations in a Saros cycle

One of the puzzles of the *Odyssey* occurs on the day the suitors are killed, when the seer Theoclymenus speaks of the horrors yet to come in words that describe a total eclipse of the sun. With a new crescent moon only a few hours away, a total eclipse would not occur at that time but Homer may have been referring to an eclipse cycle linked to the 19-year luni-solar cycle (see Appendix 3).

The Question of Chance

The probability of Homer creating, by chance, the numbers contained in the three diverse quotations about goats, suitors and plants is remote in the extreme. Nor are the current groups in isolation, and it will be seen in following chapters that they are representative of other encoded data. The selection of the numbers in just one of Homer's groups brings to mind the odds facing a gambler who has to match six numbers in the range 1 to 49 with six numbers drawn in a lottery. The possibility of choosing the six lottery numbers, in any order, is in the region of 1 in 14 million.[18] In contrast, there are six numbers in the range of 1 to 52 in the counting of the suitors and their servants, which gives some 20 million different combinations of six numbers within that group. The chance of Homer choosing at random even one group of numbers which not only add up to 118, but also lend themselves to additional manipulation, are so truly enormous as to be discounted.

The Extraordinary Pig Farm of Eumaeus; Homer's Earth-centred Universe: Cycles of the Sun, Moon & Venus

Eumaeus, devoted servant and pig-keeper to Odysseus, is reunited with his master in unusual circumstances and goes on to play an important role in the last days of the *Odyssey*. After Odysseus returns to Ithaca he heads towards the pig farm, where he is offered traditional hospitality and stays as a guest for three nights during the moon's dark period. In a long conversation with his host, Odysseus spins a lying tale about his previous experiences and his disguise is so effective that he is unrecognised by Eumaeus until he reveals himself just before the terrible climax of the epic.

While still a young boy Eumaeus was abducted from his homeland by Phoenician traders and sold to Laertes, the father of Odysseus. Eumaeus says he was born on an unknown island named 'Syria lying above Ortygia … where the sun makes his turnings' (15.404). The 'sun turns', in astronomical terms, at the summer and winter solstices, and the pig-keeper makes his entrance into the *Odyssey* right on time, during the 'standstill' period before the sun 'turns' at the winter solstice. Despite being a mere pig-keeper and amongst the lowest ranks of society, Eumaeus enjoys the deep friendship of Odysseus and is a tower of strength on his master's return to Ithaca. He also holds the key to considerable calendrical knowledge and as Book 14 of the *Odyssey* opens Homer describes his pig farm in a manner rich in literary, astronomical and calendar detail.

Although translators do not always reach word-for-word agreement in their descriptions of the physical images of Eumaeus' farm, their overall accounts portray a hut in a high clearing or yard with a wide view and the boundary of the clearing marked by a wooden fence 'in a full circle'. Translators, however, do agree on the numerical data. Within the yard are 12 pigsties, each containing 50 sows, and beyond the fence are 360 boars guarded by four savage dogs trained by Eumaeus. The following extract is from Richmond Lattimore's translation:

> [Odysseus] found [Eumaeus] sitting in front, on the porch [of his hut], where *the lofty enclosure* had been built, *in a place with a view on all sides*, both large and handsome, *cleared all about* … Outside he had driven *posts in a full circle*, to close it on all sides … Inside the enclosure he made *twelve pig pens next to each other*, for his sows to sleep in, *and in each of them fifty pigs* … *the males lay outside* … *they numbered three hundred and sixty*, and *four dogs*, who were like wild beasts, forever were lying by them. These *the swineherd, leader of men, had raised up himself*. (14.5 ff)

Eumaeus also has his own servant (14.449) and, considering his position in life as a lowly swineherd, the description of his house with a porch and well-ordered stockyard suggests that he was living in circumstances above his humble station. That is until the quotation is read as astronomical metaphor, which has been summarised in Fig. 5.6.

- Eumaeus' house = the earth at the centre of the universe.
- A lofty enclosure and view on all sides = the dome of the heavens.
- Posts in a 'full circle' = the ecliptic, the apparent path of the sun during the course of a year.
- 12 pig pens = the 12 zodiacal constellations through which the sun appears to pass during a year.
- 360 boars + 5 add-ons of 4 dogs plus Eumaeus = the 365 days of the solar year.

The profound idea of linking a humble pig farm with the path of the sun and the passing of time on earth is only the beginning of the astronomical and calendrical lore attached to Eumaeus. There is sufficient data in the quotation to define the lunations in the eight-year and Olympiad luni-solar cycles and to make it possible to extrapolate a cycle of 96 years connected with 12 Venus periods, 12 x 8 solar years, and 12 x 99 lunations. The extrapolated 96-year cycle makes it possible, in modern terms, to calculate the exact number of lunations during a solar year. In addition, there is an intriguing, but as yet unresolved, link with the catalogue of ships in Book 2 of the *Iliad*.

Days of the year: The reason Homer defines the 365 days of the solar year as 360 + 4 dogs and one pig-keeper lies in his continuing arithmetical ingenuity: the 360 boars are in number the same as the degrees in a circle or the ecliptic. With the 12 pens representing the months in a solar year, then by dividing 360 by 12

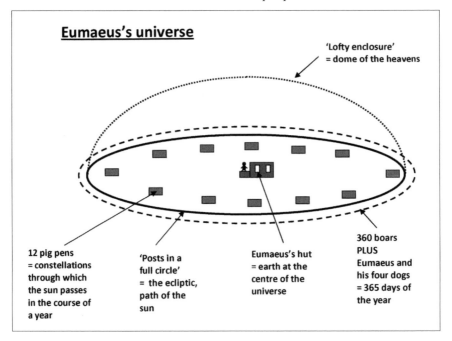

5.6 The pig farm of Eumaeus as metaphor for an earth-centred universe.

gives an answer of 30, which was the number of days allotted by the ancients to a solar month. This would have enabled Homer to further define the sun's annual journey as a solar year of 12 months each of 30 days, plus five extra [epagomenal] days, giving a total of 365 days. The idea of reckoning the solar year at 360 + 5 days, or 12 30-day months plus five extra days is not controversial and is known to have been used both in Egypt and post-Homeric Greece.[19]

Sows and cycles: It is not coincidence that Homer is specific about the gender of the pigs on the farm, for the boars are related to solar data but the sows are related to lunations. In each of Eumaeus' pens are 50 sows and each one represents one lunation. As with the intervals between the rows of vines in the orchard of Laertes, it is reasonable to propose that Homer included in his calculations similar intervals between the sleeping sows, making 49 spaces in all:

50 sows + 49 intervals = 99 = the number of lunations in 8 years.

Homer has again determined the 50 and 49 lunations of the four-year Olympiad and the 99 lunations of the eight-year cycle, during which there are five Venus cycles.

Detail of the careful husbandry of Eumaeus contains yet more numbers which provide interesting results. Each of the 12 pens in his stockyard accounts for the 99 lunations in two Olympiads, one eight-year solar cycle and one eight-year period of Venus, and leads to the calculation:

12 (pens) x 99 lunations	=	1188 lunations
12 x 8-year Venus periods	=	96 years
12 (pens) x 8 solar years	=	96 years

These cycles point towards the coming together of the moon, Venus and the sun at the end of 96 solar years, during which there are 1188 lunations and 12 x 8-year Venus periods. If, in Homer's times, calculations of the sun and moon were based on a 29.5 day lunar month and 365-day solar year, the long-term view would have indicated a luni-solar difference of only about six days in almost a century. In reality, and using accurate values for a lunation and solar year, the discrepancy is 18.6 days between the cycles of the sun and moon.

Nor is the calculation of the 12 Venus periods quite accurate, for the synodic appearance of Venus in the longer term would occur some 46 days before the new synodic cycle of the moon; that is in the 1186th lunation and not the 1188th. In the Catalogue of Ships in the *Iliad* Homer gives the total number of vessels in which the Greek regiments sailed to Troy as 1186, which matches the 12 Venus periods in 96 years. The catalogue of ships contains other numerical data and this link with the *Odyssey* suggests it is an area worthy of more investigation.

Nor is this the end of the potential calendrical riches of the pig farm, for by dividing 96 years into 1188 lunations, the number of lunations in one solar year, in decimal terms, can be deduced:

1188 lunations ÷ 96 solar years = 12.37 = the number of lunations in a solar year.

0.37 of a lunation is 10.9 days which, added to the lunar year of 354.36 days, gives a very close comparison to the 365.24 days of the true solar year:

354.36 + 10.9 = 365.26 compared to the true value of 365.24 days in a solar year.

In the absence of Homer using fractions of whole numbers, it does not seem likely that his calculations would have reached this level of sophistication, but at least the potential was there.

In addition to the description of the homestead of Eumaeus, there are other numbers concerned with life on the farm and the wealth of Odysseus. These include three of Eumaeus' men out herding pigs and a fourth sent to town with a boar to feed the suitors, while Eumaeus is shaping sandals for his feet. (14.23), a metaphorical act that possibly suggests the impending new moon. There is a further tantalising suggestion of calendrical matters when Eumaeus despairs about the many beasts the suitors eat daily: 'For as many as are the nights and the days from Zeus, on not one of these do [the suitors] dedicate only a single victim, nor only two' (14.94).

Eumaeus describes Odysseus as being enormously wealthy, with his value being that of 20 men rolled into one (19-year cycle?), and goes on to list his possessions: 12 herds of cattle on the mainland, 12 flocks of sheep, 12 herds of pigs, 12 goat herds, and, in addition, 11 scattered flocks of goats. In total the herds of animals are 59, the number of days in one hollow and one full lunar month, but their wider purpose, if any, is elusive. Nor is it yet known if the three men herding the animals and the single man sent with a boar to feed the suitors have a secondary purpose.

Of the numerical data in the rest of the *Odyssey*, there is one outstanding exception not yet linked to calendrical or astronomical matters. At 3.2ff Homer records that the people of Pylos gathered on a beach to sacrifice black bulls to Poseidon and were divided into 9 groups, each of 500 men, with each division providing nine bulls. With other such detail throughout the *Odyssey* being closely linked to calendrical matters, it suggests there is interesting material yet to be found in this huge gathering.

Data & Knowledge

Although presented in this chapter as extracts quite separate from their place in the story of Odysseus, the introductory examples of embedded data have illustrated how the following knowledge can be extracted from narrative:

A 12-month lunar year of 354 days divided into three 'seasons', each of 118 days (*Goats, suitors, trees and vines*).

'Full' lunar months of 30 days alternating with 'hollow months' of 29 days to give an average lunation of 29.5 days (*Suitors*).

99 lunations made up of two Olympiads of alternating 50 and 49 lunations (*Rows of vines*).

235 lunations of 19-year luni-solar cycle (*Fruit trees and men*).

223 lunations of a 'Saros' eclipse cycle (*Fruit trees and men*).

View of an earth-centred universe (*Eumaeus' enclosure*).

A solar year of 360 days + 5 days (*Eumaeus' herd of pigs*).

The extrapolation of data to project a lunar-solar cycle of 1188 lunations or 96 years that is linked to a series of 12 Venus periods, and possibly associated with the number of ships listed in the Catalogue of Ships (*Eumaeus' herd of pigs*).

Following on …

In the following chapters we give an astronomical/calendrical reading of the *Odyssey* in the order in which it was composed by Homer. It begins with the 40 'real-time' days of Book 1, when the gods decide to free the warrior-king and let him leave the island of Calypso. After his arrival on the island of the Phaeacians there follow five chapters in which Odysseus' accounts of his adventures after leaving Troy are linked to astronomical detail. Readers wishing to follow his travels through the night skies may find useful a guide such as *Philip's Star Chart*. The *Odyssey* then reverts to 'real-time' days and Odysseus' return to Ithaca. Before the climax of the epic, Odysseus again recalls historic events and includes, for the first time in either the *Iliad* or the *Odyssey*, the day that he left home to fight at Troy; in doing so he sets the parameters of the beginning and the end of the 19-year cycle. These chapters also include interpretation of other data from the *Odyssey*.

A projected day-by-day account of Odysseus' journey from Troy to Calypso's island is found in our projection of a Ship's Log in Appendix 1. The hypothetical log was constructed to test the idea that lunar months and phases of the moon could be linked to the rhythms of Odysseus' adventures during the course of one solar year.

Notes

1 *Homer's Secret Iliad*, p. 47, other notes on the arts of memorisation are on pp. 46–8 & 219–21.
2 Graves, R., *The Greek Myths: 1*, (Hamondsworth: Penguin, 1965), p. 21.
3 Heubeck, A., West, S. & Hainsworth, J.B., *A Commentary on Homer's Odyssey* (Oxford: Clarendon Press, 1989) Vol. 2, xvi, line 247; Russo, J., Fernández-Galliano, M. & Alfred Heubeck, Vol. 3, xxii, line 241.
4 Schultz, Joachim, *Movement and Rhythms of the Stars* (Edinburgh: Floris Books, 1986), pp. 217 & 219, gives comparisons between 235 synodic months and 19 tropical years.
5 Venus, known as the Morning and the Evening Star, reflects the times when the planet can be seen, but ancient observers may not have realised they were viewing the same object.
6 See detail in Chapter 9 of the number of men in Odysseus' fleet when he sailed from Troy.
7 Aveni, Antony, *Stairways to the Stars* (New York: John Wily & Sons, 1997) gives a more expansive account of cycles of the sun and moon and the rhythms of Venus.
8 An analysis of the eight-year cycle is found in Chapter 14, in the chart 'The House of Atreus'.
9 Butler, Samuel (trans), *The Odyssey* (New York: Barnes and Noble, reprint 1992), p. 301.
10 Chambliss, C.G. & Muchovej, R.M., *Cover Crops* (Florida: Institute of Food and Agricultural Service, May 1997, revised April 2003). 'Cover cropping in rows of vines (and other crops) continues today; for example, in Malta '… the health of the soil is of paramount importance and … other crops between the vines, like barley and vetch, and even weeds, can improve the quality of the soil' (www.maltatoday.com). In Madeira, '… vines are planted in lanes that incline to follow the natural declivity of the slopes … and distanced to permit other crops to grow between them' (www.madeirawine.com).
11 Judith Swaddling writes 'that the central day of the Olympic festival always coincided with the second or third full moon after the summer solstice'. *The Ancient Olympic Games* (London: British Museum Press, 1999), p. 4.
12 Converting, 0.086 to hours and minutes. There are 1440 minutes in a day; one-tenth of a day = 144 minutes; one-hundredth of a day = 14.4 minutes; one-thousandth of a day =

1.44 minutes. The difference is (eight-hundredths = 115.2 minutes) + (six-thousandths = 8.64 minutes) = 123.84 minutes rounded up is 124 minutes = 2 hours 4 minutes.

13 North, John, *Astronomy and Cosmology* (London: Fontana, 1994), p. 35.

14 See http://www.phys.uu.nl/~vgent/eclipse/eclipsecycles.htm.

15 Hawkins, Gerald, in collaboration with White, John B., *Stonehenge Decoded* (London: Souvenir Press, 1965), Chapter 9, pp. 132–48.

16 Source NASA, quoted at: http:www.space.com/scienceastronomy/solarsystem/solar_eclipse_facts.html.

17 *Encyclopaedia Britannica* (UK) Ltd, 2000.

18 http://mathforum.org/dr.match/faq/faq.prob.world.htm [url no longer functioning].

19 For Homer the 365-day year created problems when it came to calculating the number of days over periods of years. The solar year is about a quarter day longer, or 365.242 days in more exact terms, and how Homer accommodates the accumulated extra days over a 19-year cycle is seen in Chapter 12.

6

ODYSSEUS FREED TO RETURN HOME

If ever it needs to be emphasised that bad and dismal times in the *Odyssey* occur against a background of the diminishing crescent of the waning moon, then look no further than the first six of the 40 'real-time' days in Books 1–4. The doleful events of those times include the gods bickering amongst themselves, turmoil in Ithaca, Telemachus failing to exert his authority and the seer Halitherses threatened with exile. In addition, Penelope, her trick of weaving and unpicking a shroud for Laertes exposed, is forever weeping and having nightmares; Nestor and Menelaus recall the sorrowful homecoming and brutal murder of Agamemnon and the boastfulness of Great Aias which led to his downfall. The mood during the opening days reflects, too, Odysseus' own fortunes, as he is held captive by Calypso, pining for his wife and still far from home. Amidst all the gloom, however,

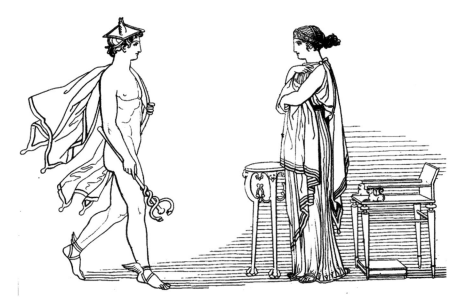

6.1 Hermes tells Calypso the gods have decreed that Odysseus should be freed and allowed to return home. (John Flaxman, 1755–1826)

there is a hint on Day 6 of the impending appearance of a new crescent moon by references to two weddings which traditionally took place at the beginning of the lunar month. Penelope is told she should make ready for her wedding to one of the suitors and in Lacedaemon Menelaus and Helen are holding a feast in preparation for the forthcoming marriages of their two children.

In this chapter we examine narrative for calendrical content from Days 7–33 of the 40 'real-time' days. Odysseus first makes his appearance in the epic on Day 7, when the moon is in its dark period he weeps in despair on the shores of Calypso's island where he has been held captive for almost eight years. With the new crescent imminent, the mood lightens as Hermes, messenger of the gods, arrives and tells Calypso to set Odysseus free. With Calypso's help, Odysseus builds a raft and sails from Calypso's island on Day 12, as the sun moves towards Capricornus. In the evening of Day 31 of the 'real-time' days Odysseus arrives on Scherie, island home of the Phaeacians, and Homer transposes his story from the zodiacal band to the glories of the Milky Way and its star-studded constellations. We now follow Odysseus' progress from when he is freed by Calypso to the court of King Alcinous and the evening of Day 33, when he recalls his adventures following the fall of Troy.

Day 7, Dark Moon: Hermes Tells Calypso to Free Odysseus

Despite Athene's pleas to the gods to free Odysseus from captivity on the opening day of the *Odyssey*, Hermes reaches Calypso's island only seven days later. The delay has been attributed to Homer's literary skill in heightening suspense, but the seven days have calendrical significance in that they represent the number of days between the moon's third quarter and its dark phase. Hermes meets Calypso and finds a large fire blazing in the hearth of her cave as she sings and sits at her loom, weaving with a golden shuttle. Homer creates an astronomical metaphor in these words:

> The cave was sheltered by a copse of alders and fragrant cypresses, which was the roosting place of wide-winged birds … whose business takes them down to the sea. Trailing round the mouth of the cavern was a thriving garden vine, with great bunches of grapes; from four separate but neighbouring springs four crystal rivulets were channelled to run this way and that. (5.63 Rieu)

At this time of the year the sun has left Sagittarius and Homer's lyrical description of Calypso's home becomes a splendid metaphor for the heliacal rising of beautiful Sagittarius and the glittering Milky Way. The 'loom and shuttle' suggest the more familiar 'bow and arrow' of Sagittarius, while the cave is proposed as the asterism, known in more modern terms as the 'teapot' or 'milk ladle'.

The seashore is the Milky Way and the four rivulets are represented by four stars from which can be traced four bands of the Milky Way. Homer's description of the lush garden is similar to that he later uses to describe the palace and garden of Alcinous, which are also in a star-studded area of the Milky Way.

Odysseus does not enter into active narrative at the meeting of Calypso and Hermes, but instead stands well apart from them crying at dark of moon on the seashore (the Milky Way). Although Calypso must ultimately let Odysseus go, they retire that night to the dark depths of her cave and sleep together (5.226). Her cave, like that of one-eyed Polyphemus, symbolises the dark period when both Odysseus and the moon are hidden from view.

Table 1. 'Real-time' Days 7–12

Day of the month, Phase of the moon	Position of the sun	Day of the *Odyssey*	Odysseus enters the story and builds a raft	2296 BC
27 Dark ●		7	Odysseus takes no part in the action except to sleep with Calypso.	8 Dec
28 Dark ●		8	(1) Odysseus begins to build his raft; cuts and trims 20 trees.	9
29 Dark ●		9	(2) Constructs decking, mast and rudder.	10
1 Crescent ☽		10	(3) Makes the sail from the white cloth given to him by Calypso.	11
2		11	(4) Completes the sides and rolls the raft to the sea.	12
3	β Capricorni	12	(5) Calypso bathes Odysseus and gives him new clothing before he spreads the sail and without closing his eyes, sails for seven days and ten, carefully keeping a watch on the stars.	13

Days 8–12, Waxing Crescent Moon: Odysseus' Raft & Navigation by Stars

There he sat [Odysseus] never closed his eyes in sleep, but kept them on the Pleiads, or watched the late-setting Boötes slowly fade, or the Great Bear, sometimes called the Wain, which always wheels round in the same place and looks across at Orion the Hunter with a wary eye. It was this constellation, the only one which never sinks below the horizon to bathe in Ocean's stream (5.270 Rieu).

Now eager to return home, Odysseus begins to build a raft to carry him away from Calypso's island and as the new crescent moon waxes so does his craft grow in size. The raft is finished on the fourth day, and after Calypso has bathed him, given him a new suit of clothing and told him how to navigate by the stars, he sails away on the fifth day. Odysseus resumes his homeward journey where it left off almost eight years earlier before he was captivated by the seductive charms of Calypso.

Odysseus sails through the night even if it may have been more reasonable for him to avoid navigating during the hours of darkness and put into a safe harbour to wait for sunrise. Homer, though, had good reason for sending Odysseus out to sea at night for, amongst other things, it enabled him to remind sailors how stars could be used as pointers to find the north celestial pole (see Fig. 6.2), a prime aid for navigation.

The Pleiades in Taurus, Boötes, the Great Bear and Orion contain a wealth of guidance for the astronomer, calendar maker and navigator. In order for Odysseus to follow Calypso's instructions all four of the constellations would need to be visible during most of the night – as they were in the winter months c.2300 BC. The Bear is circumpolar, as is part of Boötes. Both the Pleiades and Orion are in the sky when Odysseus sets off on his sleepless voyage, the Pleiades setting at about 2 a.m. and Betelgeuse, the red star in the shoulder of Orion, at about 4 a.m.

It is surprising that Calypso does not mention Gemini, for with the sun on the borders of Sagittarius as Odysseus leaves Calypso, Gemini rises at nightfall and its stars shone throughout the night in the winter of 2300 BC. Bearing in mind Gemini's ancient links with ships and the sea, and how easy it is to make the constellation shape into a raft, Edna Leigh explored the idea that Gemini was a symbol for Odysseus' raft and the 20 trees he used to build it being Gemini's 20 brightest stars.

The Pleiades & the Spring Equinox

The asterism of the Pleiades holds a special place in folklore all over the world. Many stories have been woven around that group of stars from ancient China to the Americas, and from the ancient civilisations of the Near and Middle East to the aborigines of Australia. In Greek mythology, the Pleiades were known as the 'Seven Sisters' but since only six are easily seen legends arose about the 'missing' seventh sister, which is only visible to those with keen eyesight. R.H.Allen wrote:

> The Pleiades have everywhere been among the most noted objects in the history, poetry, and mythology of the heavens. Homer's reference to them is amongst the first recorded in the western world, but Chinese astronomers noted them in 2357 BC and at that time the brightest star of the group, Alcyone, η Tauri, marked the spring equinox.[1]

On a practical note, Hesiod advised that the Aegean sailing season should begin only when the Pleiades appeared at their heliacal rising, just before dawn at the spring equinox. The Pleiades have a significance beyond their intrinsic beauty and are just one small part of the jigsaw puzzle which makes up the astronomical metaphors of the *Odyssey*. If Troy fell on or about 1200 BC, as is commonly assumed, then the equinoctial point lay between Aries/Cetus and no significant star marked its position. However, if Homer sings of a far older Troy that 'fell' at about 2300 BC, the sun would have been in the Pleiades at the spring equinox.

It is easy enough to determine which stars rise with the sun at any time of year: the zodiacal constellation rising in the east as the sun sets directly opposite in the west is the constellation in which the sun rose six months earlier and which will rise with the sun again in a further six months. When the Pleiades set with the sun at the spring equinox, the zodiacal constellation rising in the east would have been Scorpius, the constellation in which the sun would lie at the autumn equinox. Even this simple method gives a calendar of sorts; by knowing in which constellation the sun is at one time, it is a simple matter to forecast the changing of the seasons.

Late-setting Boötes & Arcturus

The second constellation listed by Calypso is Boötes, a constellation with a neck but no head, powerful shoulders, thin waist, long legs, ankles and a staff (see Fig. 2). In much earlier times Boötes was partly circumpolar and, although stars in the waist and legs dipped below the horizon, the neck, shoulders and upper torso never did and consequently, in Homer's words, the upper part of the constellation 'set late' only as the sun rose. Arcturus, α Bootis, the constellation's brightest star and the second brightest in the northern hemisphere, is also known as the 'Wanderer', for over the centuries it has slowly drifted lower in the constellation and nowadays appears to be nearer to its ankles. Arcturus, which in 2300 BC would have been nearer to Boötes' waist,[2] appears to follow the Great Bear around the North Pole and its name means 'Bear Watcher'.

The Bear or Wain

In referring to Ursa Major as a 'bear' or a 'wain', Homer acknowledges there are different perceptions of the man-made patterns of stars called constellations. The seven dominant stars of the Great Bear can take the form of a wain or wagon or be perceived as part of the body and tail of a bear. In modern times those stars are commonly known as the 'Plough' or the 'Dipper'. Homer says the Bear 'wheels around the same place' – the North Pole – and never drops below the horizon. The star closest to the North Pole *c.*2300 BC was Thuban, α Draconis, the brightest star in the constellation of Draco and far removed across the sky from the present pole star, α Ursae Minoris. By Homer's own era, *c.*750 BC, the North Pole was no longer close to Thuban but lay in a rather undistinguished area of sky between Draco and Ursa Minor, with few prominent stars. Thuban then would have been useful in giving only a rough guide to where the North Pole lay.

Pointers to Thuban, the North Pole Star

The easiest way to find today's pole star, Polaris, α Ursae Minoris, from amongst the stars that rotate around the hub of the heavens is to draw an imaginary line between β and α Ursae Majoris in the Great Bear and extend it out into space directly to Polaris. This method would have been wildly inaccurate *c.*2300 BC, but using pointers to find the pole stars of different epochs is ages old and Homer gave Odysseus two ways of locating celestial north by using stars in the Bear and Boötes. One method would have been by projecting an imaginary line from two 'pointer' stars in the rear of the Great Bear, γ and δ Ursae Majoris (see Fig. 6.2). A second way could have used the stars of Boötes and Odysseus would have found the reddish bright star Arcturus, α Boötis, easy to locate, as the three bright tail stars of the Bear draw the eye towards it. In Fig. 6.2 an imaginary line is drawn from Arcturus, via the stars in the staff, towards Thuban. A third way of finding the North Pole will be found in the story of Elpenor's funeral mound in Chapter 10. With two methods of finding north, Homer is indeed sending Odysseus home with a 'happy heart' as he sails due east keeping the pole star 'on the left hand'; not only is he returning home but he has an accurate navigation system to steer by. Sailing through the night, Odysseus would see both the Pleiades and Orion, which in turn would transit the meridian giving a competent navigator the additional information in which direction south lay.

Orion, the Hunter

In her sailing instructions to Odysseus, Calypso says that the Bear keeps an eye on Orion the Hunter, the most strikingly brilliant of all constellations, with his shining shoulders, tapering waist, battle sword at hip, spears or club in one hand and a bow in the other. One ancient myth records that after Orion was killed by the sting of a scorpion he was placed in the heavens far away from the scorpion; in other words, as any ancient astronomer would have known, Orion sets as Scorpius rises. While the pole star is vital to earth-bound sailors, the stars of Orion can be used to navigate around an area of the heavens that includes the constellations of Taurus and the Pleiades, Gemini, Auriga and Canis Major

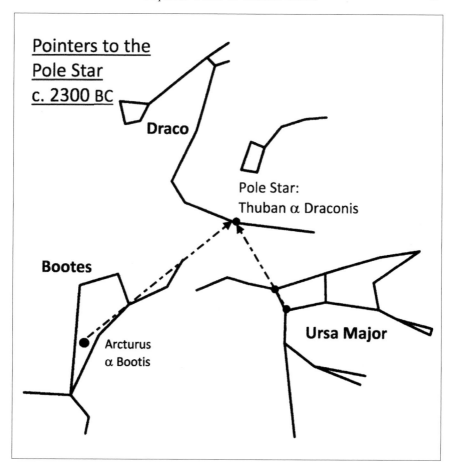

6.2 A line projected along γ and δ Ursae Majoris directs the eye towards Thuban and the North Pole *c.*2300 BC. Similarly, a line drawn from Arcturus, α Boötis, and using stars in the staff of Boötes as guides, also points to towards Thuban.

(see Fig. 6.3). An imaginary line running through the belt of Orion points in one way to Sirius, α Canis Majoris. The same line extended the opposite way runs close by Aldebaran, α Tauri, and on towards the Pleiades. Another line projected from the left side of the belt and through λ Orionis, in the 'neck' of Orion, runs on to Capella, α Auriga. The star Castor, α Geminorum, is found by running a line from the star on the right side of Orion's belt, Mintaka, ζ Orionis, and through the bright red star on the left shoulder, Betelgeuse, α Orionis.

Star-hopping in this manner has a long tradition and it is our belief that in naming four specific constellations in Calypso's sailing instructions Homer had a much wider purpose than merely enhancing narrative. Throughout the *Odyssey* (and *Iliad*) each of the constellations he names directly or metaphorically has an important bearing on the construction of his astronomical and calendrical treatise.

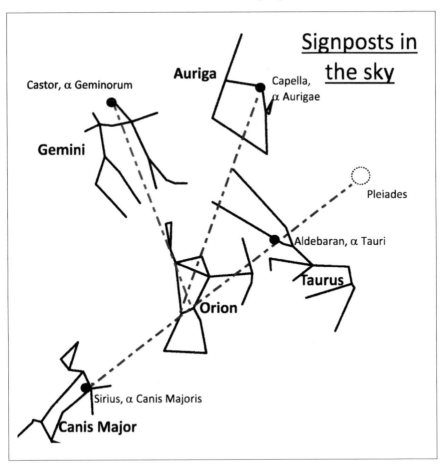

6.3 The dotted lines show how stars in Orion can be used to guide the eye to stars in other constellations.

Days 12–28, First Quarter to Third Quarter: Odysseus Leaves Calypso & Sails On

Odysseus sails without mishap for 17 days, which is the period from the moon's first quarter to its third quarter and the time of month when night sailing was easy and the face of the moon at its brightest. Translators who say that Odysseus' voyage lasts for '17' days are unaware of the importance of the phases of the moon. Older translations, such as those by Butcher and Lang and Samuel Butler, interpret Odysseus' sailing days as 'seven days and ten he sailed over the seas' (5.278). In an era long ago, the number might have been referred to as 'ten' days and 'seven'; ten days takes his journey to full moon and then seven more to the waning moon.

Table 2. 'Real-time' Days 12–33

Day of the month, Phase of the moon	Position of the sun	Day of the *Odyssey*	Poseidon destroys Odysseus' raft. The Phaeacians befriend him	2296/95 BC
4 to 20		12–28	Odysseus sails without mishap for 17 days.	13–28 Dec
21 3rd Qtr		29	Poseidon destroys Odysseus' raft but Odysseus clings to piece of timber. Athene calms the winds.	30 Dec
22		30	Odysseus drifts at sea.	31
23	β Aquarii	31	Odysseus drifts and on the twentieth day is washed up on Scherie, home of the Phaeacians.	1 Jan
24		32	Morning: Nausicaa washes clothing on the beach. Afternoon: Odysseus meets Nausicaa. Evening: Together they arrive at the palace of Alcinous.	2
25		33	Morning: the Phaeacian Games. Afternoon: Entertainment and dancing. Evening: Odysseus tells of his adventures.	3

Days 29–31, Waning Moon: Poseidon Wrecks Odysseus' Raft

Eighteen days after being freed by Calypso, Odysseus is sailing along when he spies the island of Scherie, home of the mysterious Phaeacians. The island looks to him like an upturned shield (5.280), an imaginative but not unrealistic description of the constellation Cygnus, whose stars are set against the background of the Milky Way.[3] Poseidon, angry at Odysseus for blinding his son Polyphemus, then sends a storm of raging winds. Turbulent waves wrench the rudder from Odysseus' hands and toss him into the sea; the sails, mast and half-deck quickly follow. The piece-by-piece destruction of his raft becomes a metaphor for the receding crescent of the waning moon and is strikingly similar to the way in which Odysseus will later describe the manner in which his remaining ship is also destroyed in a storm. Odysseus clambers astride a piece of timber representing the waning moon and Poseidon continues to exact his punishment and forces Odysseus to drift for two nights and two days. During his ordeal, the goddess Ino takes pity on the shipwrecked sailor and orders him to strip off the 'clothes' given to him by Calypso at the preceding new crescent and to wear a protective veil around his waist (5.345) until he reaches dry land. The 'clothes' Odysseus discards represent the passing phases of the moon.

As the waning crescent diminishes, Odysseus' strength also weakens and when he again catches sight of Scherie he is confronted with an impregnable coastline of high cliffs, the sea dashing against them (5.410). Odysseus eventually comes ashore in a river mouth, where he collapses with exhaustion. The vision of crashing foam-topped waves, surf and flying spray conjure images of an island constellation in the bright Milky Way. The metaphor continues when the naked Odysseus sleeps hidden beneath a blanket of leaves in a thicket so dense that the wind could not disturb him, nor the sun's light or rain penetrate. Meanwhile, the moon continues to wane and with the end of the final lunation, the 235th of the 19-year cycle, only eight or so days away, the sun is moving towards the winter solstice. After these tumultuous events, Day 31 comes to an end.

Day 32, Morning & Afternoon: Odysseus meets Nausicaa

A clue to the home in the heavens of the mysterious Phaeacians is found in Book 7, which opens with an elaborate history of how they came to the plentiful land of Scherie after they had been forced to leave their home in the broad lands of Hyperei, near to the land of the Cyclopes. Neither Scherie nor Hyperei can be found on earth but the migration of the Phaeacians reflects movement of some kind and an explanation can be found in constellations of the Milky Way. The origin of the word Phaeacia implies brightness, and Homer says the Phaeacians are akin to the gods and great seamen, suggesting perhaps that they 'sailed' upon that river of light from uninhabited Goat Island (Auriga and the Milky Way) to their new home in Scherie (Cygnus and the Milky Way). If such was the case then they were not alone in perceiving the Milky Way as a conduit along which to travel. Theony Condos remarks: 'Poetic fancy saw in the Milky Way a road, either the road of the gods, or the road besides which stood the palaces of the gods or the road travelled by the souls of the dead.'[4]

There is no telling what the constellation boundaries were in Homer's time, but since the Phaeacians had 'no near neighbours' (7.30), it points towards their home being in Cygnus, a beautiful constellation in which naked-eye observations are said to reveal almost 200 stars against the background of the Milky Way. The name Scherie implies 'shingle', which would be an apt metaphor for the multitude of stars in Cygnus. The Phaeacian royal family, Alcinous, Queen Arete and Nausicaa, can also be linked in myth to Cepheus, Cassiopeia and Andromeda, constellations in the same area of the Milky Way. King Alcinous and Cepheus were kings; Arete and Cassiopeia were their queens, while Nausicaa and Andromeda were their respective daughters. There is also a place in that part of the sky for the bard Demodocus who, to the music of the lyre, sang of Troy to the Phaeacian court. It is possibly no coincidence that the constellation of Lyra is adjacent to Cygnus.

Although Odysseus' stay with the Phaeacians is short in earthly terms, his time there reveals more of Homer's calendar-constructing skills. The narrative, too, is greatly enhanced by extended metaphor of constellations in the Milky Way that provide a backdrop for the epic from the time Odysseus makes his way ashore on

Scherie at the end of Book 5 through Books 6, 7 and 8, or some 1,330 lines of poetry. Until Odysseus' meeting with Nausicaa, our hypothesis that the narrative of Odysseus' adventures follows a steady rhythm linked to the phases of the moon had worked well. There the pattern suddenly appeared to change when Homer seemingly introduced several metaphorical references to a new crescent moon some seven days before it could possibly have been seen. Very early on the morning of Odysseus' arrival on Scherie, Nausicaa 'of the white arms' is told by Athene to go down to the beach and wash her 'bright' but 'dirty' clothes in a river before spreading them out to dry on the seashore, suggesting that her chore will wash away the dark of moon and herald a new crescent. Another indication of her connection with the lunar rhythm is made when she is described as Nausicaa of the 'white arms', which again creates an image of the crescent moon. With her washing complete, Nausicaa and her companions play ball and their laughter awakes the naked Odysseus. In his embarrassment he washes the salt and brine from his back, rubs himself with oil, dons new clothes given to him by Nausicaa and is magically transformed into a younger and sturdier man (6.230). When Odysseus is given new clothes elsewhere in the *Odyssey*, it also indicates the appearance of a new crescent, but on this occasion the moon is still waning. Bearing in mind these metaphorical images of the old crescent being replaced by the new, it is curious that seven days later Odysseus will throw off a beggar's disguise (22.1) and again be rejuvenated (23.155) at the appearance of a true new crescent moon.

Thoughts of weddings are also in evidence on Scherie, and Athene declares to Nausicaa that every nobleman in Phaeacia seeks her hand in marriage, for which she would need beautiful clothes (6.35) – another hint of an impending new

6.4 Nausicaa and her companions play ball on the beach. (John Flaxman, 1755–1826)

crescent moon. Nausicaa confides in her maids that her future husband should be like the rejuvenated Odysseus (6.240) and Alcinous even offers him his daughter's hand in marriage (7.310). There are yet more hints of a new crescent moon the following day when Queen Arete insists that Odysseus should again bathe and then gives him a new cloak and tunic before he cuts a slice of meat from a white-tusked boar (8.475), an ancient symbol of the winter solstice.

Such talk of washing, bathing, new clothes and a wedding imply the arrival of a new crescent, but the sequence of events on Scherie would then be out of step with the true rhythm of the moon. The new crescent will only arrive in seven days' time and the idea of Homer mistakenly recording two new moons in the space of seven days is not possible. Faced with such a puzzling situation, we rechecked translations of the *Odyssey* to discover if there were different versions of narrative, but scholars were consistent about the series of events.

We now felt we had run into a dead end and, much discouraged, put this part of the study aside. It was many months before we reconsidered the problem in a new light and realised we had been looking at Nausicaa's story only in terms of the last 40 'real-time' days and not as part of the overall 19-year calendar system. We then questioned the effect of counting a 19-year cycle in terms of alternating full months of 30 days and hollow months of 29 days. The result was surprising. If Homer had calculated that 118 of the 235 lunations were 30-day months and the other 117 were 29-day months, this would have given an average lunar month of 29.5 days. However, in modern times the lunar month is calculated at 29.531 days. The difference of 0.031 of a day multiplied by 235 (lunations) adds up to almost seven days, the length of time before the next true new crescent moon and the end of the 19-year cycle:

235 synodic months	=	6939.688 days
118 x 30 full months	=	3540 days
117 x 29 hollow months	=	3393 days
Total	=	6933 days

6939.688 - 6933 days = 6.688 days, and since Homer deals only with whole numbers this rounds up to seven days.

So, what was Homer's purpose in presenting so many false indications to the arrival of a new crescent? The conclusion of a cycle based on 235 alternating full and hollow months would indeed have occurred when Odysseus arrived in Scherie, but we propose that Homer was drawing attention to the need to account for the accumulative inaccuracy of averaging the lunar month at 29.5 days over 19 years. If this is so, it says much for his skills in calculation and observation. The narrative would also seem to support this view, for, despite previous signs of desperation by her father and his court to marry off Nausicaa, there is no further mention of her marriage. In later centuries Meton overcame the problem of adjusting the alternating full and hollow months in the 19-year cycle by arranging them in a series of 125 full months and 110 hollow months and so accounting for the seven-day deficiency.

Day 32, Evening: Phaeacians & Constellations of the Milky Way

As Odysseus makes his way to the palace and gardens of King Alcinous, Homer evokes lavish images which can be related to the Milky Way in the area of Cygnus. The palace, says Homer, was as beautiful as the sun and moon. The starry metaphors and references to the constant movement of the Milky Way continue as women folk go ceaselessly about grinding yellow corn and spinning and weaving white linen cloth, their hands fluttering like (white) aspen leaves (7.103). The king's garden is lush with pears, pomegranates, figs, apples, grapes, and fruits grow on fruits, apples on apples, figs on figs, and grapes on grapes. As if further proof were needed that Homer is constructing a metaphor for the starry heavens and not a paradise on earth, he says 'the fruits never rot nor die' and 'the flowers bloom all year'; they, like the stars, are everlasting. Similar sumptuous images of the Milky Way can be found in Homer's descriptions of Telemachus' visit to Menelaus' palace (Scorpius), Calypso's home (Sagittarius), the lush pastures of Goat Island (Auriga) and the everlasting feasting of Aeolus (Gemini) – all of them constellations in the Milky Way.

Day 33: Games & Gifts

This active day on Scherie is full of metaphorical descriptions of the Milky Way and more counting of the days of hollow and full months and the months of the year. In two short lines Alcinous compares the characteristics of the Phaeacians with the beautiful, bounteous, ever twisting and turning Milky Way. The Phaeacians, he says, are a people full of life and movement who 'can run fast … are first rate seamen … and take a delight in the feast, the lyre, the dance, frequent changes of clothes, hot baths and our beds' (8.248 Rieu). The Phaeacian games also add to the overall activity.

The day opens with Alcinous calling an assembly and sending for 52 oarsmen (8.35) from 'the town' to prepare a ship in readiness for Odysseus' departure for Ithaca. The oarsmen 'from the town' being 52 easily visible stars in Cygnus and the fitting out of the ship perhaps being a reference to the ancient constellation of Argo.

Demodocus, the blind minstrel who entertains the guests with songs of Troy, also forges a link with the night skies. Lying near to Cygnus, the bird flying down the Milky Way, is the constellation of Lyra, which celebrates the invention by Hermes of the lyre, the first musical instrument. Lyra becomes Demodocus' lyre and Vega, α Lyrae, the brightest star in the northern heavens, becomes the 'peg' from which his lyre is hung (8.68 & 8.105). Demodocus was blinded when the muse robbed him of his eyesight and there has been much discussion that Homer modelled the singer on his own conjectured blindness. Speculation that Homer was sightless would appear to have little foundation considering his vast observational knowledge of the heavens.

The brief description of the animals to be sacrificed for their meal yields the days in the month. There are a dozen sheep, eight white-tusked boars and two shambling oxen (8.58). The clue lies in the two shambling oxen, which represent two days of full moon and from that the other clues fall into place. The eight white-tusked boars have 16 tusks or 16 days of the crescent moon, and the sheep represent six days before and six days after the full moon: 8+6+2+6+8 = 30 days in a full month. However, since a month may only have 29 days that is accounted for as well. Homer names thirteen competitors in the games and later Alcinous says that, including himself, there are thirteen 'princes' and three of his sons who will donate gifts to Odysseus: the numbers 13+13+3 = 29 days in a hollow month.

Homer names each of the competitors: Acroneos, Ocyalus, Elatreus, Nauteus, Prymneus, Anchialus, Eretmeus, Ponteus, Proreus, Thoön, Anabesineos, Amphialus, Euryalus, and added to them are three of Alcinous' sons, Laodamas, Halius and Clytoneus. Etymologists have found that each name is a pun on a seafaring term[5] and once more Homer recalls that the Phaeacians are all about seas and voyages in ships that 'glide along like thought, or as a bird in the air' (7.35), a fitting description for the vessels of mariners who sail along the Milky Way. Odysseus takes part in the Phaeacian games and throws the discus further than any other contestant.

The Phaeacians are a civilised race and they press on Odysseus many parting gifts. Alcinous and 12 princes each give him a fresh cloak, a tunic and a talent of gold. One courtier, Euryalus (son of Naubolus), breaks the bounds of hospitality and disgracefully insults Odysseus' physical stature but, to make amends, he donates a 'sword of bronze, which has a sheath of newly carved ivory to hold it ... he then laid the sword with its silver mounting' (8.400). His gift can be compared with the configuration of Cygnus, or 'Northern Cross'. When Odysseus slings the sword about his shoulders it indicates that it is the time of the waning moon. Queen Arete adds a cloak and a tunic and the king himself gives a golden goblet Not only do the king and princes match in number the months of an intercalated lunar year, but they may also represent 13 constellations within the Milky Way, known as: Cepheus (Alcinous), Cygnus, Aquila, Perseus, Auriga, Gemini-Orion and Canis Minor-Monoceros-Canis Major, Argo, Scorpius-Ophiuchus, Sagittarius, Centaurus-Southern Cross, and Lupus and Ara. Arete, personified by Cassiopeia, would make a fourteenth constellation in the Milky Way.

Gifts & Days: the Lunar Months

Let us make him parting gifts, as is appropriate. Our people have for their chiefs and rulers twelve eminent princes – thirteen with myself [Alcinous]. (8.390 Rieu)

As with numbers in other parts of the *Odyssey*, the gifts given to Odysseus are linked to lunar months and years, as the following calculations show:

Gifts from Alcinous and the princes:
13 Cloaks
13 Tunics
13 Talents of gold
39 Total

From Euryalus, a competitor in the games (8.402):
1 Sword
1 Scabbard

From Arete (8.425):
1 Cloak
1 Tunic

From Alcinous (8.430):
1 Golden goblet

44 Total number of gifts

Included in this scene of friendship and generosity are 12 princes, the king and queen and Euryalus, which gives the equation:

44 gifts + 15 people = 59, which is the number of days in one hollow lunar month and one full month.

Some scholars have concluded that when Arete gives another cloak to Odysseus she had forgotten she had already given him one cloak, or that Homer had 'nodded' (13.65). On the other hand there is a calendrical answer: adding one more cloak to the total of gifts gives a tally of 60 gifts and people – and 60 is the number of days in two full months.

Day 33, Evening: Odysseus tells of his Adventures

Lavishly entertained by the Phaeacians with games in the morning, dancing in the afternoon and storytelling in the evening, Odysseus is moved to tears by memories of Troy recalled by the songs of Demodocus. When Alcinous asks Odysseus to give an account of himself, he begins to tell of the adventures that had befallen him on his ill-fated homeward journey – the exploits created to record the months of a lunar calendar. Odysseus speaks throughout the night and begins with the majestic words: 'I am Odysseus, Laertes son. The whole world talks of my stratagems, and my fame has reached the heavens ...'

Notes

1   Allen, R.H., *Star Names, their Lore and Meaning* (New York: Dover, 1963 reprint of 1899 edn), p. 392.

2   Sidgwick, J.B., *Introducing Astronomy* (London: Faber & Faber, 1961), p. 200. Arcturus has an unusually large 'proper motion' and is said to have moved 'one apparent diameter of the moon' since Ptolemy's time, 87–150 BC.

3   Moore, P., *Guinness Book of Astronomy 4th Edition* (Middlesex: Guinness Publishing), p. 193.

4   Condos, T., *Star Myths of the Greeks and Romans: a Source Book* (Grand Rapids: Phanes Press, 1997), p. 110, from 'Commentariorum in Aratum Reliquiae', p. 51.

5   Rieu, E.V. (trans.), *The Odyssey* (London: Penguin Group), 1991, p. 109.

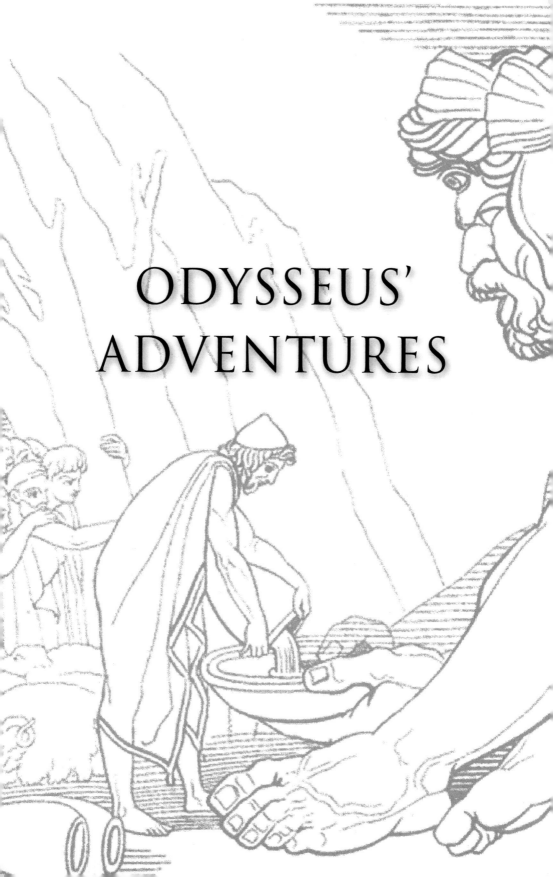

ODYSSEUS' ADVENTURES

7

TROY TO THE LAND OF THE LOTUS EATERS

Tracing the course of the tumultuous days before and after the sacking of Troy can be likened to sifting through long-forgotten items in a dusty attic. Detail of the downfall of the citadel can only be assembled in chronological order from the widely separated accounts of Helen of Troy, Demodocus and Odysseus, with supporting evidence from Zeus, Nestor and Menelaus. In Table 1, a short 'calendar' of these days begins with the tale of how Odysseus tricked a fellow soldier to give up his cloak on a cold winter's night and ends with the disastrous encounter of Odysseus and his men with the fearsome Cicones.

7.1 The wooden horse; this imposing structure is a tourist attraction at Troy. (BVDC/Fotolia)

Before the Walls of Troy: Sun in Aquarius, Waning Moon

Odysseus may be the major player in the *Odyssey* but his version of events surrounding the destruction of the Trojan citadel is considered less reliable than those
of others. During his first evening on Ithaca, while disguised as a beggar, he tells of
his role at Troy in a 'lying tale' to his friend, the pig-keeper Eumaeus. His lying tales,
often little regarded, are untrue in the sense that Odysseus is keeping his identity
secret and pretending to be someone else. Even so his stories include important
calendrical detail, which adds to knowledge found in other parts of the epic.

Odysseus spins a yarn that one night before the Greeks entered the city he
led a party of Greek soldiers who hid in reeds and brushwood beneath the walls
when the night was 'two-thirds done and the stars were past their zenith' (14.483).
A bitter north wind driving the falling snow was so cold that their shields were
coated with ice and to keep warm Odysseus used a trick to acquire a warm cloak
from one of his companions. His tale reveals not only the time of year as midwinter but also that it takes place during the last third of the hours of darkness,
with the diminishing crescent of the waning moon heralding the impending dark
period and the destruction of the city. It is easy for the eye to slip over the brief
quotation about the passing of the night hours without realising the depth of
astronomical learning required to divide night into three watches and to plot stars
across the sky over the course of a year.

Amongst the list of stars and constellations given to Odysseus by Calypso is
the (Great) Bear which wheels round the north pole, the hub of the heavens, and
never sets (5.275). Skilful stargazers can use circumpolar stars to mark the passing
of the night hours according to the positions of constellations and the season of
the year, but it is quite complicated.[1] Some long-forgotten astronomers, however,
devised an easier system of timekeeping involving stars which rise on the eastern
horizon at dusk, and cross the sky to set in the west at the approach of dawn. Such
stars would most likely have been from within the zodiacal band, an area of sky of
particular significance not only for Homer and his Greek predecessors, but also
for observers in other ancient cultures. Having identified a star or constellation
whose course could be plotted from dusk to dawn, it might appear reasonably
simple to then divide the heavens into three divisions and so calculate the passing of time. So it would have been except for two natural events. One is that the
hours of darkness vary with the seasons; in winter the nights are long and Leo,
for instance, could have been seen in the night sky for more than 13 hours. When
Regulus, α Leonis, rises just after sunset, it crosses the zenith at about midnight
and sets at dawn; the third watch of the night would then be between 3 a.m. until
the stars are swamped by the light of the sun at about 7.30 a.m. The second difficulty is that because of the changing panorama of the night sky over the course
of a year, a star rising at dusk and setting with the onset of dawn does so only for a
short time. After 10 days or so the heavens have moved on and that particular star

rises and sets later and reduces its value as a marker of time. It is then replaced by another star rising at dusk – and so on throughout the year. The ability to operate such a system of timekeeping together with their use of stars and constellations for navigation, is an indication that the Greeks were more than familiar with quite advanced astronomical concepts.[2]

When Odysseus and his companions are under the walls of Troy the waning moon appears during the third watch of the night and this observation makes it possible to deduce the phases of the moon over the following nine days until the arrival of the new crescent on the tenth, as Table 1 shows:

Table 1. The fall of Troy

Day of month Phase of moon	Position of sun	Procuring a cloak, wooden horse, Helen and the fall of Troy	Date 2305 BC
21 3rd Qtr 112th Lun.	λ Aquarii	Odysseus and fellow Greeks were stationed outside the walls of Troy. With the night two-thirds gone it was so cold that their shields were coated with rime and to keep warm Odysseus tricked a companion out of his cloak.	20 Jan
22		Menelaus, Diomedes, Odysseus and others climbed inside the wooden horse. Agamemnon set fire to the Greek camp and put out to sea leaving only the horse on the beach. The Trojans suspected it might be a trap and quarrelled amongst themselves about whether they should burn it or take it into the citadel.	21
23		Greed overcame caution and the horse was dragged into Troy.	22
24		During their first night inside the horse, Helen walked around it mimicking the voices of the wives of the Greeks. Although tempted to reply, the Greeks remained silent.	23
25		Helen cried out again for the second night running.	24
26		For a third night the Greeks heard Helen's sorrowful cries until at last they received a signal to leave the wooden horse and open the gates of the city for their comrades.	25
27 Dark ●		Troy fell easily and the city was burned. At sunset the Greeks feasted and celebrated, but Agamemnon and Menelaus argued for they had drunk too much wine.	26
28 Dark ●		The next morning half the fleet sailed homeward with Menelaus. On reaching Tenedos sacrifices were made but Odysseus returned to Troy to honour the gods.	27
29 Dark ●	β Piscium	Odysseus left Troy for the second time and the wind blew his fleet to Ismarus, land of the Cicones, where there was more booty to be had. Odysseus ordered his men to cease looting but they ignored him.	28
1 New crescent ☽		The Cicones slay six men from each of 12 ships. Odysseus and his remaining men set sail.	29

Wooden Horse: Dark of Moon

The last days of the ninth year of the siege are complex and involve much activity: Odysseus' secret reconnaissance beneath the walls; the wooden horse being taken into the city; Helen walking around the horse three times; the city falling; arguments between the Greek leaders; and finally warfare with the Cicones. All of this discord is in keeping with waning and dark periods of the moon. The story of how, towards the end of the ninth year of the siege, the cunning Greeks built a wooden horse in which was hidden a party of soldiers needs little retelling. Odysseus claimed to have devised the stratagem that led to the city's destruction but it is Demodocus who tells in some detail how the Greeks sailed away beyond the horizon and left behind the wooden horse they had built as a 'gift' for the Trojans. Some Trojans argued that the horse should be destroyed but eventually they sealed their own doom and dragged it into the city. Inside the walls, Helen was suspicious of the gift and three times walked around it and three times cried out to try and expose the men inside, but no one replied. Then, in the dark of a moonless night, the Greek fleet returned and soldiers emerged from the horse to open the city gates and let in their army; soon the citadel was burning and the Trojans put to the sword. With the constellation of Pegasus, possibly the inspiration for Homer's wooden horse, poised over the constellation of Aquarius (Troy), the city would certainly have 'burned' as the setting sun disappeared below the horizon (see Fig. 4.6).

With Troy destroyed and Helen reunited with Menelaus, the moon is still in its dark period and the Greeks, 'heavy with wine', hold an acrimonious meeting. Menelaus wants to sail home at once but his brother, Agamemnon, is adamant they should offer sacrifices to appease the anger of Athene (3.142), but this would delay them until the appearance of the first crescent moon after the winter solstice, which marks the beginning of a new year. Menelaus, once more happily reunited with his beloved Helen, may have felt a pressing need for a speedy departure for 'some god has made good the cavernous sea'. His urgency may have been heightened by knowledge of the fabled 'halcyon days', a period of some two weeks of calm weather around the winter solstice when in myth the halcyon bird laid its eggs in a nest of fish bones on the sea.[3] Odysseus was also anxious to leave for home before sacrifices were made and he sets sail for Tenedos in dark of moon. He soon repents and returns to Troy to honour the gods and make his peace with Agamemnon – but leaves again before the new crescent for a disastrous encounter with the Cicones. Agamemnon, Nestor and Diomedes, who had stayed behind to make sacrifices, sail away in the tenth year.

The point in the 19-year cycle at which Troy fell and the appearance of the first new crescent moon after the winter solstice was revealed by making a chart of the 235 lunations during the entire cycle (see Appendix 2). Twenty days after the winter solstice the sun now lies below the ring of stars in the Southern Fish, known as the 'Circlet of Pisces', a convenient home in the heavens for the

Cicones. At first all goes well and Odysseus' men sack Ismarus and seize Cicone womenfolk. His men ignore a plea for them to cease their looting, a further reflection of discord shown at dark moon. On the following morning, before the sighting of the new crescent moon, Odysseus' fortunes are reversed when Cicone reinforcements arrive 'as thick as leaves that bloom in summer', but his men hold their own until the time 'when the ploughman unyokes his oxen'. Odysseus' darkest moment comes when he loses six men from each of his 12 ships, a total of 72, shortly before the sighting of the new crescent. Metaphorically, if the 72 men represent 72 days, Homer is combining the lunar and solar calendars by counting the days from the appearance of the current new crescent to the new crescent at the spring equinox – 72 days away:

January	2 days remaining
February	28 days
March	31 days
April	11 days (the spring equinox on 11 April)[4]
	72 days in total

For Homer to have used a method of prediction combining the lunar and solar calendars only once would have been an interesting but singular event, but he uses a similar technique of foretelling the number of the days to equinoxes or solstices on three more occasions: Odysseus' encounters with Polyphemus, the Sirens and the monstrous Scylla. Seventy-two is a number with several implications: the sun processes 1° along the ecliptic every 72 years; there are 72° in each angle of a regular pentagon; and 72 divides a circle neatly into five parts – which is not to say that Homer necessarily knew of these matters.

Odysseus Sails Homewards: Tenth Year Begins

With the appearance of the new crescent heralding the 'the tenth year', Odysseus flees Ismarus and mournfully sails away on the first of the adventures that will mark the monthly lunations of an annual calendar. A projection of how lunations can be linked to the passage of the sun along the ecliptic are seen in the model in Fig. 4.3.

Calendars in the Greek city-states in the centuries long after Homer began with the sighting of a new crescent moon after either the winter or summer solstices. In Athens, for instance, the year began at midsummer but in Boeotia it began at midwinter.[5] Homer does not directly give the name of any month in the *Odyssey* but it is clear that Troy falls in the bitter cold weather of midwinter; half-way through the year is the heat of midsummer when he arrives on Circe's island, and on his return to Ithaca it is again midwinter and the longest night.

As can be seen in our projection of Odysseus' Ship's Log (Appendix 1), each monthly section has a heading that includes the month's sequential number in the year, the constellation in which the sun lies and the adventure experienced by Odysseus. For instance: 'Third month, sun in Taurus, Goat Island and Polyphemus', 'Fourth month, sun in Gemini, King of the winds'.

In the rest of this chapter and to the end of Chapter 11, Odysseus' adventures are presented as calendrical metaphor in the order in which he encounters them and which, in turn, follow the sequential order of the months of the year. His adventures can also be plotted along the ecliptic of a modern star chart.

First Month, Odysseus' fleet Hit by a Hurricane; Sun Passes Northern Fish (Pisces)

With the arrival of the new crescent Odysseus sails away from the Cicones and the sun moves through Pisces. The constellation of Pisces can be divided into the Southern Fish and Northern Fish, which are held together by a rope 'knotted' at α Piscium, the brightest star in the constellation. Although an inconspicuous constellation in terms of bright stars, Pisces stretches a considerable distance along the ecliptic and it takes the sun almost 45 days to pass from the mouth of the Southern Fish, γ Piscium, to α Piscium. During the sun's course through Pisces, one lunation of Odysseus' voyage is completed and the moon waxes to full moon in a second lunation before the sun leaves the constellation some 15 days later.

In the rhythm of Odysseus' adventures he commonly faces dire events as a lunation draws to a close and as the moon approaches the dark period at the end of the first lunar month in Pisces he might be expected to face hardship – and, of course, he does. No dramatic star myths are associated with the stars of Pisces, but in his *Phaenomena* (*c.*270 BC) Aratus described the constellation as belonging to the 'watery' area of the sky and during this part of his journey Odysseus certainly suffers while sailing the stormy seas. Zeus sends a hurricane which buffets the ships and tears the sails to shreds as the crescent of the waning moon diminishes. The ragged remnants are stowed in the holds of the ships as the crews take up their oars and row hard towards an unnamed land in an unknown location (9.75). Odysseus takes shelter for two days and two nights and the moon enters its dark phase as the fleet arrives on the unknown island. The sun now lies below the 'Northern Fish', which would make a convenient safe haven for the ships. (There are similar dramatic incidents such as when Odysseus is battered by storms at sea: at 12.314 he loses the last ship in his fleet and at 5.293 his self-made raft is deconstructed at the time of the waning moon.)

Although descriptive in narrative, Odysseus' experience with the hurricane takes only ten lines and does not seem to have aroused great interest amongst scholars who perhaps tend to move quickly on from Odysseus' woeful encounter with the Cicones to his arrival in the land of the Lotus Eaters. Its significance may have been underrated, too, because even Odysseus does not mention the incident when he later relates his experiences to his wife, Penelope (23.310). On the third day, at the appearance of the new crescent moon, Odysseus and his sailors raise the masts and set the sails to continue on their way.

Second Month, Cape Malea & Lotus Eaters: Sun Passes Pisces, Aries & Cetus, Moon Wanes

Odysseus' fleet sails safely on until the moon's third quarter foretells of further disaster and the fleet is hit by a second storm as it tries to round Cape Malea, a place of perilous cliffs and dangerous winds at the foot of the Peloponnese (9.80). It was from this adventure that our notion arose that Homer uses brighter stars on or near the zodiacal band as 'stations of the sun' rather than just plotting the path of the sun along the ecliptic and through a zodiac of 12 divisions. Although the stars along the ecliptic from Pisces to Taurus are relatively insignificant, there are two or three bright stars in Aries above the ecliptic, whilst below is one bright star in Pisces and the group of stars which make the head of Cetus. During the tale of the Lotus Eaters, which begins when Odysseus is blown off course at Cape Malea and sent past the island of Cythera, Homer quite logically would have used stars from Pisces, Aries and Cetus. As Odysseus sails down the Aegean, the sun lies between the 'head' of Cetus and the 'horn and muzzle' of the Ram, the star pattern of the latter creating a reminder of Cape Malea. Once more the waning moon is marked by stormy seas; as Odysseus commences the tricky sailing manoeuvre of rounding the Cape he is driven off course by foul winds for nine days, as the moon continues to wane and goes into its dark period. On the tenth day Odysseus leaves the familiar lands and seas on earth and enters the mystical world of the Lotus Eaters, the fearsome Cyclopes and other terrible hazards. In other words, as the sun enters Aries, Odysseus' voyages are transmuted from the 'wine-dark seas' to the 'wine-dark skies'. That there is something unusual in Odysseus undertaking a nine-day terrestrial voyage from the region of Cape Malea across the Mediterranean to the land of the Lotus Eaters has not gone unnoticed. For centuries questions have been asked about how fast Odysseus' fleet sailed and in what direction and which winds and currents may have influenced them. Ernle Bradford, for instance, said during those days Odysseus could have sailed some 650 miles to Djerba, an island off the north coast of Africa.[6]

In calendrical terms the nine-day voyage, and his arrival with the Lotus Eaters on the tenth, is the period from the third quarter of the waning moon to the appearance of the new crescent. The storm he encounters was another important clue that helped to link the adventures of Odysseus to the rhythms of the moon.

On arrival at the land of the Lotus Eaters, Odysseus sends out a reconnaissance party of two men and a herald (9.85 ff), each man possibly representing three dark nights of a monthly lunar cycle, which is then coming to an end.[7] Here Odysseus faces a peril of a different order for the lotus flower on which the natives live is 'so delicious that those who ate of it left off caring about home and did not even want to go back'.

Where Homer's land of the lotus can be found, and whether there ever was a lotus flower with the magical or narcotic qualities attributed to it, are questions which have long puzzled scholars and scientific researchers. Perhaps the answer lies in the dangerous allure of a tranquil resting place after the storms of winter and a long and arduous voyage through Pisces. Odysseus' men would have been eager to delay their homeward journey and succumb to a life of ease and the temptation of the mythical lotus flower while awaiting the calmer weather of approaching spring. Odysseus, however, pressed by the relentless march of the lunation, orders the three sailors sent out on the scouting mission to be dragged back to their ship and tightly bound beneath the rowing benches. At the appearance of the new crescent moon the fleet sets sail and carries Odysseus onwards to his dramatic encounter with the Cyclops, Polyphemus.

Notes

1   Rey, H.A., *The Stars, a New Way to See Them* (Boston: Houghton & Mifflin Co., 1962), pp. 124–5. First published 1952, and republished many times, the latest being 2008. Rey illustrates how the Dipper and circumpolar Cassiopeia can be used as a celestial clock.

2   How the Greeks of Homer's times created a 'star chart' through the medium of storytelling is explored in *Homer's Secret Iliad*, Chapters 4 & 5.

3   *Webster's Third New International Dictionary* (Springfield MA: G. & C. Merriam & Co., 1966).

4   Because of changes in the obliquity of the earth's axis, the date of the spring equinox *c.*2300 BC is different from that of today (see Chapter 5, p. 90).

5   Hannah, R., *Greek and Roman Calendars*, p. 42.

6   Bradford, E., *Ulysses Found* (London: Hodder & Stoughton, 1963), pp. 38–9.

7   On several occasions, Homer appears to use the number three as a reminder of the days of the dark period of the moon: when Helen walks three times round the wooden horse; when Odysseus three times offers a cup to Polyphemus; when Menelaus picks his three best men; when Eumaeus' treacherous nurse picks up three cups; when Odysseus stays three nights in the hut of Eumaeus; when Penelope lights three braziers; and when Eumaeus picks his three best pigs.

8

GOAT ISLAND & POLYPHEMUS

With a single round eye in his forehead, the monstrous Polyphemus vies with the wooden horse of Troy as the most unforgettable image in the *Odyssey*. Not only is Odysseus' encounter with the Cyclops one of the most enthralling stories in all mythology, but it opens for the astronomer, calendar maker and mathematician a wonderful vision of the achievements of the pre-literate Greeks. Odysseus' present adventure begins with a goat-hunting trip on a strange uninhabited island and then moves on to the grisly details of Polyphemus eating six of Odysseus' men, the drilling out of the Cyclops' eye and the subterfuge which Odysseus devises so that he and his men can escape.

In earthly terms the escapade begins when Odysseus and his fleet arrive at Goat Island and ends when the ships sail away from the island of the Cyclopes; it

8.1 Odysseus pours wine for Polyphemus. (John Flaxman, 1755–1826)

occupies five days of the lunar cycle from old moon to new crescent. During his encounter with Polyphemus the sun is in Taurus, the constellation of the spring equinox for more than 2000 years. More specifically *c*.2300 BC, the equinox was in the Pleiades,[1] an asterism of six or seven stars that lie at a distance from the main body of Taurus.

Third Month, Goat Island & Polyphemus: Auriga & Sun in Taurus

Homer introduces what might at first appear to be a low-key diversion when he tells of Odysseus' hunting expedition on a verdant but uninhabited island over-run with wild goats. The island lies 'not quite close but still not far off' from the land of the Cyclopes, which, as can be seen on any star chart, describes the same relationship in the heavens that Auriga has with Taurus, home of Polyphemus. Homer describes Odysseus' arrival on Goat Island with a metaphorical picture of

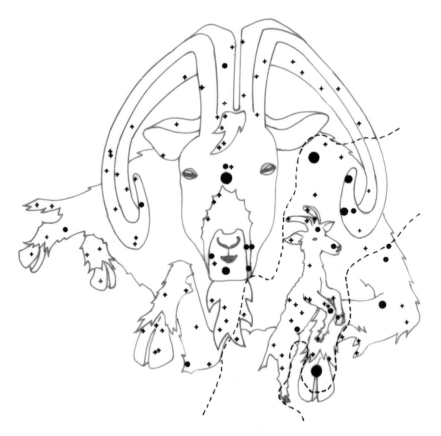

8.2 An image from Goat Island created from the stars of Auriga, a constellation long associated with goats in Greek mythology. (By GG-R)

rustic abundance which reflects the bountiful stars of the Milky Way and other celestial features that enhance Auriga.[2] There are strong similarities in the description of Goat Island with those of Calypso's island and Alcinous' palace, which we also place in the Milky Way and star-filled parts of the sky. Odysseus beaches his fleet on Goat Island in a good natural harbour, at the head of which there is a spring of clear water coming from a cave with poplars growing all round. Meadows are well watered and full of succulent grass, 'while grapes would flourish and level land for ploughing would provide bountiful harvests' (9.130 Butler).

In Greek mythology Auriga had a long connection with goats and in myth was said to be the goat that suckled the infant Zeus. The yellowish star Capella, α Aurigae, the brightest in the constellation, is known as the 'goat star' and three other stars are known as the Kids. Running diagonally across the lower part of the constellation is the Milky Way likened metaphorically in the *Odyssey* to 'water meadows' and 'lush grass', while brighter stars set against its background suggest an image of grapes. 'Ploughed land' creates an excellent simile for the dark sky in the upper portion of the constellation, and Capella becomes a 'safe harbour', with the nearby stars of the Kids as 'poplars growing all round'. A band of the Milky Way which runs close by Capella becomes an apt metaphor for the 'spring of clear water'. The Milky Way also runs through the upper region of Taurus and Homer uses similar lush pastoral imagery to describe the homeland of the Cyclopes, the race of one-eyed giants who 'neither plant nor plough', and live on wild wheat, barley and grapes which yield them wine (9.109). Such extravagant images of an agricultural paradise would have appealed to ancient farming communities and it can hardly be a coincidence that Odysseus' adventures in Auriga and Taurus occur just after the spring equinox, with its suggestions of perpetual bounty.

When Odysseus arrives at Goat Island he says 'not a gleam of the moonlight could be seen through the clouds', which is hardly surprising for on that murky night the waning moon is close to entering a dark period and would have risen in the early hours of the morning. It was the tally of Odysseus' ships and men and the 118 goats killed on the island that led to the discovery of the crucial role that embedded data plays in Homer's calendar making. After enjoying the pleasures of Goat Island and replenishing their stocks of meat, Odysseus and his men feast on the sea shore (the Milky Way), where they can see the campfires and hear the deep voices of the uncultured, uncivilised and lawless tribe of one-eyed Cyclopes on the nearby land. Seeking to satisfy his curiosity, Odysseus leaves Goat Island the following day with a party of 12 men but meets calamity at the hands of Polyphemus as the moon enters a dark period. His bleakest moment occurs when he can see no way of escaping from the cave of Polyphemus, but as the new crescent approaches he devises a cunning stratagem and on the day of the arrival of the new crescent moon he sails on towards his next adventure. As the intricate story of Odysseus' confrontation with Polyphemus develops, calendrical, astronomical and arithmetical metaphors unfold.

One-eyed Polyphemus: Moon in Dark Period

The common image of the stars of Taurus lend themselves to be redrawn as the monstrous Polyphemus, for the constellation's attributes match those of the Cyclops as much as they do a bull. Polyphemus' bent foreleg and long-striding legs, large arms and hands can be compared to the legs and horns of the bull. His single eye and face twisted to the side is that of the profile of the bull whose single eye, like that of Polyphemus, is represented by the bright red star Aldebaran, α Tauri, the brightest in the constellation. Homer adds to the imagery by including the asterism of the Hyades as a grisly representation of the vomit of the drunken monster.

> As [Polyphemus] spoke he reeled, and fell sprawling face upwards on the ground.
> His great neck hung heavily backwards and a deep sleep took hold upon him.
> Presently he turned sick, and threw up both wine and the gobbets of human
> flesh on which he had been gorging, for he was very drunk. (9.375 Butler)

Another outstanding feature of Taurus are the Pleiades, a long regarded asterism of six or seven stars that lie at a distance from the main body of the constellation. Homer refers to their position when Odysseus lies to Polyphemus that his ships have been lost: 'Poseidon,' he says, 'sent my ship on to the rocks [the Pleiades] at the far end of your country [constellation of Taurus], and wrecked it' (9.284).

Leaving behind 11 ships and their crews, Odysseus and his 12 companions arrive in the land of the Cyclopes and enter the empty cave of Polyphemus, son

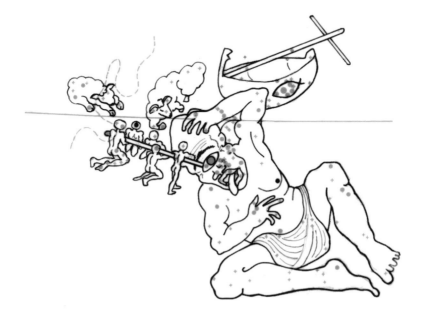

8.3 Polyphemus as a grotesque figure and the stars of Taurus. (By GG-R)

of the sea god Poseidon. When Polyphemus returns, his actions reflect that it is now the dark period of the lunar month and also describe a possible solar eclipse. Polyphemus blocks out light from the entrance to the cave (representing the sun) with a large stone (the moon) that was so huge it could not be moved by 22 four-wheeled wagons. The numbers embedded in these events will be seen to have more importance than merely adding detail to narrative.

Later, when questioned by Polyphemus, Odysseus replies with one of the best-known lies in literature and says his name is 'Noman' (9.365), which nevertheless is apt because neither the moon nor Odysseus, the lunar icon hidden in the cave, would have been visible at that time. Without further ado, Polyphemus eats two sailors for supper, followed by two more for breakfast the next day. While Polyphemus is away tending his sheep, Odysseus devises a cunning plan for the survivors to escape by blinding their tormentor with a fire-hardened pole of green olive wood. On Polyphemus' return in the evening, he takes his flock into the cave and snacks on two more unfortunate sailors. Odysseus plies the monster with drink and as Polyphemus falls into a drunken stupor, he and four crewmen plunge an olivewood pole into his eye and twist it around so fiercely that the giant's blood boils and dreadful screams are heard by his fellow Cyclopes, who cry out and ask what is happening. Out of the cave came mighty Polyphemus' voice in reply: 'O my friends, it's Noman's treachery, not violence, that is doing me to death' (9.408). His brother Cyclopes then go away blaming the shouting on a strange illness. At dawn, when Polyphemus removes the boulder to let his sheep out of the cave, Odysseus and his surviving men escape by clinging under the bellies of three thickly fleeced rams lashed together. Safe on board his ship, Odysseus taunts Polyphemus, who in a rage throws a massive stone into the sea and their ship is swept on to Goat Island, where the rest of his fleet is moored. They share their spoils and the next day Odysseus sails onward to his next adventure with Aeolus, King of the Winds; from this point it will be 88 days before he begins his stay with the witch Circe.

A Wealth of Concealed Learning

Polyphemus may be a member of a race of uncivilised and brutal people but his story conceals a wealth of concealed knowledge. A seemingly random assembly of numbers and images point towards Homer's understanding of π, the ratio of the diameter of a circle to its circumference. A collection of four-wheeled wagons contains data about the lunar calendar and a possible eclipse cycle. The number of victims and survivors amongst the men in this episode has implications for the ratio of cycles of the sun and Venus, while Homer also expresses an awareness of the precession of the equinoxes, an ancient meteor shower and the heliacal rising of Aries.

Homer & π in the Sky

In the story of Odysseus' encounter with Polyphemus there are many images of 'circles' and 'roundness' and if these are combined with numerical data embedded in the incident they give an insight into the mathematical skills of the pre-literate Greeks. It is not only the large round eye in the middle of Polyphemus' forehead that gives an image of a circle, another arises when the Greeks blind Polyphemus by taking a pointed pole of olive wood and *rotating* it in his eye socket. And if that were not enough, the name 'Cyclops' implies roundness, circular or revolving. Other images of roundness that Homer lists in the adventure with Polyphemus include wagon wheels, a boulder, a silver mixing bowl, jars of wine, baskets laden with round cheeses, open bowls of whey and milk, and an olive wood bowl. Also included are the numbers 3, 7, 21 and 22, with 3 being repeated several times:

- Odysseus received three gifts from Maron the priest.
- Polyphemus keeps his lambs and kids in three separate pens.
- Each sailor escapes by clinging to the bellies of three black sheep lashed together.
- An olive bowl offered to Polyphemus is filled with wine and emptied three times.
- After milking, Polyphemus divides the milk into three parts (milk to drink, cheese curds and whey).
- Polyphemus seals and opens the cave three times, and three times repeats the name 'Noman'.
- Three times Polyphemus eats two of Odysseus' men, and his encounter with the Cyclops takes place over three days.

There is further astronomical symbolism in other of Maron's gifts, where the silver bowl may be seen as the moon and 12 jars of wine may mark the months of the lunar year. Nor must a suggestion of the full round moon be disregarded.

   Homer is determined that his audiences should constantly bear in mind images and numbers that lead to an understanding of a topic which has greatly taxed inquiring minds from very ancient times: π, the ratio of the diameter of a circle to its circumference. The ratio can be expressed in simple terms as 'three times the diameter of a circle gives (approximately) the length of the circumference'. π is a number without end for it has infinite numbers to the right of the decimal point and it has intrigued mathematicians for thousands of years, including Archimedes (c.287–212 BC), the greatest mathematician of antiquity. Babylonians, Egyptians and Hebrews all made calculations to determine a value for π, which today is stated in brief as π = 3.142, but for many 22/7 may still lurk in the memory from schooldays. Fascination with π continues and in 2009 Daisuke Takahashi at the University of Tsukuba in Japan calculated it to 2.6 trillion digits. Author David

Blatner says that probably no symbol in mathematics has evoked as much mystery, romanticism, misconception and human interest as π.[3]

Pi, π, has many uses in mathematics, engineering and construction, and while Homer's introduction of the idea of 22 four-wheeled wagons on the island of the Cyclopes may seem curious, they are a reminder that the wheelwrights of his age would have found an empirical knowledge of π useful to centre the axle of a wheel. Odysseus takes with him to Polyphemus' island a goatskin of Maron's wine and recalls that the priest himself drank it when mixed with 20 parts of water, giving a total of 21 parts. Other gifts from Maron are seven talents and when seven is divided into 21 (parts of wine and water) the answer is three, an approximation of π that may have satisfied an ancient wheelwright and one known to the Babylonians and Hebrews. These observations suggest that Homer is hinting at something other than a mixture of wine and water that was so weak and tasteless it would have been rejected in disgust by the lusty hard-drinking warriors of the *Odyssey*.

The pursuit of accuracy in defining π has its origins in antiquity and although three may have been adequate for less demanding purposes, the Babylonians and Egyptians were sufficiently skilled to have calculated a more precise figure. Two numbers included in the episode of Polyphemus' cave point to Homer also knowing that the true definition of π was a fraction more than 3. One number is 22 (the number of wagons that would have been needed to move the boulder from the entrance of the cave) and the second is seven, which is stated when Odysseus flees the cave with six surviving companions. This gives the calculation: $22 \div 7 = 3 \, 1/7$.

Secrets of the Wagon Wheels

> [Polyphemus] rolled a huge stone to the mouth of the cave – so huge that two and twenty strong four-wheeled wagons would not be enough to draw it from its place against the doorway. (9.240 Butler)

On the face of it, Homer's choice of numbers in this quotation would seem to have little literary importance beyond giving an impression that the stone blocking Odysseus' escape route from Polyphemus' cave was indeed enormous. So huge is the stone blocking the sunlight streaming through the entrance that it could only be moved by the supernatural powers of Polyphemus. Calendrically it is a different story that begins with a simple calculation: 22 (wagons) x 4 (wheels) = 88

Eighty-eight is the number of days in two hollow months and one full month, or the interval between four new crescent moons. The Ship's Log reveals that from when Odysseus sails away after his disastrous confrontation with Polyphemus there are 88 days before the appearance of the first new crescent moon after the summer solstice. Homer has already matched the 72 men taken by the Cicones

to the number of days from the first new crescent moon after the winter solstice
to the spring equinox. The number 88 will crop up again in similar circumstances
during Odysseus' adventures with the Sirens and Scylla.

As a metaphor for the moon, the huge door stone also gives a powerful image
of a solar eclipse as it blocks out the light of the sun at the mouth of the cave. It
may not be coincidence that 88 is also the number of lunations in an eclipse cycle
of 7.11 years. Only in relatively recent times was the cycle given the name 'tzolkinex', as its length is close to 10 tzolkins, each of which had 260 days and was
a feature of the Mayan calendar system.[4] An additional calculation in which 88
lunations is also taken to represent alternate full and lunar months gives the result:

44 full lunar months of 30 days	=	1320 days
44 hollow lunar months of 29 days	=	1276 days
Total	=	2596 days
2596 days ÷ 365	=	7.11 years

Using the duration of a lunar month as the more accurate 29.53 days and mul-
tiplying it by 88 lunations gives 2598.64 days, which, divided by the true solar
year of 365.24 days, gives the same result to two decimal places as the ancient
calculations:

$$2598.64 \div 365.24 = 7.11 \text{ years} = \text{a tzolkinex eclipse cycle}$$

While it is not known whether the 7.11 year eclipse cycle had been recognised at
the time of Homer, it may lead to interesting lines of inquiry in the future.

Precession of the Spring Equinox

When Odysseus puts out the eye of Polyphemus two astronomical possibilities
can be considered. In the short term, Aldebaran, α Tauri, lies near to the path of
the sun and each year its light is obliterated by the rising sun. The blinding of
Polyphemus may suggest a reference to the slow precession of the spring equinox.
Aldebaran was the marker of the equinox at about 4200 BC and the gouging of
Polyphemus' single eye would make an admirable metaphor for the passing or
precession of the equinox towards the Pleiades (*c.*2300 BC). It is as inevitable in
a yearly calendar that the Cyclops' eye should be put out as it is certain that the
point of precession moves on through the zodiac; even the injured Polyphemus
is philosophical about the inevitability of his fate for he had had a warning that a
man called Odysseus would rob him of his sight (9.511). Although Polyphemus
had expected a big strong man to carry out the deed, perhaps like precession,

Odysseus may have seemed of little consequence over the shorter term but proved inexorable over the ages.

The gouging of Polyphemus' eye could also provide a short account of the principles related to the spring equinox, which are summarised today as 'the motion of the equinoxes along the ecliptic (the plane of the Earth's orbit) caused by the cyclic precession of the Earth's axis of rotation' (*Encyclopaedia Britannica*, 2006). Homer avoids the need for this scientific explanation by telling how Odysseus takes an olivewood pole to blind Polyphemus. The pole is essentially a gigantic fire drill, an age-old method of making fire by friction, and Homer's description of the process is accurate. Fortunately for Odysseus, Polyphemus had left lying around a pole of green olivewood, a symbol of the spring equinox and in its green state a good type of wood for a fire drill. Homer's narrative also accurately reflects the sound effects of fire-making: the roots of the Cyclops' eye crackling in the heat, the hissing of hot iron in cold water and the shrieking of Polyphemus as Odysseus twirls his pole. Crackling, hissing and shrieking are the sounds heard when a sharpened stick is rapidly revolved in what is called an eye or socket.

Cycles of the Sun & Venus

The significance of why Homer says that four men plus Odysseus prepare a stake of olivewood to gouge out Polyphemus' eye was at first puzzling. It might, however, be linked to an astronomical ratio concerning cycles of the sun and Venus. The planet's 584-day synodic cycle just happens to coincide with the solar year of 365 days, in the ratio of five Venus cycles to eight solar years. Anthony Aveni says it means that any visible aspect of Venus timed relative to the position of the sun will be repeated almost exactly after eight years.[5] The ratio of five to eight is found when Polyphemus eats four men, leaving only eight of the sailors who accompanied Odysseus still alive. With violence in his heart, Odysseus hardens an olivewood stake to blind the Cyclops and four men are chosen by lot to help him. It makes in total a group of five, and so providing the numbers five and eight, which is the ratio of five Venus cycles (a Venus period) to eight solar years.

Coincidence that it might be, it is worth noting that during the historic period chosen for our model of the 19-year cycle, Venus, the Morning Star, was visible in the sky before dawn when Odysseus was in the cave of Polyphemus.

Meteor Showers & Polyphemus' Bleeding Eye

If drilling out the eye of Polyphemus was not grisly enough, Homer enhances the story by telling of the blood spurting from the giant's eye. In *Homer's*

Secret Iliad[6] similar references to bleeding or bursts of tears were considered as descriptions of meteor showers. Trying to trace the incidence of particular meteor showers in the distant past is fraught with difficulties; on the one hand because of a lack of records and on the other because of the variable nature of the showers themselves. However, the 'red hot blood' streaming from Polyphemus' eye (9.299) calls to mind the Taurids meteor shower, with its radiant near Aldebaran and known for its fireballs. Although the Taurids are now seen in November, it is thought to be a meteor shower in its 'old age', and in the eleventh century AD, is said to have been as prominent as the Perseids are now.[7]

Odysseus & his Men Escape: Heliacal Rising of Aries

The escape of the Greeks from Polyphemus' cave draws attention to another feature in the spring skies *c*.2300 BC and provides a link with the rams that concealed Odysseus and his men. At that point in the annual calendar the constellation of Aries (the Ram) made its heliacal rising on the eastern horizon at dawn, just before its stars were overwhelmed by the growing light of day. For some 40 days before, Aries would not have been visible either by day or night. It is hard to get away from the symbolism of rams in the story of Polyphemus (9.425) and Homer tells how as they leave the cave of Polyphemus, Odysseus and his men cling to the bellies of these 'thick-fleeced, fine big animals their coats of black wool'.

Eighteen rams were lashed together in groups of three to carry the sailors, an arrangement which can also be associated with the grouping of certain stars of Aries.

Odysseus is carried by the leader of the flock, and Polyphemus is puzzled why his prized ram left the cave last and not first as was usual; this draws attention to Hamal, α Arietis, which is the brightest star in Aries but not the one which leads the constellation across the sky.

Adjusting the Lunar Calendar

When Polyphemus eats six of Odysseus' men, Homer partly resolves the adjustment needed to keep the lunar and solar calendars in harmony. Without human intervention the lunar calendar of 354 days is soon out of step with the 365 days of the solar calendar. In one year there is almost an 11-day difference between the two calendars; in three years it is 33 days; after ten years this has increased to 109 days. Of the dilemma, David Ewing Duncan wrote:

The ancient Greeks and others who threw their lot in with the moon found themselves with calendars running almost 11 days fast, a misalignment that within a few years flings a calendar into disarray against the seasons, flip-flopping the summer and winter solstices in just 16 years. This situation is unacceptable to anyone using such a calendar as a guide to planting and harvesting, or for knowing the proper seasons for sailing, building houses and worshipping gods.[8]

Homer shows his awareness of the 11-day annual shortfall and two tragic episodes, one in the first half of the year and the second in the latter part, imply how the problem can be resolved. Homer does not use fractions of numbers and at the spring equinox the six men eaten by Polyphemus might be the rounded up 5½ days that the lunar calendar falls short of the solar calendar between one equinox and the next. Similarly, when Odysseus arrives at the autumn equinox, Scylla devours six more men to accommodate the further disparity of five-plus days that had arisen between the spring and autumn equinoxes. The ten goats plus Odysseus (10 + 1 = 11) serve as a reminder of the differing number of days between the lunar and solar years, as will the 11 ships that are later destroyed by the Laestrygonians. There is also an indication of intercalation, the period insertion of an extra (intercalary) month into the lunar calendar to keep it in step with the solar calendar. Apart from Odysseus, 12 men went to the land of the Cyclopes and they represent metaphorically the number of months in a lunar year. With the addition of Odysseus the party totalled 13, the number of months in an intercalated year. A reading of Odysseus' visit to Hades suggests that it takes place after an intercalary month (see Chapter 10). In Homer's era the solar year was calculated as 12 months x 30 days (360 days) plus 5 extra (epagomenal) days, to give a total of 365 days. In Chapter 5 Homer expressed this in narrative by listing 360 boars on the farm of Eumaeus and adding to them five (four dogs plus Eumaeus), to give 360 + 5 = 365. As well as this and Odysseus' five-day adventure on Goat Island and with Polyphemus, Homer also draws attention to five-day periods when Odysseus and his men arrive on Circe's island, and Odysseus' homecoming on Ithaca at the climax of the *Odyssey*. Detail of how two of these periods are linked to narrative can be seen in Table 1 (overleaf):

Table 1. Five-day periods in the *Odyssey* followed by an adventure

Climax of the *Odyssey*	Goat Island & Polyphemus
Day 1: With the last sighting of the waning moon in the morning, Odysseus arrives in Ithaca. That night he sleeps in Eumaeus' hut.	Days 1–2: Odysseus and his men arrive on Goat Island late at night. Next morning they hunt and in the evening they feast.
Days 2–3: Odysseus stays in Eumaeus' hut.	Day 3: Odysseus and 12 men row to the island of the Cyclopes and explore Polyphemus' cave. The entrance of the cave is blocked and they are trapped inside. Two men are eaten by Polyphemus.
Day 4: Odysseus makes his way to his palace and is recognised by his old nurse, Eurycleia.	Day 4: While still trapped in the cave, four more men are eaten and during the night Odysseus drills out Polyphemus' eye.
Day 5: New crescent appears on day of the Feast of Apollo. Odysseus vanquishes the suitors.	Day 5: Odysseus and his surviving men escape at sunrise and return to Goat Island.

Notes

1   See *Homer's Secret Iliad*, pp. 116–7, for another possible reference to the Pleiades being at the boundary of Taurus as perceived by Homer in the *Iliad*.

2   In the *Iliad* Homer uses similar imagery of the Milky Way to describe the Shield of Achilles. *Homer's Secret Iliad*, p. 198 ff.

3   Blatner, D., *The Joy of* π (Hamondsworth: Penguin, 1998).

4   The name Tzolkinex was suggested by Felix Verbelen (2001): see: http://www.phys. uu.nl/~vgent/eclipse/eclipsecycles.htm. See also Aveni, A., *Stairways to the Stars* (New York: John Wiley & Sons, 1997), p. 36.

5   The term 'Venus year' used in association with this synodic period, should not be confused with the 224.7 days it takes for Venus to orbit the sun.

6   *Homer's Secret Iliad*, pp. 122, 142, 145–6 & 184.

7   Bone, N., *Philip's Observer's Handbook Meteors* (London: George Philip, 1993), p. 113.

8   Ewing, D., *The Calendar* (London: Fourth Estate, 1998), p. 17.

9

KING OF THE WINDS TO CIRCE'S ISLAND

Odysseus next comes to the island of Aeolia, where he will stay for a month feasting and storytelling with Aeolus, King of the Winds. The narrative takes a curious turn and for once no ill befalls the homeward-bound Greeks. During this lunar month the sun leaves Taurus, crosses a band of the Milky Way and moves through Gemini, a constellation with a long history steeped in mythology. At the end of his month's stay with Aeolus, Odysseus bids farewell to his royal host and receives 'a bag of winds', a parting gift which brings more woe for the weary voyager.

Fourth Month, King Aeolus: Sun in Gemini

Homer's description of the kingdom of Aeolia may be short in terms of narrative, but he creates a picture of the easily discernable stars of Gemini in the two forms they have been known since ancient times: a rectangular outline set against the backdrop of the Milky Way (Fig. 9.2), and a pair of 'matchstick twins' (Fig. 9.3). As Aeolia comes into sight, Odysseus describes it 'as an island that floats upon the sea, iron bound with a wall that girds it'. When Gemini rises it gives an impression of the constellation floating on the 'seas' of the Milky Way. An imaginary line connecting the principal stars in the rectangular outline of Gemini suggests the 'iron wall', with the Milky Way, which runs diagonally through the constellation, making a fine steep cliff. Secondly, the rectangular 'island' can also be perceived as the bed in which Aeolus and his wife and family of 12 children sleep warm and snug under the 'blanket' of the Milky Way – as the following quotation shows:

> Now, Aeolus has *six* daughters and *six* lusty sons, so he made the sons marry the daughters, and they all live with their dear *father* and *mother*, feasting and enjoying every conceivable kind of luxury … but by night they sleep on their well-made bedsteads, each with his own wife between the blankets. (10.1 Butler)

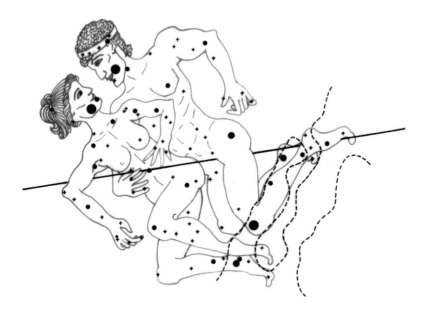

9.1 The stars of Gemini and the Milky Way make a fine bed for Aeolus and his queen. (By GG-R)

In Gemini's other familiar form as 'matchstick twins', Aeolus represents Castor, α Geminorum, once thought to be brightest star in the constellation, while his queen becomes Pollux, β Geminorum. In the leading twin, other stars apart from Castor are allotted to their six sons; in the rear twin the brighter stars apart from Pollux are allotted to their six daughters. At first we thought this a rather strange perception but it is not unique, and on Egypt's Dendera zodiac the constellation is represented by a male and female figure walking hand in hand.

That Homer should associate Gemini with the Aeolus, King of the Winds, comes with little surprise for there is a very old connection between the constellation and stormy weather. According to myth, the twins, Castor and Pollux, were placed in the heavens above a starry ship as their reward for protecting their fellow Argonauts in a storm that almost overwhelmed the good ship *Argo* during the quest for the Golden Fleece. Castor and Pollux were considered by the Greeks, and even more so by the Romans, as auspicious to mariners. The twins have also been linked to the electrical phenomenon

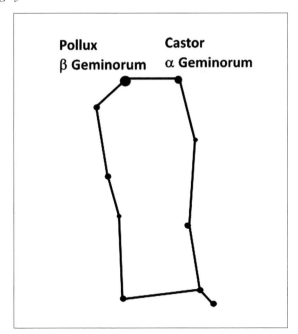

9.2 Gemini as an 'island that floats on the sea' and the bed in which Aeolus and his family sleep.

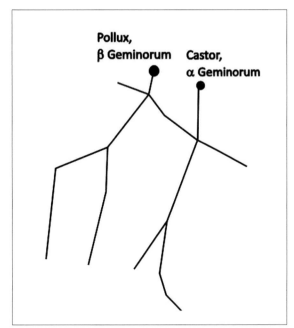

9.3 Gemini as a pair of 'matchstick' twins.

known as St Elmo's fire, common in heavy weather at sea and well known since ancient times.[1] Aeolus, King of the Winds, makes a present of 'a bag of winds' to Odysseus, which later unleashes a terrible storm when opened by his men.

Fifth Month, Odysseus Leaves Aeolus: Sun Moves from Gemini into Cancer

Odysseus' peaceful month of feasting on Aeolia (10.14) may seem at odds with the usual rhythm of his adventures because nothing untoward happens to him or his men. During their stay with Aeolus the sun moves along the ecliptic through the 'feet' of Gemini, where stars of the Milky Way reflect the bountiful image of the 'forever feasting' Aeolus and his family. Other similar generous metaphors of the Milky Way are found in the lavish descriptions of Calypso's cave (Sagittarius), Alcinous' palace and garden, the dancing and feasting of the Phaeacians (Cygnus, Cepheus, Cassiopeia) and Odysseus' adventure on luxuriant Goat Island (Auriga). Later, as Odysseus reaches Helios' island, he suffers both feast and famine as the sun crosses the bands of light and dark pools of sky in the Milky Way. On leaving Aeolia, Odysseus steers his ship single-handedly for nine untroubled days and on the tenth comes in sight of his homeland, Ithaca. Weary because of his days at the helm but comforted by the thoughts of home, he hands over command of his ship to the crew and falls fast asleep. All is not well with his seamen, however, who believing that the bag of winds given to Odysseus by Aeolus contains treasure, open the gift and instantly unleash a storm. Odysseus awakes and is so disgusted at their misdeeds that he covers his face with a cloak as the turbulent winds force the fleet back to Aeolia. The mood is now changing and Aeolus is no longer a benevolent friend and orders Odysseus, 'whom the gods now detest', to leave immediately. For six days the ships sail on and on the seventh arrive in the land of the Laestrygonians.

Odysseus' days at sea after first leaving Aeolus, sighting his homeland, the incident with the bag of winds, his return to Aeolia, his immediate expulsion and his subsequent voyage to the land of the Laestrygonians, is one of the most difficult adventures to place within a period of time. Fortunately, Homer gives several markers which make it possible to plot his journey through the lunar calendar, as can be seen in the Ship's Log (Appendix 1). On the tenth day after first leaving Aeolia, Odysseus and his shipmates can see cooking fires burning in their homeland (10.30). In earthly terms, it is a mystery of how he can be so near home and yet still face many more years of suffering before setting foot on Ithaca. Here, in less than four lines of poetry, Homer illustrates his knowledge of one of the fundamental rules of the night sky; that is, when the full moon rises in the east it is in the constellation 180° opposite that in which the sun had set in the west. In other words, as the sun leaves Gemini and moves towards Cancer, the full moon rises in Capricornus. The 'fires' the sailors can see on the horizon are the rising stars of Capricornus, the constellation in which the sun will lie when Odysseus eventually returns to Ithaca.

Events on the tenth day of his first departure from Aeolia suggest that a full moon is shining and this makes it possible to project the days of the second lunar month associated with Odysseus and Aeolus. On the tenth day Odysseus is blown back to Aeolia, which seemingly would take the same number of sailing days as before; this gives two ten-day periods on each side of a full moon, 20 days in all. Aeolus forces the fleet to leave immediately and the crews 'row' for six days as the waning crescent diminishes and on the seventh arrive in the land of the Laestrygonians, with the moon in its dark period. With the sun now in Cancer, the lunation ends in tragedy as the Laestrygonians eat one man from Odysseus' own ship and destroy the other 11 ships of his fleet and their crews. This latter incident again illustrates that the lowest part of Odysseus' adventures occur as a lunation ends. In total, almost two lunations pass from when Odysseus first lands on Aeolia to his arrival on the island of the Laestrygonians, during which the sun travels some 55° along the long stretch of open sky from Gemini to Cancer.

One puzzle remains: Odysseus' return to Aeolia after his men open the bag of winds takes ten days which seems inexplicable because you cannot travel 'backwards in time'. An answer may lie in the 19-year cycle chosen for our model calendar, when his return to Aeolia would have occurred with the heliacal rising of Gemini. By that time the sun had moved out of Gemini, so its stars, no longer obscured by the light of day, could only be briefly seen on the eastern horizon at dawn as the constellation made its heliacal rising. Odysseus' return to Aeolia (Gemini) may be a recognition of this and perhaps it is more than coincidence that he takes with him two men who sit on each side at the palace door, symbolising the two 'stick men' in the ancient concept of Gemini. Other metaphors that describe heliacal risings of constellations are found when Odysseus straps himself under the belly of a ram (Aries), in Elpenor's burial (Leo), in Odysseus' return to Charybdis (Scorpius and the Milky Way) and when Odysseus is portrayed as the greatest archer on the field of Troy (Sagittarius). Why Homer should tell such a complex story during this period is not entirely clear.

Laestrygonians, Odysseus Loses 11 Ships: Moon Dark Period

Odysseus' disastrous visit to the land of the Laestrygonians occupies only one day, the remaining hours of the moon's dark period, which is followed by a new crescent. The sun meanwhile has moved into Cancer, a rather inconspicuous constellation set between brilliant Gemini and bold Leo, but nevertheless its features are highlighted in Odysseus' encounter with the Laestrygonians. δ Cancri lies directly on the ecliptic and is a marker for a station of the sun (see Chapter 4, Fig. 3 & Table 2). For Homer it was the 'home of giants' and if the constellation is considered in human form, it appears relatively tall with ι Cancri at the head, δ Cancri at the waist, and β and α forming the feet (see Fig. 5). The wife of Antiphates, leader of the Laestrygonians, is described as a 'giantess as huge as a mountain', as are her fellow countrymen. Praesepe, or the beehive cluster, at

9.4 Disaster befell Odysseus in the land of the giant Laestrygonians, who killed most of his men and sank 11 ships. (John Flaxman, 1755–1826)

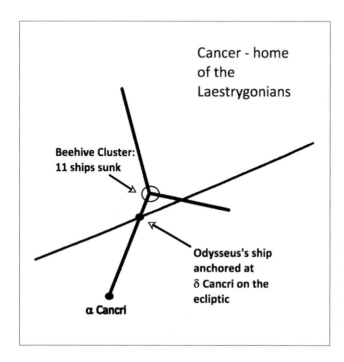

9.5 Eleven ships of Odysseus' fleet tied up at the Beehive Cluster, where they were sunk by the Laestrygonians. Odysseus moored a way off – at δ Cancri.

the centre of the constellation, becomes the harbour where 11 of Odysseus' ships come to a disastrous end.

Homer's account of the lives of the herdsmen and shepherds of Laestrygonia has always been something of an enigma for scholars:

> one herdsman, driving his flocks in hails another, who answers as he drives his flocks out; and there a man who could do without sleep could earn him double wages, for one herding the cattle, one for the silvery sheep. There the courses of night and day lie close together. (10.83 Butler)

There have been various attempts to interpret these lines and the most popular is that the land of the Laestrygonians was in the far north, where at midsummer there is daylight for 24 hours. Perhaps Homer meant nothing more than to restate that night follows day with 'cattle' representing the hours of daylight and 'silvery sheep' the starry hours of darkness. Indeed, when Odysseus eventually lands on the island of the sun god, Homer implies that cattle represent the daylight hours and the silvery sheep the hours of darkness. Odysseus sends out a reconnaissance party of three men (as in Lotus land) and one of them is immediately eaten by Antiphates. Far from welcoming Odysseus, the giant Laestrygonians throw rocks at his fleet and destroy 11 ships in a sheltered harbour – the 11 days in which the annual lunar calendar falls short of the solar calendar. To escape from the slaughter, Odysseus draws a sword from his side (marking the appearance of the new crescent moon), cuts the cable of his own ship, which is anchored at α Cancri, and orders his surviving men to row for their lives.

Venus & the Rock-throwing Giants

Odysseus' voyage home almost came to end at the hands of Laystrygonian giants. One man from his own ship was promptly eaten by the giant King Antiphates and the other giants threw rocks at the other 11 ships, killing their crews. When the fleet left Troy there had been 59 men on board each of the 12 ships, but the Cicones took six men from each, leaving crews of only 53 men. As Odysseus departed from the Laestrygonians the total number of men lost from his fleet was:

11 sunken ships x 53 men	=	583
Man lost from Odysseus' ship	=	1
Total	=	584
Number of days in the cycle of Venus	=	584

Sixth Month, Circe's Island: Sun in Leo at Midsummer

After the catastrophe at the hands of the Laestrygonians, Odysseus and his crew sail in their ship to Aeaea, the island home of the witch Circe. The sun passes from Cancer into Leo, the constellation of the summer solstice *c.*2300 BC, when Regulus, α Leonis, the brightest star on the ecliptic, rose with the sun. No doubt for both astronomical and spiritual reasons the solstice was a momentous occasion for ancient watchers of the sky and Odysseus' encounter with Circe does justice to the phenomenon; it is no surprise to learn that Circe is the daughter of the sun god Helios, who brings light to mankind.

Table 1. Five-day period on Circe's island

Days 1–2	With the last sighting of the waning moon, the mood is one of tiredness and grief as the men put ashore in silence. There is no action as the sailors rest in weariness and sorrow for two days.
Day 3	In the morning Odysseus explores the island and at midday spears a great antlered stag. On his return to camp his crew feasts until evening.
Day 4	The day is full of action and astronomical metaphor: Odysseus surveys the island and a reconnaissance party of 23 men under the command of Eurylochus is sent out to explore. When they arrive at Circe's palace she drugs their food and turns 22 of them into swine. Odysseus sets off to rescue his men and overcomes Circe's magic.
Day 5	Circe turns the swine into men again.

While surveying the lie of the land on the morning of his third day and with the moon in its dark period, Odysseus sees a column of smoke rising in the centre of the island. He does not yet know that it indicates Circe's home and in some despair returns to his ship to give his men a meal. When close to the ship he encounters a great antlered stag and, seizing the opportunity to provide food for his hungry companions, he kills the beast by striking it 'half way down the spine' with his bronze spear. Carrying the dead animal on his back, Odysseus returns to his ship where he and his crew feast on meat and wine throughout the rest of the day before sleeping on the sea shore.

In describing the killing of the stag Homer establishes important times not only in the day but also in the solar year and the 19-year cycle. The stag's death-blow comes from a bronze-tipped spear, a metaphor for the sun and one that is repeated at the climax of the *Odyssey*. The spear strikes halfway down the line of the beast's spine, which metaphorically places the sun on the ecliptic below the 'back' of Leo. It is now just halfway through the solar year. It is also the mid-point of the 19-year cycle and there are a further nine and a half years to go before Odysseus will be reunited with Penelope.

It is strange that a stag should replace the constellation familiarly seen as a lion, but such animals have a powerful and widespread image in mythology. Gavin

9.6 Odysseus carries the giant
stag back to his ship at the
halfway point of the 19-year
cycle with the sun in the stars of
Leo. (By GG-R)

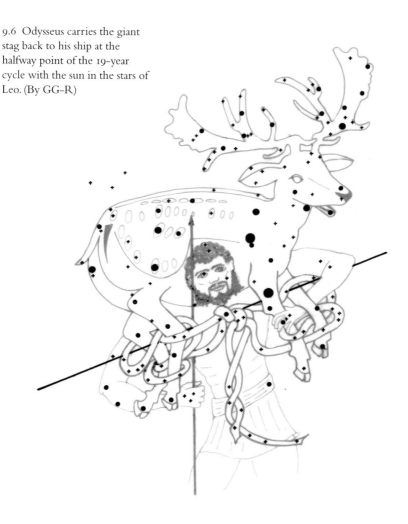

White[2] writes that early Eurasian myths and cult objects link the stag with fire, the sun and the solar chariot:

> In Greek tradition the association is reflected in the hind of Cerynia (the object of the third labour of Heracles) whose golden horns glinted in the sun. In fact, its golden horns represent the rays of the sun in exactly the same manner that the mane of the lion or horse represents the sun's radiating light.

Stags and other deer in Greek myth outside the works of Homer feature strongly in stories of Artemis, the hunter goddess, and that of Cyparissus who accidentally killed his pet stag at midday and died of grief.

At day break on his fourth day on the island Odysseus makes a strange admission to his men that they are lost and he does not know where east and west lie or where the sun rises or sets (10.190). Unless he was hiding in a cave, that statement at first seems too absurd for words, for the sun had set in the west the previous evening and had risen in the east only a short time before. In trying to explain the incongruity of how Odysseus could have lost his bearings, scholars have said that he was trying to fix the exact earthly position of the island of Aeaea so that he could plan his next strategy. A further explanation may be that at the time of the summer solstice the sun rises not directly in the east but at ENE (60°) and sets not directly in the west but at WNW (300°). Odysseus goes on to tell his men that the previous day he had discovered they were on a largely low-lying island with the sea all around and stretching away to the horizon, 'in the middle, through dense oak-scrub and forest, he glimpsed a wisp of smoke' (10.196). Since the rising smoke indicates that the island is inhabited, Odysseus may indeed have been planning his next move. In astronomical terms, and at the midpoint of the year, his bird's eye view of the island can suggest an image of the earth at the centre of the starry seas of the universe and the far encircling horizon as the ecliptic, the apparent annual path of the sun. A great circle such as the ecliptic has no beginning and no ending, and the smoke from Circe's chimney may be the point about which the heavens rotate like a great wheel. At a winter solstice a similar view of the universe is created in the description of Eumaeus' farm.

Odysseus' men are greatly disturbed by his claim that they are lost and fear an encounter similar to those with Antiphates and the man-eating Polyphemus. To quell their fears Odysseus divides his crew into two parties, each of 23 men, and sends one group under the command of Eurylochus to investigate. In the panels 'The Moon & Odysseus' Sailors' (below) and 'Venus & the Rock-throwing Giants' (above), it can be seen that this was no casual division of his crew and reveals calculations about the moon.

The Moon & Odysseus' Sailors

Exciting discoveries were made by calculating the number of sailors in the fleet of 12 ships that sailed away from Troy. Data is taken from several parts of the *Odyssey*.

Circe's island: Odysseus divides his crew into two parties each of 22 men, with himself leading one and Eurylochus the other:

22 men + Odysseus	=	23
22 men + Eurylochus	=	23
	=	**46 men**

Earlier, Odysseus had lost from his ship:

Taken by the Cicones	=	6
Eaten by Polyphemus	=	6
Eaten by Antiphates	=	1
	=	**13 men**

Odysseus' crew when he left Troy:
46 + 13 = 59

59 is the number of days in one full and one hollow lunar month

---

Sailors in Odysseus' fleet

By inference, each of Odysseus' 12 ships that left Troy had, like his own, 59 men:
12 x 59 = 708

708 is the number of days in two lunar years – or in one lunar year of
354 days and 354 nights

On encountering Circe, Eurylochus is suspicious of her motives and refuses to enter her palace where his men are wined, dined … drugged and magically turned into swine. When Eurylochus returns to tell Odysseus of the calamity, Odysseus throws his bow and 'silver studded sword of bronze about his shoulders' (10.261) and sets off to the rescue. It is now dark of moon and not a good time for Odysseus to be asserting his authority, never mind challenging the supernatural powers of a witch. Nor is his sword going to be of much help for he will be powerless to use it until the new crescent moon appears. When in Circe's palace Odysseus' sword is worn on his back before being drawn and sheathed (10.333). Similarly, his actions are restricted in his confrontations with Polyphemus (9.300), Eurylochus (10.348) and Teiresias (11.95) during the dark period before the new crescent.

Nevertheless, help is at hand and before Odysseus reaches Circe's palace: Hermes gives him a piece of herb which the gods call 'Moly' (10.30), and which will thwart Circe's wiles and magical powers. Described by some translators as having a black root with a flower as white as milk, this divine herb, in a commentary[3] by Heubeck and Hoekstra, is said to be 'black rooted with milk-white petals' and a further source[4] includes the phrase that it is still 'in the process of growing'. For almost 3000 years Moly has been sought in vain on earth, but as a lunar metaphor it creates an image (Fig. 9.8) of how a waxing crescent moon (the flower or white petals still growing) emerges from its 'black roots' (the dark period when the moon cannot be seen). Hermes forewarns Odysseus that he must draw his 'sharp sword from his side' and use the piece of Moly, and its powerful image of the growing crescent moon, when he confronts Circe. On entering the palace Circe tries to overpower Odysseus but the Moly protects him and as the new crescent has not yet arrived he puts his newly drawn sword back into his sheath. Protected by Moly, Odysseus joins the witch in bed. His powers are restored with the sighting of the new crescent moon the following day and he makes her promise to change the swine back into men.

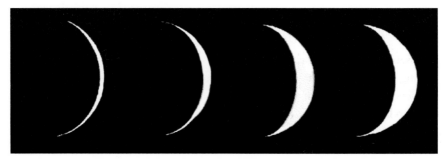

9.7 Translators describe the mysterious plant Moly with phrases that include 'black rooted with milk white petals' and still 'in the process of growing', which evoke an image of the waxing crescent moon as it comes out of the dark period.

Month Seven, Men Transformed: Sun Leaves Leo

On the morning of Day 5, Odysseus is bathed and given a new tunic but remains 'dumb' and refuses to eat, for the new crescent will not be seen until dusk. Odysseus also has an argument with Eurylochus, his second-in-command, and would like to cut off his head but in the absence of the new crescent (his sword) he cannot do so (10.439). Odysseus does not forget the men turned into pigs and he reminds Circe of her promise. At the sighting of the new crescent and the beginning of a new monthly cycle, Circe rubs the sailors with a magic salve and, like the new crescent moon, they look younger and more handsome dressed in new tunics (10.452). Then begins their year's stay with Circe. The Circe episode, like that involving Goat Island and Polyphemus, covers five days and begins with the last sighting of the waning crescent, through the period of dark moon to the new crescent.

Notes
1   Allen, R.H., *The Star Names, Their Lore and Meaning* (New York: Dover, 1963 reprint), pp. 225–6.
2   White, G., *Babylonian Star Lore* (London: Solaria Publications, 2008), p. 192.
3   Heubeck, A., West, S. & Hainsworth, J.B., *A Commentary on Homer's Odyssey* (Oxford: Clarendon Press, 1989), Vol. 2, line 302, p. 60.
4   Jones, H., *Glotta* (1973).

10

HADES & THE GHOSTS

Odysseus dallied in the arms of the witch Circe until a 'year had passed in the waning of moons and the long days' of summer had again come around. Months of idleness and good living on the island of Aeaea had left his crew homesick and eager to launch their ship and resume their voyage towards Ithaca. In the longest account of any of his adventures, Odysseus bids farewell to Circe and arrives in the land of the Cimmerians and Hades, where he meets the ghosts of the dead and then, strangely, returns to Circe's island to cremate the young sailor Elpenor. Within these tales are concealed two methods by which Homer keeps the lunar calendar in step with the solar year. The first is achieved by putting the annual calendar on hold for a year and in the second Homer inserts an intercalary lunar month into the annual calendar and, consequently, into the 19-year cycle. On Odysseus' arrival in the land of the Cimmerians and Hades, Homer displays an understanding of the movement of the heavens and on Odysseus' return to Circe's island he draws

10.1 Odysseus in the underworld and the shades of the dead. (John Flaxman, 1755–1826)

attention to the heliacal rising of Leo and illustrates how stars in that constellation can be used as a pointer to the celestial north pole. Fundamental as these concepts are they can be deduced by linking the rhythm of his story telling to phases of the moon and the lengthy journey of the sun through Leo and Virgo.

Seventh Month, Adjusting the Lunar Year (Intercalary)

When Polyphemus eats six of Odysseus' men, loses 11 ships to the Laestrygonians and later loses a further six men to Scylla, it is Homer's metaphorical reminder of the need to reconcile the 11-day difference between a lunar year and a solar year, a problem that has bedevilled calendar makers for thousands of years. Without adjustment, the lunar calendar would in only three years be out of step with the solar calendar by 33 days. In Mesopotamia, long before Homer, an extra month was inserted or intercalated into the lunar calendar in every third year to bring it back into line with the solar calendar. There is an early reference to an intercalary month, in a letter sent by Hammurabi, King of Babylon *c*.1795–50 BC, to his governors, which declared:

> This year has an additional month. The coming month should be designated as the second month Ululu, and wherever the annual tax had been ordered to be brought to Babylon on the 24th of the month Tashritu it should now be brought to Babylon on the 24th of the second month of Ululu.[1]

Then, as now, time and taxes waited for no man. With the discovery of the 19-year cycle intercalation became more sophisticated and in Babylon and Greece in the fifth century BC intercalary months were inserted into the cycle in the third, sixth, eighth, eleventh, fourteenth, seventeenth and nineteenth years.[2]

This raises the question of what Homer knew of intercalation long before the eponymous Meton (432 BC). The Ship's Log (see Appendix 1) shows that Odysseus arrives on Circe's island just after the summer solstice, towards the end of the 118th lunation. After overcoming the witch and despite their driving need to return to Ithaca, Odysseus and his crew begin their year-long sojourn with Circe with the arrival of the new crescent moon; at the same time the 19-year cycle continues to tick away. During this year nothing is recorded about the lives of Odysseus and his crew.

As we continued to record Odysseus' movements in the Ship's Log we found, much to our surprise, that when the midsummer days return the following year (10.468), a new crescent moon appears at the summer solstice when the sun rises with Regulus, α Leonis. This was one of our most exciting discoveries, for the calendar clearly showed that the new crescent appears 11 days earlier than it had the previous year. We now had a practical example, rather than dry theoretical maxim, of the number of days the lunar calendar falls short of the solar calendar. And that was not the only revelation that came with the new crescent. When Odysseus leaves Circe in his following adventure he meets with Persephone and the ghosts, which indicates that the sun will pass through Virgo rather than Leo; Persephone's many associations with Virgo are explained in the next chapter. For this to happen Odysseus would need to remain with Circe as the sun moves from Regulus for the next 30 days. How then can Odysseus be on one hand with Circe and at the same time with the ghosts in Virgo? An answer is found by declaring the 30 unchronicled days Odysseus spends in Leo with Circe as an intercalary month. Homer gave substance to our notion when at the end of the period Circe finally tells Odysseus he is free to go for 'you do not need to stay in *my house* against your will' (10.489).

Leo, as the intercalary month, would be in keeping with the time of year that an extra month was inserted into the lunar calendar in later Greek times. Homer's method of inserting an intercalary month and bringing harmony between a lunar year (354 days) and a solar year (365 days) is both simple and ingenious.

Table 1. Projected intercalary months in Homer's & Meton's 19-year cycle

Year	1	2	3	4	5	6	7	8	9	10	11	12	13	14	15	16	17	18	19
Homer	█		█			█			█		█			█			█		
Meton			█			█		█			█			█			█		█

In seeking evidence to explain this confusing situation we created a hypothetical chart of the 235 lunations during the 19 years from 2314–2295 BC, when Regulus marked the summer solstice on 14 July and the winter solstice fell on 8 or 9 January (Appendix 2). In the tradition of ancient calendar makers, we began the cycle with the appearance of the first new crescent moon after the winter solstice and found the sequence in which Homer's 13-month years fell. We were then able to compare Homer's cycle with Meton's 19-year cycle. We found that both cycles have seven 13-month years, or intercalary years, but in Homer's model cycle, these are in the sequence 1, 3, 6, 9, 11, 14 and 17, whereas in Meton's distribution the intercalary years are found in the sequence 3, 6, 8, 11, 14, 17 and 19.

Both Meton and Homer have intercalary months in the third, sixth, eleventh, fourteenth and seventeenth years, but the major difference is that Homer's cycle begins with a 13-month year, whereas that of Meton's ends with an intercalated month in the nineteenth year. As a single standalone cycle it may not seem reasonable for Homer to begin with an intercalary year, but over a period of two or more cycles it would work well. The main reason, however, for Homer using this form of distribution may be that it gives a 13-month year in the ninth year, when Hector meets his fate in the *Iliad* at a summer solstice, and allows him to describe the mechanism of inserting of an intercalary month in the adventures of Odysseus. Whether in the future other indications of intercalated months will be found remains to be seen.

Odysseus Prepares to Leave Circe: Strange Incident of a Drunken Young Sailor

After his year's stay with Circe, Odysseus' adventures resume in the dark period at the end of the intercalated month, when his men rebuke their leader for linger-ing, and he in turn reproaches Circe for failing to let them continue their voyage home. Despite their discontent, Odysseus and his crew feast before he takes Circe to bed. There is a troubled night ahead and Circe tells her lover that he has to go down to the realms of Hades, the underworld home of the ghosts of the dead. Criticism, fear of the future, separation and tales of woe are all indications that the moon is in its dark period. Tragedy follows in the morning when Odysseus learns that Elpenor, the youngest sailor on his ship, has been killed in a bizarre accident during the night. Elpenor is young and undistinguished and his fatal fall from the roof of Circe's house (10.551) after a night of heavy drinking may appear to be a strange distraction. Elpenor had climbed on to the roof to get 'some air', another indication that the hot days of summer had again come around. Metaphorically, the constellation of Leo represents Circe's enchanted palace. Only a few imagina-tive strokes of the pen are needed to turn the stars in the outline of a 'lion' into a 'palace' with a long ladder stretching from its roof to the ground, the ecliptic.

No doubt still nursing a hangover, Elpenor fell from the roof and tumbled backwards to his death. The 'neck' of Leo is marked by α Leonis and to add further to the image of Elpenor falling from the roof he could have landed on the ground at Regulus on the ecliptic. Although Elpenor may appear to be a foolish weakling and a man of little account, this is far from the case, as will be seen when Odysseus buries him with great honour. With the appearance of the new crescent Odysseus must be on his way and there is no time now to arrange a funeral for Elpenor. Odysseus, dressed in a new tunic, takes provisions on board his ship and raises the mast and sails. Circe then sends a favourable breeze and off they sail to Hades, the kingdom of the underworld.

Land of the Cimmerians: in Perpetual Darkness

When Odysseus leaves Circe, he sails 'till the sun went down, and all the ways grew dark' (11.10), and continues until the ship 'reaches the furthest parts of the River of Ocean'. Try as they may, students of the *Odyssey* have been unable to find an earthly location for the land of the Cimmerians, but a fitting destination can be found 'under the earth', where Hades is a dark shadow of the upper world amongst the constellations of the southern hemisphere. The sun has now moved through Leo to β Virginis, in the 'head' of Virgo. Until sunset, a north wind drives Odysseus' craft across 'Ocean's stream' into the stars of the southern hemisphere and the city of the Cimmerians. They live in a land of perpetual darkness which the sun does not see 'as it climbs into the sky nor as it falls back towards the earth'. Their home is always surrounded by mist, fog and perpetual night, and its people have a thoroughly miserable existence (11.13). Odysseus then moves on to Hades a place where people live as shades or ghosts in a land of darkness. Odysseus' tale has now become a story within a story, which unfolds in two places at once. While he is located in Hades, somewhere 'below the earth', the sun continues its passage along the ecliptic through the constellation of Virgo.

Circe had earlier told Odysseus he would come first to Persephone's grove of poplars and willows, then the River Archeron, and its tributaries Periphlegethon and Cocytus and he would find a large 'rock'. A metaphorical connection can be found by Odysseus sailing down the Milky Way until reaching the huge ancient constellation of Argo Navis, with its brightest star, Canopus, α Carinae, recognised as the large rock. A star chart reveals that in the region of Vela and Pupis, the Milky Way divides into several branches (the rivers) enclosing a large 'pool of sky' (the grove), with surrounding bright stars (poplars and willows). In 2300 BC Canopus, the second brightest star in the heavens, would always have been below the horizon at the latitude of Athens/Chios, and because of its position so far south would have been absent from the daytime skies; in other words, the sun could never 'shine' on Canopus. However, the Greeks of Homer's times were well established sailors and travellers, and would have known that Canopus could be seen during a part of the year from southern Crete, Cyprus and Egypt – all of them places south of 35°N and mentioned in the *Odyssey*.

Eighth Month, the Ghosts of Hades: Sun in Virgo

While Odysseus is in Hades (Argo Navis) the sun continues through Virgo a constellation steeped in myth and legend whose origins lie far back in history. Seen as a woman, but sometimes headless because of the faintness of the 'head stars', Virgo has long been linked to females and has been known as Ishtar, Demeter, her daughter Persephone, Erigone, Astrae and even the Virgin Mary. It is the constellation's association with death that reflects Odysseus' meeting with ghosts and Persephone in particular. The legendary myth wrapped around the story of Persephone is that she was abducted by Hades, King of the Underworld, but her mother, Demeter, eventually brokered a deal that enabled her daughter to spend part of the year in the upper world before returning to the underworld. The exact number of months she spends in either place depends upon the particular version of the tale.

Originally a grain goddess, Persephone's periodic release from Hades each year was associated with the harvest, and Virgo is a fitting home for she was also known as *Kore*, the Greek word for virgin. Persephone plays a prominent role in the account of Odysseus' visit to Hades and the goddess makes entrances

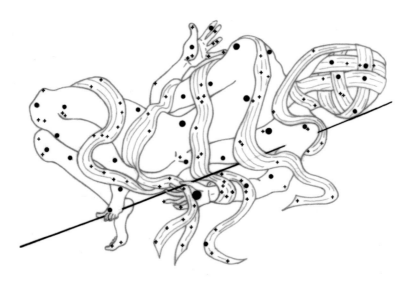

10.2 A shroud-wrapped ghost in Hades amongst the stars of the constellation of Virgo. (By GG-R)

at the beginning, the middle and the end. Before he left Aeaea, Odysseus had already been told by Circe that the sight of Persephone's Grove would mark his entrance into the Underworld (10.513), where he should pray to the god Hades and Persephone (11.47).

Odysseus makes his way to the kingdom of the dark and takes his sharp sword from his side (11.24), a hint that a new adventure is about to begin and digs a trench as 'the souls of the dead came swarming up' (11.48). Odysseus is astonished to find that the first ghost he meets is that of young Elpenor who has arrived in Hades before him.

Elpenor pleads on the lives of his companions past and present, his commander's wife (Penelope), Odysseus' father (Laertes) and son (Telemachus), that on Odysseus' return to Circe's island/constellation of Leo he should be buried with all due honour. Elpenor's awesome plea continues with his further wishes that he should be mourned, cremated with his armour and a barrow or mound built for him by the seashore so that men may learn of him.[3] It is something of a literary mystery why a sailor who died in drink and who was perhaps the least prepossessing of Odysseus' crew, requests a funeral mound equal to that of the heroic warriors Patroclus, Hector and Achilles, but Elpenor has added dimensions. Astronomically, the riddle of how Elpenor reaches Hades before Odysseus is easily solved. Elpenor tumbles to his death and arrives in Hades on the last day of a lunation, while Odysseus arrives in Hades after sailing through the first day of the following lunation.

Odysseus' mother appears but he sends her away because he must first talk to Teiresias, who warns him that the cattle of the sun god must not be eaten, and that even when he has endured all his hardships and arrived home in Ithaca, his stay there will be brief before he has to set out once more on his wanderings. Teiresias' words are also an indication of the perpetual nature of 19-year cycles and Odysseus' never-ending travels: as one cycle ends, another begins. Odysseus' mother makes a second appearance and their reunion is greatly moving, for unknown to him she had died of grief for the son she believed she had lost.

Odysseus again draws 'his long sword from his strong thigh' as the adventure continues (11.230) and Persephone sends up the ghosts of women whose often-tragic stories are revered in Greek myth. Odysseus meets 29 ghosts of women and men and, as Homer's astronomy is usually logical and simple, we suggest that each ghost is allocated to one day, so marking the passage of the sun through the constellation. Legends of the women ghosts are perhaps not so familiar today as they once were, but Homer mentions Epicaste (Jocasta), who married Oedipus, her son, and Ariadne, daughter of King Minos, also found in the legend of Theseus and the Minotaur. Soon Persephone drives away the women's ghosts and the ghosts of Greek heroes from Agamemnon to Achilles and Aias, and from Orion the Hunter to Sisyphus and Minos, then make their appearance.

As the lunation comes to an end Odysseus is ready to leave Hades, but not before his darkest hour when he is surrounded by tens of thousands of 'the tribes of the dead'. He is in desperate fear that Persephone would also send up the Gorgon's head or some ghastly monster because the constellation Perseus, holding the Gorgon's head (Algol, β Persei, the Demon Star), can be seen in the east just after sunset. Homer's introduction of the ghosts of the dead and the conversations they have with Odysseus is a chilling reflection on the mortality of mankind.

In panic, Odysseus rushes back to his ship and returns to the upper world, 'in the dwelling place of early dawn' on a sandy shore (the Milky Way), to rejoin the constellations on and close to the ecliptic. The sun has now passed Spica and is in the region of λ Virginis, and the Milky Way becomes a convenient route for his return journey as it passes 'under' the earth and eventually re-emerges in Scorpio. Odysseus and his sailors fall asleep and on awakening there is much activity before the sun rises and they return to Circe's house for the funeral of Elpenor. This is another strange event for it suggests that Odysseus does the impossible by moving backwards along the ecliptic from Virgo to Leo. Nor is this is the only time that Homer infers the sun and moon are moving in reverse; he does so after Odysseus' fleet leaves Aeolia and again in his encounter with Charybdis. One astronomical observation that links these three events is the heliacal rising of a particular constellation. In the case of Circe it is the heliacal rising of Leo that occurs at this time. Whether this will prove to be a complete answer to this unusual event remains to be seen. After Elpenor's funeral Circe reminds Odysseus and his men

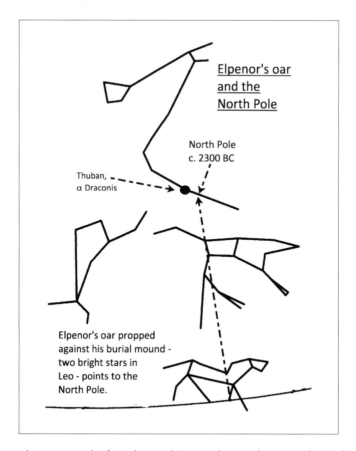

10.3 Elpenor's oar rests on the funeral mound (Leo) and points the way to the north celestial pole via Ursa Major.

that they will 'die twice' and again warns of the perils they have yet to face. As dawn breaks (12.142) Odysseus sets sail towards his new adventure.

Elpenor's Funeral Mound: Pointer to the North Pole Star

Odysseus' 'return' to Circe's island (Leo) enables him to carry out Elpenor's wishes to give him a funeral with heroic ceremony that outstrips his humble rank. As a final mark of respect to the young man, his oar is placed on the burial mound. Homer makes so much of introducing Elpenor into the *Odyssey*, giving him a prominent role in the narrative of the underworld and finally carrying out his funeral wishes, that it makes one suspect there is more to him than at first appears. And so there is. With the stars of Leo's rectangular 'body' making an admirable image of a funeral mound and with his oar propped against two bright stars, Elpenor's final resting place gives an unforgettable way of finding the north celestial pole, an invaluable guide to sailors. Fig. 3 shows that if Elpenor's 'oar' is projected from Regulus, α Leonis, on the ecliptic at the bottom of the mound, through the yellow star γ Leonis at the top of the mound, it points upwards to χ Leonis Minoris, on past the 'leg' of the Great Bear, through γ Ursae Majoris and δ Ursae Majoris, towards Thuban, α Draconis, the star that pointed true north *c*.2300 BC.[4]

The usual literary explanation of the curious digression of Elpenor is that it provides a continuous thread between Odysseus' departure from Circe's island to his arrival in Hades, and finally his return again to Circe's island. However, concealed within Elpenor's tragic tale are several layers. The first is a straightforward word picture of the constellation of Leo as a palace with a ladder leading to the roof. The second layer shows how during one lunation the sun travels through the constellation of Leo and the third layer reveals how the funeral mound of Elpenor provides sailors and travellers with an accurate and essential pointer to Thuban, the North Pole star. While Elpenor's oar would have been invaluable for pointing true north during the months of the year when both Leo and the circumpolar Bear were visible in the night sky, Homer gives alternative methods of finding true north at other times, using pointers from the constellations of Boötes and Ursa Major, as seen in Chapter 6. After Odysseus has buried Elpenor, and with the moon in its dark period, he again takes Circe to bed. During a troubled night the witch warns him of the horrors he has yet to face: the deadly song of the Sirens, the Wandering Rocks, the turbulent whirlpool Charybdis, the hideous six-headed Scylla and the temptations of the sun god's cattle. Odysseus' visit to Hades has several complex calendrical themes running through it and was not an easy adventure to interpret astronomically. Commentators have acknowledged that Odysseus' journey to Hades comes from several different sources but nevertheless the accepted literary form is believed to be a comprehensive reflection of Homer's intentions.

Notes

1 Walker, C. (ed.), *Astronomy before the telescope* (British Museum Press, 1996), p. 45.
2 Pannekoek, A., *A History of Astronomy* (London: George Allen & Unwin; New York: Dover, 1963 reprint), p. 51.
3 Edna Leigh was struck by the coincidence of warriors from other cultures and other ages being buried by the seashore, where they could be seen by future generations. Her belief that these heroes were buried where all could learn from them is one of the principal ideas underlying her astronomical discoveries of the *Iliad* and the *Odyssey*.
4 In 2300 BC α and γ Leonis, γ and δ Ursae Majoris were on or near to the 6hr line of celestial longitude. Regulus, α Leonis, rose with the sun at the summer solstice and at noon on midsummer's day reached its highest position on the celestial equator at +23° 57' 2". While Thuban at +90° was the significant star nearest to the north celestial pole and the apparent distance between Regulus and the celestial pole would be not so great as it is now. The roof, the sickle of Leo, from which Elpenor fell, would indeed appear to be in the 'roof of the heavens'.

11

SIRENS TO CALYPSO'S ISLAND

After his night with Circe, and no doubt troubled by her dire warnings, Odysseus and his men leave her island for a second time at the appearance of the new crescent moon. Their voyage will carry them past the temptations of the Sirens, the perils of the Wandering Rocks, the horrors of the monstrous six-headed Scylla, and on to the island of Thrinacia. There, Odysseus' starving crew devour the cattle of the sun god Helios and in an act of terrible retribution Odysseus' remaining ship is destroyed and all of his crew killed in a storm. As Odysseus clings to his ship's wreckage he is sucked down and spewed out by the whirlpool Charybdis before finally drifting on to Calypso's island. All of these adventures occur during four lunations, while the sun is travelling 120° along the ecliptic.

Odysseus' voyage from Circe's island was a challenging area in which to link his adventures with phases of the moon, metaphorical images of the constel-

11.1 Odysseus is tied to the mast of his ship as he endures the song of the Sirens. A number of translators of the *Odyssey* give the number of Sirens as two and not the three commonly depicted in other works. (John Flaxman, 1775–1826; Wikicommons)

lations and the sun's passage across bands of the Milky Way. One consideration arose from the modern perception of how constellations in that part of the zodiac are projected. Today, in the 30° zodiacal division of Scorpius, only one-third is made up of stars from that constellation and stars in the scorpion's 'tail' are outside the zodiacal band. The remaining two-thirds of the division contains stars of the giant amorphous constellation of Ophiuchus, whose feet lie on the ecliptic; in reality the sun spends only nine days in the stars of Scorpius before moving into Ophiuchus. To complicate matters further, in antiquity the constellation of Scorpius extended into stars of Libra, which were described as the 'Claws of Scorpius'. When Libra (the Scales) became a separate zodiacal constellation is unknown, although the Romans claimed to have introduced it into the Julian calendar, *c.*45 BC. There even may be a reference to Libra as pair of scales: in the *Iliad*, when Zeus 'sire of all the heavens balanced his golden scales' (*Iliad* 8.65). The concept of Libra as a pair of scales arises from its brightest star, α Librae, lying on the ecliptic with two other stars, δ and β Librae, on either side and almost equidistant from it, so creating an image of 'scales' or a 'balance' (see Fig. 1). Ian Redpath (*Stars and Planets*) gives a diagram showing the scales equally balanced about the ecliptic,[1] but in most modern star charts the configuration of Libra is not centred about the ecliptic.

A second issue arises because there appear to be more adventures in the narrative than possible lunations while the sun is travelling along this part of the ecliptic. Homer creates powerful images of the Sirens, the Wandering Rocks, Scylla, Charybdis and Odysseus' month's stay on Thrinacia, but if each of these incidents was allotted one lunation his homeward journey would have extended well into the following year. The 19-year cycle would then have been thrown out of step and it would have been impossible for Odysseus to have spent almost eight years with Calypso. To make matters more confusing, there are three versions of the hazards he faces; Circe's warning to Odysseus, Odysseus' warning to his men and, finally, Odysseus' own version of events, which he told to the Phaeacians.

We remained firm, however, in a belief that as a lunation comes to an end Odysseus faces disaster and with the appearance of a new crescent he sails towards his next adventure. Careful examination of each hardship and the area of sky through which the sun was travelling eventually led to a solution. We had previously realised that 'Aeolus' bag of winds' brought no real harm to either Odysseus or his men. His ship was not destroyed and men were not killed; misfortune only struck when the Laestrygonians sank 11 ships when the moon was later in its dark phase. This insight reinforced the view that it was only dark of moon that brought real suffering to Odysseus and his men and it enabled us to complete a model calendar for his remaining adventures. It also became clear that Odysseus' voyage past the Sirens, the Wandering Rocks, Charybdis and Scylla occur rapidly, one after the other, with no description of long sailing periods between them. Despite their potential danger nothing untoward happens to either Odysseus or his crew during these encounters. To make himself safe from the lure of the Sirens, Odysseus is tied securely to his ship's mast; the Wandering Rocks fail to smash his ship; and the threatening whirlpool Charybdis does not suck down his craft. Calamity only strikes when Scylla, the six-headed monster, snatches six of his men as the lunation comes to an end.

Ninth Month, the Sirens: Sun Leaves Virgo, Passes into Libra-Scorpius

Circe had warned Odysseus that the unwary would be lured to their deaths by the enchanting singing of the Sirens and despite their subsequent fame, Homer takes only 35 lines of the *Odyssey* to tell their story. Forewarned is to be forearmed, and Odysseus cleverly safeguards himself and his crew from the Sirens' deadly song. As the sun leaves Virgo it passes through the Claws of Libra, where three stars, α, β and σ Librae, make an excellent 'island' home for the temptresses; the brighter stars α and β Librae also offer a reminder that Homer refers only to two Sirens (12.54), and not the three found in other myth and art (see Fig. 1).[2] As Odysseus' ship sails towards the Sirens, the wind drops, the sails of the ship are stowed in the hold and the crew rows so hard in their hurry to reach home that they churn the water white with their blades. To ensure that his crew does not come to any harm, Odysseus warms 'a great round cake of wax' or 'a large wheel of wax' (12.174) and cuts it with his sharp sword into earplugs for his crew, so preventing them from hearing the Sirens' song. The 'great round cake' metaphorically represents the honey-coloured disk of the full moon and Odysseus' sharp sword provides another image of the waxing or waning crescent moon.

We were well versed by now in the important role that encoded numbers had in the structure of Homer's calendar and calculated how many pieces of wax would have been needed to plug the ears of the crew. The result had calendrical implications: when Odysseus' ship left Circe's island there were 45 men, including Odysseus on board. To block the ears of the 44 crewmembers Odysseus had to use 88 pieces of wax. At this point in our model calendar, 88 is the number of days from the waning moon as he passes the Sirens to the waning moon when his remaining ship is destroyed.

Odysseus, on the other hand, wishes to hear the song of the Sirens and he is put out of harm's way when he orders his men to tie him to the mast and not to release him no matter how much he pleads. 'You must bind me very tight, standing me up against the step of the mast' (12.158). The metaphorical image of Odysseus tied to the mast in an upright position draws attention to stars in Libra, which lie directly on the ecliptic: α, κ and λ Librae become the mast which ends in the 'step or block' to which it is fixed, the asterism β, δ, ν, ω¹ Scorpii (see Fig. 11.1).

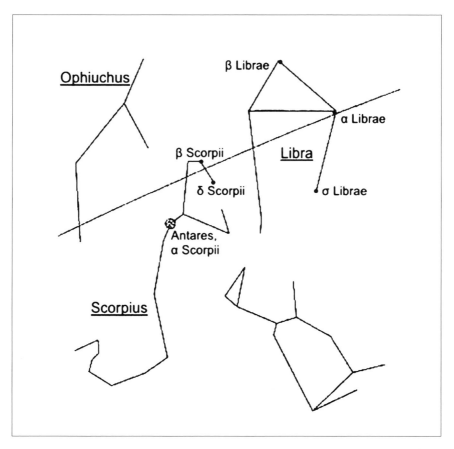

11.2 The path of the sun crosses α Librae in Odysseus' encounter with the Sirens, and between β Scorpii and δ Scorpii as his ship runs the gauntlet of the Wandering Rocks.

The Sirens sit in a grassy meadow and the star β Librae is said to have a green-ish tinge, although it is not certain whether it can now be seen with the naked eye, it may have been brighter in antiquity.[3] Homer's references to a 'pile of bones' and the 'mouldering skeletons' of the Sirens' victims may well indicate stars of lesser magnitude found in the region of γ Librae, close to the ecliptic.

The Wandering Rocks: the Autumn Equinox

As the moon moves into its dark period Odysseus passes the Wandering Rocks, espies the whirlpool Charybdis, and meets tragedy with the six-headed monster Scylla. He undergoes these daunting challenges in only one day, as the sun passes through the autumn equinox and moves towards the bright Milky Way. At c.2300 BC the autumn equinoctial point lay between Libra and Scorpius, and although there is no convenient star to act as an exact marker for the point, the stars β and δ Scorpii that straddle the ecliptic are well placed to represent it. Just as precession can cause the equinox to 'wander' over time, so can β and δ Scorpii be designated as the 'Wandering Rocks' and indicate Homer's awareness of the phenomenon of the precessional equinoctial point. At the same time the path of the sun between the two stars becomes the narrow gauntlet through which Odysseus' ship metaphorically must run (see Fig. 11.2).

The spring and autumn equinoxes lie directly opposite each other on the celestial globe, and when the autumn equinox lay in Scorpius, the spring equinox lay in the Pleiades. Homer emphasises the equinox when Odysseus compares his current plight with his experiences shortly after the spring equinox and his encounter with Polyphemus. Of the many myths surrounding the Pleiades, one

11.3 Stars of Scorpius and the six-headed monster Scylla. The line running left to right is the ecliptic. (By GG-R)

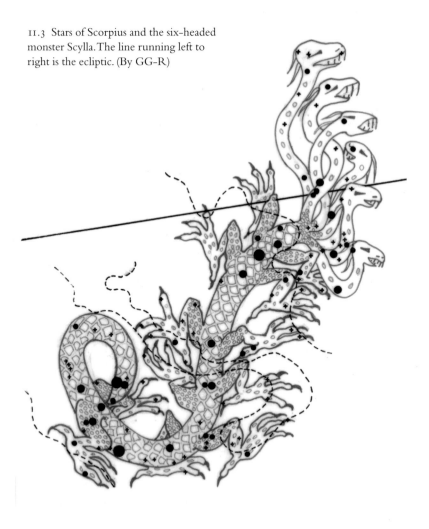

likens them to a flock of birds, and a possible reminder of the opposing positions of the equinoxes on the ecliptic is brought to mind when Homer says of the Wandering Rocks: 'Here not even a bird may pass' (12.61). The most famous ship in Greek mythology is *Argo*, the vessel which carried Jason and the Argonauts in search of the Golden Fleece. Jason's story was told by Apollonius of Rhodes (*c*.260 BC), but he acknowledged its far older origins 'as former bards relate'. The legend was certainly known in Homer's time for Circe warned Odysseus that *Argo*, guided by some mysterious power, was the only vessel to have sailed through the dangerous Wandering Rocks (12.72).

Odysseus and his men face two hazards whilst sailing through the narrow passage: on one side there are cliffs (the Milky Way) and on the other there are two overhanging rocks – one of them described as a towering peak is designated as Antares, α Scorpii, and the other as σ Scorpii. In her warnings to Odysseus, Circe had given another clue that the sun would here be approaching the Milky Way by references to Amphitrite, goddess of the sea, sending in her 'great breakers thundering in', and stirring up the 'roaring seas'.

As the sun continues its course through Scorpius, Odysseus spies Charybdis which for the present does them no harm. The whirlpool Charybdis is a metaphor for the Milky Way and can be seen throughout the night twisting and turning across the heavens, an observation that can be replicated with the 'time skip' feature on modern computer programmes.

Odysseus & Scylla: Sun in Scorpius, Dark Moon

We place the monstrous six-headed Scylla amongst the stars of Scorpius, the constellation long associated with death. As Scorpius rises in the east, Orion sets in the west, a phenomenon of the heavens that is well preserved in mythology. Although the myths surrounding these two constellations may vary in their details, they follow the same general pattern. Orion the Hunter is fatally stung by a scorpion, and after his death the gods place Orion and the scorpion at opposite ends of the heavens so they could never meet again. As a metaphorical description of Scorpius, Homer's imagery of Scylla's head protruding menacingly out of her cave is reflected in the same proportions in which Scorpius seems to rise out of the Milky Way. As Odysseus passes through the narrow strait between β and δ Scorpii, he is surrounded by danger before being pounced upon by Scylla. So smooth is the cliff on which she lives that even a man with 20 hands and 20 feet could not scale it. We designate the brighter stars in Libra, the one-time Claws of Scorpius, as the six heads and necks of Scylla. Scylla's 12 feet waving in the air protrude from the constellation's 'body' and tail stars, while her waist is deep in a cave centred at about α Scorpii in the Milky Way and reaching below the zodiacal band (Figs 11.3 & 11.4). Hugging a cliff on Scylla's side of the channel,

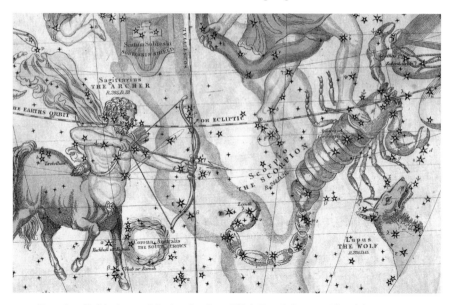

11.4 Scorpius, Ophiuchus and Sagittarius from Elijah Burritt's 1835 *Atlas of the Heavens*. For Homer, Scorpius became the monster Scylla. The feet of Ophiuchus can be seen touching the ecliptic.

Odysseus makes as much haste as possible but at dark of moon Scylla strikes and devours six of his sailors who 'screamed and stretched out their hands to me in their mortal agony'.

  As with the six men eaten by the Cyclops at the spring equinox, these six victims are important in balancing the days of the solar and lunar years and also in the calculation of how many sailors Odysseus initially had under his command. In the absence of Homer using fractions of numbers, Scylla's six victims, as with those of Polyphemus, can be seen as the rounded-up five and a half days that the lunar calendar falls short of the solar calendar between one equinox and the next.

From Autumn Equinox to Winter Solstice

Odysseus' passage through the steep-sided strait and his deadly encounter with Scylla (12.76) contains encoded calendrical data which adds up to 88, as can be seen in the panel 'Phases of the Moon and the Counting of Days. Eighty-eight is the number of days in the annual calendar between the new crescent moon which appears as Odysseus sails away from Scylla at the autumn equinox to the new crescent at the winter solstice. Although the constellation boundaries in ancient times are not known, an extended constellation of Scorpius-Claws, with Scorpius lying against the background of the Milky Way, provides an ample number of stars for the body parts of Scylla.

Phases of the Moon & the Counting of Days

88 is the number of days in one full and two hollow lunar months and this period can be calculated from three incidents in the *Odyssey*. On each occasion 88 is the number of days between significant phases of the moon. The number 72 is also invoked once for a similar purpose.

Polyphemus

The entrance to Polyphemus' cave was sealed by a stone so heavy that 22 four-wheeled wagons could not move it:

$$4 \times 22 = 88$$

Here, 88 is the number of days between four new crescent moons from the time Odysseus leaves Polyphemus to the time he begins his stay with Circe.

The Sirens

To prevent his crew of 44 men from hearing the deadly song of the Sirens, Odysseus plugs each of their ears with wax:

$$2 \times 44 \text{ pieces of wax} = 88$$

At this point in narrative, 88 is the number of days from the waning moon as he sails past the Sirens to the waning moon when Odysseus' remaining ship is destroyed.

Monstrous Scylla

The numbers defined in Odysseus' encounter with Scylla at 12.76:

20 hands and 20 feet	=	40
6 necks + 6 heads	=	12
6 mouths x 3 rows of teeth	=	18
misshapen feet	=	12
crewmen taken by Scylla	=	6
Total	=	**88**

88 is the number of days from the crescent moon of the autumn equinox to the crescent moon of the winter solstice.

The Cicones and 72 hostages

The Cicones seized six men from each of Odysseus' 12 ships:

$$6 \times 12 = 72$$

72 is then the number of days from the crescent moon of that adventure to the full moon of the spring equinox.

As the moon comes out of its dark period at the end of a lunar month, Odysseus sails onwards with the new crescent and they next arrive in Thrinacia, the island of the sun god, Helios, where Eurolochus is adamant that they should anchor and not roam over the seas during the night because that is when storms spring up. Sure enough, a storm rises during the night and provides a calendar marker for the waning moon.

Tenth Month, Cattle of the Sun God: Sun in Ophiuchus & Sagittarius

No doubt shaken by the terrible events in Scylla's realm and grieving the loss of six men, Odysseus sails towards Thrinacia and his encounter with the cattle of the sun god. Long before Odysseus approached the island, he had been warned of the perils of eating the cattle by both Teiresias and Circe. So dire were the consequences of his crew defying these warnings that the subsequent deaths of Odysseus' foolish men are told in the opening lines of the *Odyssey*. Odysseus is reluctant to land on the island, but the pleas of his men force him to change his mind; however in turn they swear not to eat any cow or sheep. Odysseus moors their ship by a stream of fresh water, the Milky Way, and after supper the crew's mood is sombre as they remember their dead shipmates and they fall into a fitful sleep. In the 'third watch of the night when the stars had shifted their places' and the time that the waning moon rises, fate intervenes in the form of a terrible hurricane. In the morning, Odysseus beaches his ship and again forbids his men to eat the cattle of Helios. An on-shore wind blows for a month and makes it impossible for them to leave the island.

In their early days on Thrinacia, Odysseus and his men eat the ship's stores and then turn to fishing and catching birds for food. As the game runs out, they starve and so desperate is Odysseus that he goes off to pray and returns only to discover that his men have killed Helios' cattle. They feast for six days on the forbidden meat before a favourable wind at last allows them to leave the island on the seventh. Homer does not say for how many days the ship's stores lasted, nor for how long the crew hunted and starved, nor for how long Odysseus withdrew from his men. He does state, however, that Odysseus arrived on the island in the 'third watch of the night' (12.312) and a storm blew up and these off-shore winds kept him there 'for a whole month [as] the south wind blew without a pause' (12.325). This provides enough information to draw up a chronological timetable for Odysseus' stay on Thrinacea by plotting the phases of the moon, the passage of the sun along the ecliptic and the rhythm of narrative.

Odysseus' previous adventure ended when Scylla snatched six men at dark moon and, with the appearance of the new crescent, he sailed to Thrinacia where the waning moon signalled troubled times ahead. Meanwhile, the sun travels along the ecliptic for 21–22 days through a relatively starless patch of sky and across two bands of the Milky Way until it reaches the 'right knee' of Ophiuchus, η Ophiuci. Odysseus' stay on Thrinacia begins with the waning moon and a month later he and his crew leave at the time of the next waning moon when Zeus conjures up a storm. During his month on the island, the sun travels through Ophiuchus, a constellation that defies visual association with man, god or beast, and then onwards to λ Sagittarii. The dominant feature of the Milky Way, with its beauty and abundance of stars, also lends itself to a metaphorical image of Thrinacia, reflected in narrative concerning the sea and seashore. While the boundaries of the Milky Way cannot be defined precisely it divides into two bands which enclose a dark starless patch of sky between Ophiuchus' 'right heel', 51 Ophiuchi, and a star in Sagittarius' bow, λ Sagittarii (see Table 1).[4]

After feasting for six days, and as the moon wanes, Odysseus and his men cast off from Thrinacia on the seventh and sail through open seas (12.400 ff).

Table 1. Feast and famine on Thrinacia

Phase of moon	Sun's position (approx.)	Milky Way	Food supplies	No of Days
Waning	η Ophiuchi	Band of Milky Way	Eat ships' provisions. Search game, fish or fowl	11
New Crescent				
Full	51 Ophiuchi λ Sagittarii	Pool of dark sky	Starvation looms	12
Waning	σ Sagittarii	Band of Milky Way	Feast on Helios' cattle	6
	π Sagittarii		Leave island	1
Total				30

Days of the Lunar Year: Helios' Cattle

In the description of Helios' domain, a calendrical answer can be found to an extract from narrative that has long puzzled scholars, when Homer expands upon his theme of 'the cattle of the sun god' and in doing so again defines the number of days in a lunar year:

> Here you will see many herds of cattle and flocks of sheep belonging to the sun-god; *seven* herds of cattle and *seven* flocks of sheep, with *fifty* head in each flock. *They do not breed, nor do they become fewer* in number, and they are tended by the goddesses *Phaethusa* and *Lampetie*, who are children of the sun-god *Hyperion* by *Neaera*. (12.130 Butler)

Helios has 350 cattle (7 x 50) as well as 350 sheep (7 x 50). Strangely, the number of animals never changes and nor do they breed or die. The cattle and sheep total 700, not a figure with obvious astronomical or calendrical connotations.

But Homer helps us along this tricky path when Hyperion declares that Odysseus' men have killed his cattle, 'in whom I always delighted, on my way up into the starry heaven, or when I turned back again from heaven toward earth' (12.380). In other words, the sun god suggests that the 350 cattle represent the hours of daylight on 350 days; by implication the 350 sheep would then represent the hours of darkness on 350 nights.

'In the 700 sheep and oxen the ancients recognised the 700 days and nights of the lunar year[5] and Aristotle is said to have recognised the 350 cattle as the days of a lunar year.'[6] In calendrical terms neither of these references is accurate for the lunar year has 354 days and there appears to be a shortfall of four days. Homer, however, has not quite finished with his calculation and again uses the add-on technique of memory in which he adds a smaller number (four) to a larger collective one (350). He says that Hyperion's cattle and sheep are tended by Phaethusa and Lampetie, the children of Hyperion by Neaera – a total of four characters – which leads to the calculation:

700 cattle and sheep = 700 days and nights	=	350 days
Plus: Phaethusa, Lampetie,		
Hyperion and Neaera	=	4
Total	=	354 days in a lunar year

Odysseus Reaches Calypso's Island: Sun in Capricornus

After being marooned on Thrinacia for a month, the storm abates and Odysseus and his men leave the island and sail for a further month while the sun proceeds 30° along the ecliptic from π Sagittarii to θ Capricornii. A star chart will show that the sun is now passing through a relatively starless part of the sky and Homer records that 'no other land, or anything but sky and water, was to be seen'. As the moon wanes Odysseus again faces disaster when Zeus takes revenge for the killing of Helios' cattle and creates another storm. A dark cloud sits over Odysseus' ship, which is battered by a hurricane before being destroyed by a bolt of lightning and all the crew except for Odysseus are killed.

Homer again describes how a ship breaks apart as the forestays snap, the mast falls and crushes the pilot's skull, sulphur and lightning are in the air, men are tossed into the sea to their deaths and the ship's ribs separate from the keel. To save himself, Odysseus binds together a makeshift raft from the debris, but to his dread the wind 'blows him back' through the night and at sunrise he finds himself at Scylla's rock, where Charybdis, the deadly whirlpool overhung by a giant fig tree, 'was beginning to suck the salt water down' (12. 428). In 'blowing back' his hero, Homer creates a colourful image of the heliacal rising of Scorpius at sunrise against the background of the Milky Way.

Amidst the star-studded region surrounding Scorpius, Antares (α Scorpii) makes a fine foothold in the fig tree to which Odysseus clings like a bat. The long branches above his head represent the 'branches' of the Milky Way and the glittering stars in the tail of Scorpius are the roots far below him. Charybdis, the turbulent whirlpool, again suggests the wonderful sight of the Milky Way, which during the course of a night appears to wind around the sky as the earth turns. After Odysseus' raft is sucked down by the whirlpool some timbers resurface and Odysseus clings to them and drifts for nine days until he reaches Calypso's island. With the appearance of the crescent moon the following day, he begins his almost eight-year stay with the enchantress.

In plotting the passage of the sun along the ecliptic and linking it to Odysseus' adventures, we found that after his adventure in Hades, the sun travels almost 120° along the ecliptic from Libra, Scorpius, Ophiuchus, Sagittarius and into Capricornus; that is, the sun travels from the 'foot' of Virgo, λ Virginis, to β/α Aquarii.

Counting the days during this period gives:

Odysseus leaves Circe and encounters Scylla (dark moon)	=	29 days
From the new crescent to the waning moon	=	20 days
On Thrinacia from waning moon to waning moon	=	29 days
Odysseus sails with only 'sea and sky' in sight	=	30 days
Storm destroys ship (waning moon) Odysseus drifts for nine days	=	9 days
Odysseus arrives on Calypso's island	=	1 day
Total	=	118 days

It was an unexpected surprise that the counting of the days came to 118, the same calendrical division of one-third of a lunar year found also in the lists of goats, list of suitors, and the trees and vines in Odysseus' orchard.

Return to the 40 'Real-time' days: Days 33 & 34

Odysseus abruptly ends his long night's storytelling and reminds Alcinous' court that it was only the previous day that they had learned of his departure from Calypso in 'real-time' days, of the catastrophic storm sent by Zeus, of being almost drowned by the vengeful Poseidon and of how he was washed up on the shores of Phaeacia. Odysseus had begun his stories on the evening of Day 33 and he says 'it is tedious for me to repeat a tale.' The court is overwhelmed and sits in silence until Alcinous speaks of the pressing need to get Odysseus on the move again and calls for preparations to be made for his guest's departure for Ithaca. In the morning Odysseus is impatient to begin the final leg of his journey home and to settle his account with the suitors at the end of one 19-year cycle and the beginning of

11.5 As the Phaeacians prepare a ship for a voyage to Ithaca, the sighting of a waning moon just after dawn creates a memorable image of Odysseus looking over his shoulder at the rising sun and wanting to be on his way. (Own photo)

another at the appearance of a new crescent. As the Phaeacians make ready a ship, the waning moon would have been visible in the morning sky and 'Odysseus kept on turning his eyes towards the sun, as though to hasten his setting, for he was longing to be on his way' (13.29 Butler). After sunset, the Phaeacians row their ship away from Scherie and speedily carry the sleeping Odysseus overnight to the shores of Ithaca, where he is left with gifts of treasure shortly before the dawn of a new day. The last vestiges of the waning moon are still visible in the pre-dawn sky, as is Venus, 'the brightest of all stars ... which often ushers in the tender light of early dawn' (13.94).

The Phaeacians set about their return journey to Scherie immediately but are struck by disaster when, in retribution for their help to Odysseus, Poseidon strikes and transforms their ship into a rock firmly anchored to the sea-bottom (13.160). Like Jason's ship *Argo*, the Phaeacian vessel was also a magical vessel for 'not even the wheeling falcon, the fastest creature that flies, could have kept her company' on that overnight voyage. *Argo* was so famous in Greek mythology that like many mortal heroes a place was found for it amongst the stars in the southern hemisphere against the background of the Milky Way. In ancient times *Argo* was the largest constellation but in the nineteenth century AD it was divided into Vela (the sails), Puppis (the poop) and Carina (the keel). It is proposed that

Homer places the Phaeacians' magical ship in the same area of sky, which, like its counterpart *Argo*, could be said to be firmly fixed in the seas of the Milky Way. In 2300 BC, from the location of Chios, 38°N, and at about the time of the winter solstice, Argo (Vela, Puppis and the upper parts of Carina) were visible during the night hours, with Vela, like the ship that carried Odysseus, slipping below the horizon just before dawn and disappearing before the eyes of the waiting Phaeacians. Canopus, the brightest star in Argo, however, was not visible from Chios but would have been visible from Ur in Mesopotamia, 33°N, and Cairo in Lower Egypt, 30°N.

Notes

1   Redpath, I., *Stars and Planets, Eyewitness Handbooks, Star Charts by the Royal Greenwich Observatory* (London: Dorling Kindersley, 1998), p. 105.

2   Murray, A.T., Fitzgerald, R., Butler, S., Butcher & Lang, A. are amongst those who put the number of Sirens at two. Rieu, E.V. & Fagles, R. do not give a number.

3   Moore, P., *The Guinness Book of Astronomy* (London: Guinness Publishing 4th Edition, 1992), p. 162.

4   Redpath, I. (ed.), *Norton's 2000.0, Star Atlas and Handbook, Maps 12 & 14* (Essex: Longman, 1996).

5   *Harper's Dictionary of Classical Literature and Antiquities* (New York: Cooper Square Publishers, 1965), pp. 779–80.

6   Rose, H.J., *Handbook of Greek Mythology* (London: Routledge & Kegan Paul), p. 23.

12

ODYSSEUS:
THE INVISIBLE HERO

With Venus, the Morning Star, shining brightly in the sky, Odysseus awoke on the shores of Ithaca after sleeping deeply whilst the Phaeacian ship carried him overnight to his island kingdom. It now would seem reasonable for the grand climax of the epic to have occurred on the first or at least the second day of Odysseus' return, with the devoted husband and father dashing off to his palace to reclaim his heritage and be reunited with his wife after 19 years away. Instead it takes five days and 5000 lines of poetry before Odysseus is triumphant. Athene acknowledges the extraordinary situation when she tells Odysseus: 'Any other man on returning from his travels would have rushed home in high spirits to see his children and wife. You, on the contrary, are in no hurry even to ask questions' (13.333).

Athene infers that Odysseus wants to check on the fidelity of his wife, and even though the goddess confirms that Penelope has been truly faithful, Odysseus goes

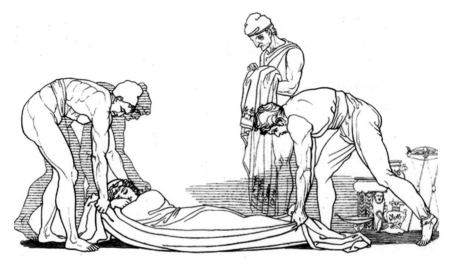

12.1 Sleeping Odysseus is taken ashore on Ithaca by the Phaeacians. (John Flaxman, 1755–1826)

into hiding. Nor are doubts of Penelope's devotion ever raised again. The absurdity of Odysseus' delay suggests a deeper purpose insomuch that Homer needs to account for the moon's dark period at the end of the 19-year cycle. His solution is eminently simple: as the moon cannot be seen when it is in conjunction with the sun, then Odysseus, the great lunar icon, is hidden when Athene, with a touch of her magic wand, transforms him into a beggar:

> she withered the smooth skin on his supple limbs, robbed his head of its dark locks, covered his whole body with an old man's wrinkles, and dimmed the brightness of his fine eyes. And she changed his clothing into a shabby cloak and tunic, and filthy rags grimy with smoke. Over his back she threw a large and well-worn hide of a nimble stag; finally she gave him a staff and a poor, shabby knapsack with a shoulder strap. (13.430 Rieu)

Odysseus' disguise is a metaphor for the dark of moon, but as the year draws to an end Homer may well have also intended to present the ragged old man as an image of Old Father Time, whose origins can be traced to Kronos and the oldest Greek creation myths. Later, as the old year ends and a new one begins, Odysseus/Father Time is transformed into a youthful specimen of manhood.

After Athene disguises Odysseus as a beggar his character is removed from the action. Except for his magical meeting with Telemachus, he stays secure in Eumeaus' hut for three nights and makes his way to his palace in the late afternoon of the fourth day. So effective is Odysseus' disguise that while he stays in the hut of his friend, the pig-keeper never suspects the real identity of his guest. Even later, when Odysseus comes face-to-face with Penelope and spins a long yarn,

12.2 When Eurycelia washes the feet of Odysseus he is still disguised as a beggar and looking, not unlike Old Father Time himself. Detail from an Attic drinking vessel.

she believes she is talking to a stranger. Homer creates powerful images of the impending new crescent when his aged nurse recognises a scar on his thigh made by the crescent-shaped white tusk of a wild boar. Later he shows the scar to the faithful Eumaeus and comrade-in-arms Philoetius as 'proof' of his identity before the contest of the great bow takes place.

During the days and nights which follow Odysseus' arrival in Ithaca, Homer gives a good indication of the times of day when events occur and none more so than in the last hours of the dark period and the moment when the new crescent moon appears in the evening sky. It is then that Odysseus throws off his beggar's rags and is transformed into a warrior-king, who leads the destruction of the suitors who had been harassing Penelope. After the slaughter of suitors and maids, and when the palace has been cleansed, Odysseus and Penelope retire to bed on the longest night of the year.

There are good calendrical reasons for Odysseus being cloaked as a down-and-out and hidden in Eumaeus' hut:

- From the moment Odysseus is disguised to when he is revealed as a glittering warrior defines the days of the lunar month from the beginning of the dark period to the appearance of the new crescent.
- To accommodate an error of almost five days in the 19-year cycle when the solar year is calculated as 365 days instead of 365.242 days.

The Dark Period & New Crescent

Just how long the moon remains in its dark period and when the first sighting of the new crescent can be made depends on a number of factors and would have been as familiar a problem to Homer as it is today. There is no absolute answer as to how long the dark phase of the moon lasts and Joachim Schultz states that 'when the moon passes into the direct vicinity of the sun [it] remains invisible for three or four days'.[1] Duncan Steel also writes of the uncertainty of making the first sighting:

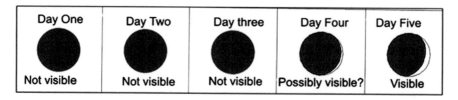

12.3 The 'dark' period of any lunar month is not a fixed interval of time. In this sample diagram from 'TheSky' the waning moon would be seen at dawn on Day 1 but would not be visible that night or the following two nights. On Day 4 the sliver of the new crescent moon may be too slender to be seen with the naked eye at dusk. On Day 5 it would be clearly visible at dusk.

At new moon it is glimpsed very soon after sunset and just before it dips below the western horizon. The amount of time after conjunction before the new moon can be seen depends upon a number of factors, including the latitude of the observer, the time of year, and the location of the perigee in terms of both celestial latitude and longitude.[2]

The problem was recognised in ancient times and, according to Geminus of Rhodes, (fl. first century BC), 'The new moon is visible at the earliest one day, at the latest three days after the conjunction'.[3]

Days of the Solar Year

Defining the solar year at 360 days + 5 additional days was common in antiquity, and in Egypt it was enshrined in the story of the goddess Nut, who married her twin brother Geb. So angry was the god Ra at their union that he decreed Nut could not bear a child in any month of any year. Sympathy for Nut's plight came from Thoth, god of wisdom, and while playing draughts with the moon he won a part of its light, which he used to create five new days. These were added to the 360 days of the official year and it was on each these days that Nut's five children were born.[4] In ancient Greece the time for the beginning of a new year varied and might be marked by the winter or summer solstices, or the spring equinox.

Adjustments to the 19-year Cycle

If Homer had not made adjustments to the calendar system it would soon have been obvious to ancient observers watching the skies after 19 'years' of 365 days that something was very wrong. For after 365 days the moon, instead of being a new crescent, would still have been waning and visible only in the early morning. The sun too would not have reached its position at the winter solstice. Only five days later, at the winter solstice, would the new crescent be seen against the same background of stars as it was when the cycle began. Five days are required to make up the shortfall before the current cycle ends, and the sixth day marks the first day of the following 19-year cycle.

The discrepancy is illustrated in Figs 4 and 5, and although it shows a cycle between 2314 and 2295 BC, it is typical of a 19-year cycle that begins and ends with the appearance of a new crescent moon at a winter solstice. In Fig. 4 the new crescent moon at the beginning and the end of the cycle is in Pisces, but in Fig. 5, and after 19 years of 365 days, the old moon is still waning and lies between Sagittarius and Capricornus. Five days later, 19 years of 365.24 days have passed and harmony is restored; the moon's 19-year synodic cycle is complete and it is

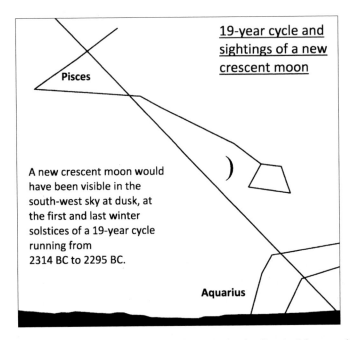

12.4 & 12.5 These two drawings show why Odysseus had to be disguised for several days before the winter solstice. The drawing on the left shows a new crescent moon at both the beginning and end of 19 years of 365.24 days. The drawing on the right shows that after 19 years of only 365 days observers would see the still waning moon and that it would be a further five days before the solstice.

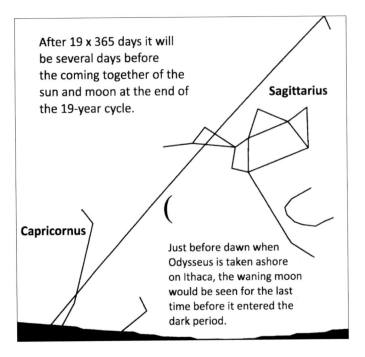

seen against the same background of stars in Pisces and at the same phase as when the cycle began.

The sun, too, has reached its position in Aquarius at the winter solstice at which it was when the cycle began.

Evidence of a 19-year Cycle

Evidence to support the view that the final days of the *Odyssey* are dictated by phases of the moon is found throughout the *Odyssey*. Examination of narrative was hampered by constant flashbacks, reminiscences, lying tales and other events which make it difficult to put into chronological order the events of the remaining days of the 40 'real-time' days and bring the 19-year cycle to a close. Nevertheless, careful reading provides sufficient evidence to determine when Odysseus left Ithaca, the number of years he spent besieging Troy, the duration of his long journey from Troy and his eventual return home. While Books 13 to 23 of the *Odyssey* are devoted to marking the end of the luni-solar cycle, it is only in Book 19 that Homer, for the first time in either the *Iliad* or the *Odyssey*, describes the day that Odysseus left Ithaca at the beginning of the cycle. In doing so, he brings together the parameters for the 19 years that bind the epics together. To establish the validity of Odysseus' 19-year absence being marked in lunations, the following questions need to be answered from narrative:

Does Homer expound upon a 19-year luni-solar cycle?
Does he give the phase of the moon at the end of the cycle?
Does he give the phase of the moon and the time of year when the cycle begins?
Does he point to the precise day of the year the cycle ends?

It is not just literary emphasis that leads Homer to repeat five times that Odysseus would 'return home in the twentieth year', that is after 19 complete years. As the *Odyssey* gets underway, the seer Halitherses tells of a prediction he made when the Greeks first set out for Troy and that after much hardship Odysseus would come home in the twentieth year and no one would know him (2.175). Odysseus later reveals to Telemachus that he has, after 'long wandering', arrived home in the twentieth year (16.206). In his beggar's disguise Odysseus lies to Penelope about the twentieth year (19.222) and makes a similar declaration to his father (24.322). Before the great contest with the bow, Odysseus tells Philoetius that 'at last, in the twentieth year, I am come back to my own country' (21.206). The confusion of how arriving home 'in the twentieth year' marks the end of 19 solar years is explained in Chapter 4.

Phase of Moon at the End of the Cycle

There are several references to the phase of moon at the end of the cycle. On the first night of his return to Ithaca, Odysseus shelters in the hut of Eumaeus and in a lying tale says that his 'master' (himself) will return 'between the waning of the old moon and the waxing of the new' (14.160). This is clearly a reference to the disguised Odysseus' return during the dark period of the moon and the failure of the pig-keeper to recognise him. A further hint of the end of the 19-year cycle and an impending new crescent occurs when Penelope first meets her disguised husband and fails to recognise him. In a lying tale he consoles her with the words that 'Odysseus is alive and near' and 'this very month … will be here between the waxing and the waning moon' (19.306). No doubt the deception between man and wife would have caused great amusement to those ancients who knew the *Odyssey* only as a source of literature, but in its wider sense Homer is again forecasting that the monthly, annual and 19-year cycles are coming to a conclusion. As if these two hints were not enough, Homer repeats the message in the early morning hours before the *Odyssey* reaches its climax, when Penelope dreams she 'saw Odysseus by me in bed looking exactly as he looked when he sailed away with his army, and my heart leapt up, because I took it for no dream but reality' (20.87). Far from being the cries of a deeply troubled woman, Penelope is foretelling that soon the new crescent moon will appear in the shape of a rejuvenated Odysseus, looking as he did 19 years earlier – and that is exactly what happens.

Beginning of the Cycle: Odysseus' Departure for Troy

There is ample evidence in the final days of the *Odyssey* concerning the momentary 'coming together' of the sun and moon at the end of a 19-year cycle. That being so, it points to the undeniable conclusion that 19 years earlier, when the cycle began, there would also have been a new crescent moon against the same background of stars at a winter solstice. This introduces something of a mystery about the *Iliad* and the *Odyssey*, for logically it might have been more reasonable of Homer to include Odysseus' departure for Troy in its chronological place in the *Iliad*. Narrative describing Odysseus' departure from Ithaca comes only on Day 38, amidst the dramas and deceits of his homecoming. Curious as it may seem, this juxtaposition enables Homer to show that the phase of moon and time of year when Odysseus first left home were the same as those he is describing at the end of the *Odyssey*, so defining the beginning and end of a 19-year cycle.

When disguised Odysseus reaches his palace, Penelope does not recognise him and eagerly questions the apparent stranger for news of her husband. During their conversation Penelope recollects the day that Odysseus left for war:

Odysseus wore a *thick, double, purple cloak*, displaying *a golden brooch with a pair of sheaths* into which the pins fitted. There was a device on the face of it: *a hound holding down a dappled fawn in his forepaws* and *ripping* it *as it scrabbled* … and the whole thing done in gold. (19.225 Rieu)

A clue to the chilly time of year is given by the 'purple double-lined cloak', and there are two metaphors for the new crescent moon – the golden brooch and the hound seizing a dappled fawn. The warm purple cloak not only indicates that Odysseus left home in midwinter but it is also creates a splendid image of the night sky against which the golden brooch shines as brightly as did the new crescent moon[5] on that long-ago day. The brooch has two prongs with which to fasten it, and it is not too great a test of imagination to picture these as the twin points or horns of the crescent moon. The intricate design of the face of the brooch is described in detail: a dog holds a spotted fawn between its forepaws and strangles it as it struggles. The death of a fawn is a strange choice of subject with which to adorn a brooch given to a loved one as a tender farewell memento, but a comparison with the crescent moon provides an astronomical reason.

At the time of the new crescent, sunlight reflected from the Earth gives a faint illumination to those parts of the surface of the moon still in shadow. The phenomenon is known as 'earthshine', or more poetically as the 'old moon in the new moon's arms'. What a wonderful image it creates if Homer's hound were a metaphor for the bright crescent of the new moon gripping the fawn, whose dappled markings are the earthshine shadows of the moon's craters. No matter how much the fawn struggles to escape the clutches of the dog, as the moon

12.6 New crescent moon and earthshine. (Steve Jurvetson/ Wikicommons)

waxes earthshine is obliterated by light and the fawn disappears. Would a dog and fawn be any more unusual than the figures created in other cultural imaginations from amongst the shadows and outlines of the moon's surface? 'The human imagination has seen many things lurking in [the moon's] markings,' wrote Roger Highfield.[6] 'Some cultures see a woman weaving, an elephant launching off a cliff, or a girl with a basket on her back. Others a rabbit, or even a four-eyed jaguar. We see the Man in the Moon, a face consisting of dark eyes and mouth, with bright forehead, cheeks and chin.'

Another metaphor for earthshine is given when Homer describes Odysseus' tunic: 'As for the shirt that he wore next his skin, it was so soft that it fitted him like the skin of an onion, and glistened in the sunlight to the admiration of all the women who beheld it' (19.233). On the day Odysseus boarded his ship and began his 19-year voyage over the wine-dark seas of the sky, earthshine could well have been said to reflect both the shape and colour of an onion skin. When Homer says the shirt glistened in the sunlight, it poses the question of whether he knew that it is the reflected light of the sun that illuminates the moon.

If Homer's intention is to emphasise the beginning of a cycle, what better way than to use a memorably decorated brooch as a simile for the new crescent moon, to hearken twice to the effect of earthshine and to remind us of the cold weather and dark skies at the winter solstice by the gift to Odysseus of a double-lined purple cloak? Only a few lines later, Homer draws further attention to the phase of moon when Odysseus spins a yarn to Penelope and describes his squire, Eurybates:

> He had a servant with him, a little older than himself … his shoulders were hunched, he was dark, and he had thick curly hair … Odysseus treated him with greater familiarity than he did any of the others, as being the most like-minded with himself. (19.244 Butler)

This sudden and unique reference to Eurybates and his close resemblance to Odysseus suggests yet another metaphor for the dark of moon that precedes the arrival of the new crescent.

The Day the 19-year Cycle Ends

The climax of the *Odyssey* occurs on Odysseus' fifth day in Ithaca and the 39th of the real-time days, with Odysseus still disguised as a beggar during the morning and early afternoon. With the arrival of the new crescent he throws off his disguise and rids his palace of the plague of suitors. Penelope at last recognises her husband and if further confirmation were needed that it is the shortest day and the longest night, Homer describes the reunion of Odysseus with his wife in these words:

Indeed [Odysseus and Penelope] would have gone on indulging their sorrow till rosy-fingered morn appeared, had not Athene determined otherwise, and *held night back in the far west*, while she would not suffer Dawn to leave Oceanus. (23.243 Butler)

While the quotation has overtones of the supernatural, it was Homer's memorable way of marking the longest night, when the sun rises late. Earlier that day another indication of the winter solstice was given when Athene changed herself into a swallow, the bird that symbolises the solstice:[7] 'she herself taking the shape of a swallow, darted aloft to perch on the smoky main beam of the hall' (22.238). Nor is it a coincidence that the feast of the archer god Apollo (21.259) is celebrated on that day, for Sagittarius, constellation of the bowman, rises majestically in the sky before dawn. Following our overview of the crucial astronomical and calendrical events of the days leading up to the climax of the *Odyssey*, the next chapter gives a more detailed examination and interpretation of narrative during the same period.

Notes

1 Schultz, J., *Movement and Rhythm of the Stars* (Edinburgh: Floris Books), p. 75.

2 Steel, D., *Marking Time, the Epic Quest to Invent the Perfect Calendar* (New York: John Wiley & Sons, 2000), p. 396.

3 Bickerman, E.J., *Chronology of the Ancient World* (Ithaca NY: Cornell University Press, 1964), p. 18.

4 Stuart, G., *Encyclopedia of Myth and Legend* (London: Headline, 1993), p. 339.

5 When the moon first rises it can appear to be orange or yellow – or golden. This effect is caused by the atmosphere, which contains tiny particles of dust. When the moon and sun are close to the horizon their light passes through more of the atmosphere than when they are high in the sky. Atmospheric particles let through red light, which gives both heavenly bodies their distinctive and changing colours. See http://home.hiwaay. net/~krcool/Astro/moon/moonorange/.

6 Roger Highfield, Science Editor, *Sunday Telegraph*, 12 January 2003.

7 An earlier reference to the swallow at the time of the winter solstice is made when Odysseus tests the string of his great bow 'which sang as he plucked it with the note of a swallow' (21.411).

13

ODYSSEUS TRIUMPHANT

During its final six days, the *Odyssey* reaches a tremendous climax both in literary and astronomical terms, and so important to Homer is this relatively brief period of time that he devotes to it almost half of the epic, from Books 13 to 24. The countdown begins on Day 35 of the 40 'real-time' days, when Odysseus is left sleeping on a beach on Ithaca by the Phaeacians. It ends on Day 40 when Athene brings the *Odyssey* to a close and harmony has been restored both in terms of calendars and literary matters. We will now show how Homer weaves into narrative the momentous astronomical events that occur during the last days of the epic.

13.1 When Eurycleia recognises a scar on the leg of Odysseus he prevents her telling of her discovery until the next day – when a new crescent will be clearly visible. (Christian Gottlob Heyne, 1729–1812)

Table 1: Odysseus and the final days of the *Odyssey*

Day of the month, Phase of the moon	Position of the sun	Day of the *Odyssey*	Events in narrative	2295 BC
27 Waning moon in the morning sky. Venus visible. No moon at night	Capricornus–Aquarius	35	Odysseus arrives in Ithaca and Athene disguises him as a beggar. He stays with Eumaeus whom he deviously tells that 'his master will return between the old and the new moon'.	5 Jan
28 Dark moon		36	Odysseus remains hidden in Eumaeus' hut.	6
29 Dark moon		37	Odysseus remains hidden in Eumaeus' hut.	7
30 Moon emerging from its dark period at the end of the 19-year cycle		38	Odysseus, still in disguise, goes to his palace where his old nurse, Eurycleia, recognises a scar on his leg. No one else 'sees' him at this hint of the impending new crescent. Odysseus, in a lying tale, assures Penelope that 'her husband will return between the old and the new moon'.	8
1 New crescent appears marking the beginning of a new year and new 19-year cycle	Aquarius (Winter Solstice)	39	Feast of Apollo. Solar eclipse? Odysseus reveals his scar to companions before stringing his great bow. After his bronze-tipped arrow flies through 12 axe-heads he throws off his disguise, kills the suitors and beds Penelope.	9
2		40	Odysseus visits Laertes and encounters relatives of the dead suitors. The *Odyssey* ends in harmony … before Odysseus resumes his wanderings.	10

Day 35, Dark of Moon: Odysseus Returns

As dawn approaches, Odysseus awakes and Venus and the last sliver of the diminishing crescent are in the sky. Athene, whose beauty compares to the brilliant Morning Star, appears in disguise and Odysseus tells her a lying and boastful tale. She quickly reveals her real identity and warns Odysseus of the trials he faces and they discuss the downfall of the suitors. As the moon enters its dark period, she transform Odysseus into an aged beggar dressed in rags. With sunrise, the waning moon, like disguised Odysseus, can no longer be seen and the prophecy that he would return home between the waning of one moon and the arrival of the next has been fulfilled.

Meanwhile, Athene goes to Menelaus' palace in Lacedaemon to tell Telemachus that it is time to return home and warns him of a suitors' plot to ambush and kill him. Telemachus is eager to leave, but it is a dark and moonless night and his friend, Peisistratus, says they should begin their homeward journey in daylight (15.51). Scholars have noted here an apparent discrepancy in narrative: Athene leaves Odysseus in Ithaca in daylight but arrives at Menelaus' palace while it is still dark. Lacedaemon is to the east of Ithaca and in strict terms the sun would have risen there some nine minutes before it did on Odysseus' island. This confusion has been suggested as one of the times when Homer 'nodded'.

Later that morning Odysseus arrives at the home of his old friend and servant, the pig-keeper Eumaeus, who is so confounded by the disguise that he believes he is befriending a stranger. That night the weather is foul and raining and, while inside the pig-keeper's hut, Odysseus spins a tale of his adventures. Homer clearly states 'there is no moon' (14.457) and eventually the pig-keeper goes out in the cold dark night to guard his animals, and slings his sword around his shoulder, a sign that the new crescent has not yet appeared.[1]

Day 36, Dark of Moon: Odysseus Stays in Hiding

How Odysseus and Eumaeus spend their time during the daylight hours of the second day is not recorded, but in the evening they again talk and Eumaeus confirms that it is midwinter and 'the nights are very long [and] give one time to listen and be entertained' (15.392). Eumaeus tells of his earlier life and his native island of Syrie that lies in the direction of Ortygia, where 'the sun turns its course' (15.403). It is a recognised interpretation that Eumaeus is drawing attention to the place on the horizon where the sun rises at the winter solstice. Meanwhile, Telemachus continues his homeward journey and as the sun sets and darkness spreads over the seas he sails to Ithaca during the moonless night and avoids a party of suitors lying in ambush. The suitors felt, perhaps with some justification, that some god had a hand in Telemachus' escape (16.356).

Day 37, Dark of Moon: Odysseus & Telemachus Meet

With the moon in conjunction with the sun, Odysseus remains disguised in beggar's clothes, but with the assistance of Athene he has a magical encounter with Telemachus. After breakfast his son arrives at the pig-keeper's hut but fails to recognise his father until Eumaeus is sent on an errand and Athene briefly transforms Odysseus to his true self (16.172). After an emotional reunion, father and son plan the destruction of the suitors on the day after Odysseus will return to his palace – another intimation of the forthcoming new crescent moon. Telemachus is urged to keep his father's arrival secret and in another touch of sorcery Athene again hides Odysseus in the rags of a beggar so that when Eumaeus returns he is still unaware of his guest's identity. Telemachus goes to the palace, where he finds the troubled situation unchanged, the suitors pursue his mournful mother and he returns to spend the night with Odysseus in Eumaeus' hut.

Day 38, Dark of Moon: Odysseus Goes to the Palace

In the morning Telemachus goes to his father's palace where, in keeping with the dark phase of the moon, there is an air of gloom; Eurycleia and Penelope are in tears and the suitors have malice in their hearts. Odysseus and Eumaeus follow in the late afternoon as it becomes colder (17.191) but the pig-keeper is still unaware of the identity of his companion. As the pair make their way towards the palace they meet a goat herder, a familiar figure in Ithaca both in Homer's times and today. The goat herder, Melanthius, is singled out in Homer's song of the heavens when he comes face to face with Odysseus and makes a sneering attack on the 'beggar' dressed in rags and tatters (17.215). As literary narrative, this may seem just another incident in which Homer emphasises the hostility facing Odysseus as he seeks to reclaim his wife and inheritance. So important is Melanthius to the story, however, that he makes four appearances before meeting his death in a particularly gruesome manner.[2]

When the 40 'real-time' days of the *Odyssey* begin, the sun lies between Sagittarius and Capricornus and by the time Odysseus arrives in Ithaca, some 35 days later, it has moved through most of Capricornus and is approaching Aquarius (see Fig. 2). In their modern configuration, and very probably in Homer's, stars

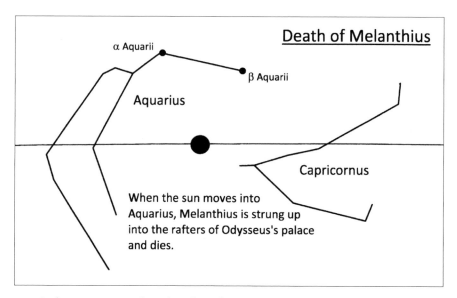

13.2 As the sun progresses along the ecliptic from Capricornus to Aquarius it seals the fate of Melanthius.

from these two constellations overlap, and the sun appears to arrive at β Aquarii before it passes δ Capricorni, the constellation of the fish-tailed goat. Odysseus meets the goatherd on the road to the palace late in the afternoon, as the sun is about to move from Capricornus to Aquarius at the winter solstice. So angry is Odysseus at the manner in which he is humiliated by Melanthius that he debates whether he should kill the goatherd with his long staff, a metaphor for the impending new crescent. As on similar occasions in the *Odyssey*, it is still dark of moon and until the new crescent is sighted he is powerless to act (17.235) and Melanthius is temporarily reprieved.

The concept of Capricornus as a goat is very ancient and Richard Allen writes: 'Although we do not know when Capricornus came into the zodiac, we may be confident that it was millenniums ago.'[3] The constellation makes a fine home for Melanthius, but in later Greek mythology Capricornus acquired a fish tail when the goat-like Pan changed his lower half into a fish to escape the sea monster Typhon.[4] In dramatic terms it may be that Homer considers Melanthius as the man who tried to stop Odysseus, the lunar icon, in his tracks – a metaphor perhaps for the futility of trying to halt time itself.[5]

After their confrontation with Melanthius, Odysseus and Eumaeus continue to the palace, where Odysseus is recognised by his faithful dog, Argus, which promptly expires. When Odysseus arrives at the palace he is aggressively accosted and humiliated by the suitors, another sombre event reflecting the dark of moon.

New Crescent Moon Imminent: Eurycleia Recognises Odysseus' Scar

> Odysseus was sitting by the fire, but now he swung abruptly round to face the dark, for it had struck him suddenly that … [Eurycleia] might notice a certain scar he had, and his secret would be out … Eurycleia then came up to her master and began to wash him. At once she recognized the scar, the one Odysseus had received years before from the white tusk of a boar. (19.389 Rieu)

The meeting of Odysseus and Eurycleia occurs in the evening after Penelope tells the nurse who had known Odysseus since childhood to wash the feet of the 'stranger'.

When Eurycleia recognises an old scar on the thigh of Odysseus, he seizes her by the throat and swears her to keep his identity secret for his time is not yet come. Eurycleia sees the scar when Odysseus turns away from the fire, in the manner that the crescent moon appears to turn away from the sun as it came out of conjunction. Odysseus' white scar as a metaphor for the new crescent moon turning away from the fire, the sun, suggests again that Homer knew that the moon is illuminated by reflected sunlight as was indicated when Odysseus' shirt

13.3 This helmet in the museum at Olympia, Greece, is decorated with curved boars' tusks.

Odysseus's scar and a new crescent moon

The boar's scar recognised on Odysseus's thigh by Eurycleia is a metaphor for the impending new crescent moon.

The 'fire' from which Odysseus turns away is the setting sun just below the horizon and whose light illuminates the new crescent.

13.4 As the moon comes out of conjunction, Odysseus 'turns away from the fire' in the same way that the new crescent moon 'turns its back' on the sun. His 'scar' from the curved ivory tusk of a boar reflects the shape of the imminent crescent.

was compared with an onion skin (see Chapter 12). It is likely, too, that Homer deliberately attributed Odysseus' scar to the tusks of a boar rather than an injury inflicted in battle, for the animal's curving white tusk evokes a striking image of the new crescent and these beasts have been associated with the winter solstice. Strangely, the scar is seen only fleetingly by the nurse and not at all by Penelope, who is in the same room, and there is a degree of uncertainty about Homer's intentions in Eurycleia's recognition of Odysseus. As the moon emerges from the dark period only a very slim crescent, some 4.4 per cent, would be illuminated and it is unclear whether Homer is hinting at the approach of the new crescent or if he is saying that under some conditions a new crescent could have been visible. What is certain is that on the following evening 7 per cent of the new crescent would have been clearly visible and Odysseus finally recognised as he cast off his beggar's clothes.

Penelope's Nightmare: Aquila Stands Above Capricornus

Odysseus' identity remains concealed even when he meets Penelope, who tells the 'beggar' of a strange nightmare in which 20 geese feeding at a trough were killed by the crooked beak of a great eagle which swooped down from a mountainside (19.541). The eagle reappears and tells the frightened Penelope not to fear for the eagle is really her husband and the geese are the suitors who are doomed soon to die. An explanation for Penelope's nightmare can be found in the skies directly above Capricornus, where lies the constellation of Aquila, the Eagle. Altair, α Aquilae, is the brightest star in the constellation and as a simile for the giant bird's beak it points towards Capricornus. The great 'mountain' down which the eagle 'flies' is the Milky Way, and when it later 'perches on a projecting rafter', it is possibly yet another reference to the Milky Way. Although Capricornus is not an outstandingly bright constellation, there are 20 easily visible stars in that part of the sky and the trough for the geese can be seen as the ecliptic. As the sun passes from Capricornus into Aquarius and reaches the winter solstice, so too will Penelope's nightmare have a happy ending.

Day 39, New Crescent Moon: Odysseus Triumphs

The literary and calendrical strands of the *Odyssey* come together on the penultimate day of the epic, when a feast in honour of Apollo celebrating the appearance of a new crescent moon is held. On this occasion it is also a winter solstice, when a new 19-year cycle and new year will begin. In view of Odysseus' forthcoming great feat with his bow, it is pertinent that at the winter solstice *c.*2300 BC Sagittarius, the brilliant constellation of the archer, made its heliacal rising about two hours before dawn and could be seen in all its glory on the eastern horizon.

   All is bleak on the morning before the new crescent moon becomes visible in the late afternoon and there are troubled events at the palace. Penelope awakens and cries out that she has seen Odysseus by her bedside looking just as he did when he set off for Troy 19 years before. In the palace only one woman is found grinding corn on a quern, whereas normally there would be 12; it is another indication that the sun is now in the final constellation of the solar calendar and when she has finished her chores then a year will have come to its end. The inexorable passing of time represented by grinding mills is rooted deep in mythology.[6] Odysseus is still a stranger to Penelope, his supporters and his enemies. The suitors, preparing for the Feast of Apollo at midday, are as disagreeable as ever and Telemachus clashes again with them as they gather in the banqueting hall. There follows a curious incident when the seer Theoclymenus addresses the suitors in terms that set the mood for the imminent scene of bloodshed and slaughter. In describing the fearful omens associated with a total solar eclipse, he says that 'the Sun is blotted out from heaven, and a foul mist has crept upon the world' (20.351). He paints a horrifying picture of the evil associated with eclipses, the crying suitors covered in darkness, wailing voices, walls and beams dripping with blood, and ghosts making their way to hell. An eclipse would have been a disturbing phenomenon for both man and beast in those times, but powerful as these words are, they present something of an astronomical mystery. A total solar eclipse could not have taken place so soon before the rising of the new crescent moon and if one had occurred it would have been at least a day earlier, when the sun and moon were in direct conjunction (see Appendix 3).

At this critical point just a few hours before the crescent moon appears, disguised Odysseus reveals himself to his friends Eumaeus and Philoetius and confirms his identity by showing them the boar's tusk scar (21.217) and warns of the ordeals soon to come. There is great emotion from Eumaeus and Philoetius at his revelation but Odysseus calls a halt to the weeping and wailing lest it be 'prolonged until sunset' when the new crescent moon appears. Odysseus and his comrades next secretly gather arms together and make their preparations to destroy the suitors. In the climax to the *Odyssey*, Homer describes an exercise in archery that would be highly improbable on earth, the violent slaughter of the suitors and an act of brutality against 12 women that is unforgettably outrageous. So extraordinary are these events that they suggest Homer had in mind other matters as well as those involving mortal heroics and violence. The archery contest takes place after Penelope issues the challenge that she will marry the man who can string the great bow that Odysseus left behind on leaving for Troy, and then perform a highly unlikely feat of skill.

> Penelope: I intend to propose a test using the very axes which he [Odysseus] sometimes set up here at home, twelve in a row like props under a new keel. Standing a good way off, he could shoot an arrow through them all. (19.572 Rieu)

At Athene's prompting, Penelope fetches the bow from a storeroom and Telemachus digs a trench in which to place the 12 axes. Naturally, none of the suitors manage to string the bow and the story continues when Penelope agrees to let disguised Odysseus take up the challenge. Nevertheless, she will not marry the 'beggar' if he succeeds but instead promises him new weapons and a set of new clothes, just as the moon will soon be dressed anew. Penelope orders the bow to be given to Odysseus and says: 'This stranger is strong and well-built … give him the bow and let us see whether he can string it or no' (21.334).

In another indication of the ending of the 19-year cycle, Telemachus has now come of age and asserts his authority. He banishes his mother from the ensuing drama, saying that what follows is men's work, and Penelope tearfully goes to her bedroom. Telemachus tells Eumaeus to give the bow to Odysseus who, to cries of derision from the suitors and a heaven-sent roll of thunder, fires a bronze-tipped arrow through the 12 axe-heads, as the new crescent moon appears in the evening sky. '[Odysseus] picked up this shaft [arrow], set it against the bridge of the bow, drew back the grooved end and the string together, all without rising from his stool and with a single aim, shot. Not a single axe did he miss' (21.416 Rieu).

Scholars have given much thought to the remarkable feat of archery and there is disagreement through which part of the axe the arrow might have passed. Robert Fitzgerald translates it as going through the 'socket ring'; E.V. Rieu says the bolt went through the 'handle ring'; while Richmond Lattimore states that Odysseus 'let the arrow fly, nor missed any axes from the first handle on, but the bronze-weighted arrow passed through all, and out the other end'. Discussion has speculated on how far apart the axes might have been placed and even the effect of gravity on the trajectory of a flying arrow. Such a feat would almost certainly be impossible in mortal terms and by concentrating on how Odysseus might have achieved it the true significance has been obscured. As metaphor it provides three striking calendrical images of the passing of a year:

1. The bow, described at 21.363 as 'curved' by Rieu and Lattimore, and 'horned' by Fitzgerald, is readily associated with the new crescent moon.[7]
2. The bronze-tipped arrow represents the sun.
3. The trench represents the ecliptic, and as the arrow passes through each of the 12 axes it records the passing of the sun through each month of the year.

As the arrow reaches the twelfth axe the new crescent moon appears in the sky and marks the coming together of the sun and moon at the end of the last year of the 19-year cycle. With a new crescent visible in the sky, Odysseus throws off his disguise and declares 'The mighty contest is at an end'. This bold cry was quite correct, for as he and his comrades slaughter the panicking suitors without mercy, the conflict between the sun and moon was, for the moment, at an end and the 19-year cycle was in harmony. So important is the image of the coming together of the sun and moon that after the suitors have been killed Homer repeats its message in brutal detail when Telemachus hangs 12 maidservants who had enjoyed the favours of the suitors.

13.5 Odysseus looses his arrows at the suitors at the bloody climax of the *Odyssey*. (Gustav Schwab, 1882; Wikicommons)

> He took a cable … made one end fast to a high column in the portico, and threw the other over the round-house, high up, so that their feet would not touch the ground … the women's heads were held fast in a row, with nooses round their necks, to bring them to the most pitiable end. (22.465 Rieu)

The execution of the maids fulfils both a literary purpose by shocking the reader and an astronomical purpose in creating images that again memorably mark the passing of the last year of the 19-year cycle. The line fetched about the roundhouse indicates the ecliptic, with the 12 months represented by the 12 hanging maids; as each maid dies so too does a month pass as the sun journeys along its annual path.

The sun now having passed out of the stars of Capricornus into Aquarius, is marked by another vicious act of revenge when the goat herder Melanthius, who had taunted the ragged Odysseus, is 'strung up from a high pillar till he was close up to the rafters' and then has his nose cut off, his vitals drawn out and given to the dogs. In a final fury, his hands and feet are cut off (22.474). It is a terrible end for the man who challenged Odysseus and time itself.

The Winter Solstice: Secret of the Marriage Bed

With the arrival of the new crescent, Odysseus, keeper of the luni-solar cycle that has just passed, is also rejuvenated by divine intervention and given a new tunic and cloak. Athene transforms him so that he is taller and stronger, with thick hair on his head and 'he came out of the bath looking like one of the everlasting gods' (23.163). Penelope, however, prolongs her husband's desires and puts him further to the test by saying he is hardly the man he was 19 years ago and tells the nurse to make up his bed outside the room. Odysseus becomes angry and says the bed could be moved easily only by a god before describing how the bed was built:

> A great secret went into that complicated bed; and it was my work and mine alone. Inside the court there was a long-leaved olive-tree which had grown to full height with a trunk as thick as a pillar. Round this I built my room of compact stonework and when it was finished, I roofed it over. (23.182 Rieu)

The 'olive tree' is a symbol for the winter solstice, while the 'room' points to Aquarius, the constellation in which the sun is now lying. At last Penelope acknowledges that Odysseus is indeed her husband and they retire to bed for lovemaking and the recalling of Penelope's travails at home in Ithaca and Odysseus' tales of his adventures. It is indeed the winter solstice and on the longest night Athene 'kept golden-throned Dawn waiting' during their prolonged reunion (23.344).

By now Homer has accounted for the five days needed to adjust the 19-year cycle: 19 years each of 365 days (6935 days) plus 5 'extra' days, make a total of 6940 days – the number of days in 19 solar years. So too have been completed the 235 lunations which balance the 19 solar years.

Day 40: Odysseus Visits Laertes

The final day of the *Odyssey* is something of a curiosity in literary terms and it has been suggested that a writer other than Homer added it. Compared to the tempestuous events of the previous day it may appear to be a low-key ending to the epic, but astronomically the day is important.

Not only does it illustrate the continuity of the ever-repeating 19-year cycle but it is also the day on which Homer describes the orchard of Odysseus, which reveals high-level data concerning cycles of the sun, moon and Venus (see Chapter 5). Even as the epic draws to a close there is a flourish of more calendrical data at 24.275, when Odysseus tells his father, in a lying tale, that he gave a stranger (himself) the following gifts: 7 talents of gold (the sun), 1 silver wine bowl with a floral design (the moon), 12 cloaks, 12 rugs, 12 robes and 12 tunics with the add-ons of 4 serving women. This data leads to the following calculations about the sun and moon:

Cloaks, rugs, robes and tunics (4 x 12)	=	48	
Talents of gold	=	7	
Silver bowl	=	1	
Serving women	=	4	
Total	=	60 (days in two full lunar months)	

Cloaks, rugs, robes and tunics total 48 plus 4 serving women = 52

52 x 7 (talents of gold) = 364

364 + 1 (silver bowl) = 365 (the number of days in a year).

There is more magic when Odysseus' father is transformed: 'Athene came and filled out the limbs of … [Laertes], making him seem taller and sturdier than before, so that as he stepped out of his bath his own son was amazed to see him looking like an immortal god' (24.366 Rieu).

Father, son and grandson now represent the enduring nature of the 19-year cycle; the rejuvenated Laertes and Odysseus are icons of two cycles past, while the youthful Telemachus carries calendrical wisdom forward as a new cycle begins. The family series of three cycles could be extended to four by the inclusion of Autolycus, the grandfather whom the young Odysseus was visiting when wounded in the boar hunt. Those 4 x 19-year generations would give the same number of years as the cycle of 76 years introduced by Callippus of Cyzicus (*c*.370–300 BC), which further improved calendrical accuracy, although there seems to be no indication that this extension has any special significance in the *Odyssey*. Odysseus' family cycles and others are explored in Chapter 14.

Later, on their way home to the palace, Odysseus and his small party are attacked by townspeople in revenge for the killing of the suitors, but Athene orders them to cease fighting and declares peace between the two sides (24.545). Indeed, harmony had been restored between the warring factions on earth, and the conflict between the lunar and solar calendars was also momentarily at an end.

These events may have brought the *Odyssey* to a close but they were not the end of Homer's calendrical concerns. The tribulations of Odysseus were to continue in the future, and it was not for him to enjoy the pleasures of kingship and a loving family. As Telemachus led the people into a new 19-year cycle, Odysseus was doomed to fulfil a prophecy by the soothsayer Teiresias. His fate was to leave Ithaca carrying an oar, until he came to a country where the people thought it was a winnowing shovel, had never heard of the sea, did not mix salt with their food, and knew nothing about ships. To the seafaring Greeks such a destination would have been a place of fantasy and Odysseus' search for it would have been as endless as time itself. Odysseus' death, predicted Teiresias, would be peaceful and come from the sea, metaphorically – perhaps the same wine-dark seas of the heavens that Odysseus had sailed on his lunar adventures.

Notes

1   Edna Leigh wrote: 'Years ago I should have known an ancient astronomer when I met
    one in the pages of the *Odyssey*, in spite of Homer's decking him out to look like a
    swineherd setting forth to guard pigs on a winter's night. Why, for example, does Homer
    make such a point of Eumaeus', Odysseus' swineherd, dressing in his heaviest garments
    and going out to watch pigs in their mountain top shelter on a cold winter's night in
    the rain with a north wind blowing; what marauding animal would be likely to leave
    its lair to attack one of the boars or to climb the stockade and attempt to carry off a
    piglet before being put to flight or killed by fifty irate sows in any of a dozen pens?
    As the most complacent of contemporary swine can be most fearsome beasts when
    disturbed, what watching do Odysseus' razorbacks really need? If not pigs, what is the
    swineherd watching? Why is Eumaeus watching from a mountain top in the first place?
    Rough and rocky as the island of Ithaca is said to be, surely pigs would thrive in a more
    sheltered location?' She went on to suggest that the 'pigs with shining teeth' (Lattimore),
    which Eumaeus went to observe, could have been the Hyades, the asterism in Taurus
    known in antiquity as the Little Pigs and which at around midnight *c.*2300 BC were
    close to setting in the western sky. See also Hinckley, Allen, *The Star Names, Their Lore
    and Meaning* (New York: Dover, 1963 reprint), p. 388.

2   The references to Melanthius are: 17.212, 20.173, 20.253, 21.265, and where he meets his
    gruesome fate at 22.135.

3   Allen, R.H., *Star Names, Their Lore and Meaning* (New York: Dover, reprint 1963), p. 139.

4   Ridpath, I., *Stars and Planets* (London: Dorling & Kindersley, 1998), p. 75.

5   Foolish Pandarus in the *Iliad* tries to halt time by killing Menelaus but fails (*Iliad* 4.127)
    and, like Melanthius, he also met his own death (*Iliad* 5.291). See *Homer's Secret Iliad*,
    pp. 209–10.

6   de Santillana, G. & von Dechend, H., *Hamlet's Mill* (Boston: Godine, 1977), pp. 290.

7   Many centuries after Homer, Shakespeare created a similar image in *A Midsummer Night's
    Dream* when he described a new moon as a 'silver-bow new-bent in heaven'.

14

CYCLES WITHIN CYCLES: PENELOPE, HELEN & HEROES

Odysseus is the undoubted focal point of the calendar system spanning the *Iliad* and the *Odyssey*, but other leading characters also have their parts to play in Homer's 19-year and eight-year cycles of the sun and moon. When the solstices and rites of passage such as births, comings of age, marriages, kingship and the finality of death are linked to Penelope, Helen of Troy, Laertes, Telemachus, Agamemnon and Menelaus, some very interesting patterns emerge. As our researches expanded we found concealed in the layers of Homer's epics examples of other cycles and cycles running within cycles.

Weeping Penelope & the 19-year cycle

Throughout literary history Penelope has been depicted as the beautiful, grieving and ever-faithful wife of Odysseus and the protective mother of her only child, Telemachus. So powerful are the dramatic perceptions of her female strengths and

14.1 Athene tells the sleeping Penelope that Telemachus has returned home. (John Flaxman, 1755–1826)

emotions that her role in the larger calendrical model was for long obscured. Until the moment Penelope finally acknowledges her husband, she often cuts a sorry figure: forever weeping and bemoaning the absence of Odysseus, being much disturbed by terrible dreams and when marriage to one of the suitors looks inevitable, wishing for an early death. On the other hand she is admired for her cleverness even by suitors whose approaches for marriage she fended off for almost four years with the trick of weaving a shroud for Laertes by day and unpicking her work by night. Odysseus, too, is impressed by her ability to say one thing and yet mean another (18.281), a passing reference perhaps to her mortal and astral roles.

No other character in the *Odyssey* reflects the dreary times of the waning moon more than does Penelope. She makes her debut on Days 1 & 2 of the 40 'real-time' days, when the waning moon heralds a period of gloom and misery. On Day 6 she makes another appearance and her despair is marked by a dream that is as dark and disturbing as the moonless night. A month later, on Day 37, Penelope appears again at dark of moon and has another nightmare. So deep now is her anguish at the prospect of marrying a suitor and her fears that Odysseus will never return, she says: 'I wish Artemis would let me die so sweetly now at this very moment, that I might no longer waste in despair for the loss of my dear husband' (18.202; 20.61 Butler). Late in the afternoon of Day 38, disguised Odysseus makes his way to the palace and although in the evening even he talks to Penelope at length; she fails to recognise him – and will not do so until the new crescent moon appears the following day. It was from her meeting with the 'beggar' that Penelope's metaphorical role became clear.

As already noted, a curiosity in the structure of the *Odyssey* is that details of Odysseus' departure from home are revealed by Penelope only after he has returned to Ithaca and are not mentioned at all in the *Iliad*, which chronologically is the first of the two epics. The literary device of Penelope being present at both the departure and return of Odysseus establishes the parameters of the beginning and end of the 19-year cycle. From Book 16 to the climax of the epic in Book 23, Penelope comes into her own and there are five places in the narrative indicating her involvement with the cycle.

Penelope's farewell gift to Odysseus of a brooch with its imagery of a new crescent moon marks the beginning of the 19-year cycle at a winter solstice (19.226).

When Telemachus returns from Lacedaemon he asks Penelope if she has married and taken someone to her marriage bed, which had lain 'without bedding and covered with cobwebs' (16.34) since Odysseus went to war. She had, of course, not chosen a new husband and the bed that Odysseus had so skilfully made on the occasion of their marriage (23.188) would remain dusty and unused until the appearance of the new crescent at the end of the cycle. Only then, with the moon at the same phase and in the same position against the background of stars as it had been 19 years earlier, would Odysseus and Penelope be reunited in their rejuvenated marriage bed.

On Day 39, the climax of the *Odyssey*, Penelope must confront her worst fears and decide which of the suitors she will marry. Athene directs her to fetch Odysseus' great bow and its quiver of arrows from a storeroom, whose bronze key and handle of ivory presents another image of the new crescent moon. The bow, which had lain unused for 19 years, had prestigious origins and once belonged to Eurytus, who in turn was killed by Apollo the archer god for his boastfulness. Eurytus' son, Iphitus, inherited the bow and gave it to Odysseus before he was killed by Heracles, a demi-god noted for his archery skills (21.15ff). Consequently, the bow and quiver were precious to Odysseus and it would seem out of character for him not to have taken them to Troy where, with the exception of Philoctetes, he was regarded as the best Greek archer (8.215). Before leaving for Troy, Odysseus had fired an arrow through 12 axes set up in the palace but this feat had not been seen for at least 19 years.

In earlier appearances in the *Odyssey*, Penelope had repeatedly stated that she had not had a night's sleep since Odysseus left home, for 'when night comes and we all of us go to bed, I lie awake thinking, and my heart becomes prey to the most incessant and cruel tortures' (19.520). Only after retiring to her room, when Odysseus fired the fateful arrow, did she at last fall into a deep slumber as the cycle ended.

In the *Odyssey* there are powerful images of Penelope, which set the opening and closing parameters of the 19-year cycle. Her gifts to Odysseus on his departure for Troy to the point on his return, when she only recognises him after the sighting of a new crescent moon, make Penelope herself a personification of the luni-solar cycle.

Penelope & Gifts from the Suitors

Ten lines of poetry from Book 18.290 to 18.300 set the scene for Penelope's link with the annual lunar calendar, when she tells the suitors in some anger that they should not be eating her out of house and home but instead presenting her with gifts. In response she is given a gown, 12 brooches, a gold chain and a pair of earrings, all of which are metaphorically evocative. On the embroidered gown of beautiful material were attached 12 golden brooches 'each fitted with a pin with a curved sheath' (Rieu) or fitted with 'curved clasps' (A.T. Murray). If the golden brooches are metaphors for the sun and the curved clasps for the new crescent, then Homer may be indicating the 12 solar months and 12 crescent moons of the lunar calendar set against the background of the heavens.

The suitor Eurymachus presents Penelope with a golden chain strung with amber beads 'that gleamed like the sun', which is similar to the golden chain with amber beads stolen by the pirates when Eumaeus was kidnapped by pirates (15.460). Both occasions reflect troubled times and in the case of Penelope the moon is in its dark period – when total eclipses of the sun are possible.

The golden necklace of 'amber beads' creates an image of the effect known as 'Bailey's Beads', when the moon blots out the sun with the exception of a thin rim broken up into 'beads' of light. It would, however, have been more likely for a solar eclipse to occur when Penelope receives her gifts on Day 38, rather than in the morning of the following day as described by Theoclymenus (20.351). Metaphors of the moon continue when two squires give Penelope a pair of earrings 'each with three drops shaped like mulberries'; these are similar in description to the earrings which Hera wore in the Robert Fagles' translation of the *Iliad* (14.170) and which were likened in *Homer's Secret Iliad* (pp. 166–7) to three prominent and easily observable features on the surface of the moon (see Fig. 12.6). A fourth gift described as a necklace of great beauty is still puzzling.

Penelope & Odysseus Reunited

Even when Penelope returns from her room after the suitors are killed and the maids are hanged, she claims to be unsure that Odysseus is her husband and persists in making him prove his identity. This interlude gives Homer the opportunity to portray the rejuvenated Odysseus in glittering terms and the marital bed he had made with his own hands is described in narrative rich in allusions to the winter solstice. Quite soon Penelope is convinced and 'she flew weeping to his side, flung her arms about his neck, and kissed him. Do not be angry with me, Odysseus,' she cried, 'you, who are the wisest of mankind' (23.205). Reunited at last, she and Odysseus retire to the now restored marriage bed on the longest night of the year. After Athene delays the arrival of dawn and Odysseus later goes to meet his father, Penelope plays no active role in the epic. She is, however, doomed to suffer further loneliness, for with the beginning of the new 19-year cycle and the relentless passage of time, Odysseus must again set off on his wanderings to fulfil the prophecy made by Teiresias.

Helen of Troy, Aged 48½

Helen of Troy is the most celebrated women in Greek myth and legend and her story tells of vanity and love, unfaithfulness and reconciliation, and the smouldering anger of a husband whose revenge led to the destruction of the Trojan city. She has a surprising role to play in Homer's calendrical masterpiece. Helen sowed the seeds of the Trojan War when she fled from her doting husband Menelaus and fell into the arms of Prince Paris of Troy. Her destiny had been decided in a squabble between the goddesses Hera, Aphrodite and Athene after Eris, the god of discord, threw a golden apple, inscribed with the words 'For the Fairest', into a crowd of guests at a wedding. Each of the trio of gods believed the apple was meant for her but, unable to agree, they asked Paris, younger son of the King of Troy, to decide

14.2 Detail from Helen of Troy, by Evelyn de Morgan, 1898. Note the new crescent moon with a faint outline of earthshine.

who should receive it. In exchange for Paris' vote Hera offered a bribe of power, Athene offered wisdom and Aphrodite offered him the hand of the most beautiful woman in the world. Paris made his choice and, guided by Aphrodite, he met Helen and together they fell in love and ran away to Troy. Humiliated in front of his fellows, Menelaus called on his brother, Agamemnon, to raise an army and besiege Troy to restore his honour – and his wife to their bed.

Homer neither acclaims Helen as the beauty 'whose face launched a thousand ships',[1] nor in the *Odyssey* does he give her age, but there are clues which make it possible to calculate her advancing years. The first hint is found in the *Iliad*, where amidst the Trojan mourning and weeping after Hector has been vanquished at midsummer by the Greek warrior Achilles, Helen is full of sorrow and wails that 'it is now the twentieth year' since she had arrived in Troy (*Iliad* 24.765). Helen's anguished cry is an indication that a 19-year cycle has passed since she left Menelaus' kingdom in Lacedaemon. There are, though, two important differences between her absence from her husband's home and Odysseus' 19-year absence from Penelope. The first is that Helen's cycle begins at the summer solstice and Odysseus' begins at the winter solstice. In the *Iliad*, when Achilles kills Hector, brother of Paris, the time of year is clearly marked when the goddess Hera brings the longest day to a close by commanding 'the lingering sun to set' (Iliad 18.239). In the *Odyssey* Athene marks the longest night at the winter solstice as she 'holds back dawn' when Penelope and Odysseus are united in bed. Homer so sets the parameters for Helen's 19-year cycle running between summer solstices, while Odysseus' cycle runs between winter solstices. Homer has also shown that more than one cycle can be in operation at any one time and that luni-solar cycles are continuous and one follows the other as certain as night follows day. The second difference between Helen and Odysseus' cycles is that her 19-year cycle begins a decade before Odysseus leaves to fight at Troy. Helen's slighted and besotted husband, Menelaus, and his brother, Agamemnon, had taken ten years to assemble the fleet that sailed there. Revenge may be 'a dish best served cold', but the fires of passion in the breast of Menelaus must surely have long since turned to cold ashes.

Helen Through the Years

When Homer records such lengthy periods of time as Helen's 19-years in Troy, Odysseus' year-long stay with Circe, his almost eight years with Calypso and the four years in which Penelope fooled the suitors, nothing is recorded of events during those periods. These long intervals are, however, of great importance in setting the parameters for luni-solar cycles and marking the passage of time within cycles. With this in mind, we assembled references to Helen in chronological order and placed known facts about her within the timescale of other events in the *Iliad* and the *Odyssey*. The results gave interesting conclusions about Helen's age.

Revealing Helen's Age

On Helen's abduction		= 19 years old
After 19 years in Troy	= 19 + 19	= 38 years old at a summer solstice
At fall of Troy	= 38 + 6 months	= 38½ years at a winter solstice
Return to Lacedaemon	= 38½ + 9½	= 48 years at a summer solstice
Climax of the *Odyssey*	= 48 years + 6 months	= 48½ years at a winter solstice

When Paris abducted Helen she was a young wife with a baby daughter, Hermione, whom she left behind with Menelaus. Considering the overwhelming importance of luni-solar cycles to Homer, it seems reasonable to suggest that this young mother was 19 years old when she arrived in Troy. Nineteen years later Hector was killed at midsummer and Helen had then lived through two 19-year cycles and would be 38 years old; six months later, when Troy fell, she was 38½. Menelaus then reclaimed his bride and they lived happily ever after. While heading for home in Lacedaemon fierce winds divided Menelaus' fleet and he and Helen were driven to the shores of foreign lands. Eventually the reunited couple found themselves in Egypt where they made a fortune and after eight years they were allowed to sail back to their homeland at the annual flooding of the River Nile, which occurs at about the time of the summer solstice. The lives of Helen and Menelaus once more touch Odysseus' when his son, Telemachus, visits their palace in search of news of his father. Helen makes her final appearance a month before the midwinter climax of the *Odyssey* 10½ years on from the dramatic midsummer of the *Iliad*. Helen's age then can be calculated as being 48½ years old.

At the end of the *Odyssey* Helen's allure is undiminished but she is then a woman of maturing years whose independent astronomical cycles point to a complexity of other interwoven cycles based on human lives. Just how intricate these cycles can be was discovered when delving into the stories of the wider family of Odysseus (the House of Laertes) and of Agamemnon (the House of Atreus).

Odysseus & the House of Laertes

The four generations of the House of Laertes with which we are concerned are found at 16.118, when Telemachus identifies his great-grandfather, grandfather and father: 'Laertes was the only son of Arceisius, and Odysseus only son of Laertes. I am myself the only son of Odysseus.' At 4.145 it is also learned that Telemachus was a baby at his mother's breast when Odysseus left for war, but 19 years later he had come of age, assumed manly responsibilities and grown a beard. If the lives of Helen and Telemachus can be measured in 19-year periods then it would be logical to consider that the lives of Laertes and Odysseus were involved in a similar pattern. It then became possible to project the length of time that both Laertes and Odysseus reigned as kings of Ithaca and to recognise the significance of each of them abdicating and passing on the throne to his son.

That Odysseus should become king while his father was still alive is unusual and no reason is given for Laertes' abdication and retirement into obscurity, although it can be deduced that it was driven by the calendrical necessity of continuous cycles. In turn, at the end of the *Odyssey*, Odysseus continues the custom of abdication and on resuming his wanderings leaves Telemachus, newly come of age, to rule in his place. Such a smooth transmission of power is both unusual and sometimes foolish, as Shakespeare points out in the tragedy of *King Lear*.

Although Arceisius is recognised as a King of Ithaca, Homer gives no details of his reign, but the increasing old age of his son, Laertes, is stressed as the years go by and he becomes more and more decrepit. When Odysseus leaves for Troy, both Laertes and his mother Anticleia, are 'at the 'threshold of old age' and some 12 years later, Anticleia's ghost tells Odysseus that 'old age is pressing hard' on his father. A little more than eight years later the 'flesh lies withering on his bones', and his age and infirmity are again highlighted when Eumaeus discovers Laertes' ancient mouldering shield that had lain unused for many years. In brief, Laertes is very old.

On the final day of the *Odyssey* three generations of the royal family are brought together in a touching bucolic scene, which opens with Laertes as a frail and forgetful old man, revitalised Odysseus in the prime of life, and the youthful Telemachus having just achieved maturity. At this cyclic anniversary, Athene magically rejuvenates the old and feeble Laertes into a tall and sturdy man in the prime of life (24.366, 520) and so unites cycles past with cycles yet to come. The chart, 'Lives of principal characters: lunations and 19-year cycles', illustrates the interwoven 19-year cycles of these three important characters.

Odysseus: A Hero in Middle Age

The focal cycle in the life of Odysseus begins when he leaves Ithaca to go to war and ends on his reunion with his wife 19 years later. His story, however, begins two 19-year cycles before then. At his birth, Odysseus' maternal grandfather, Autolycus, instructed Laertes to send Odysseus to visit his grandparents when he has 'grown up', a phrase implying the visit took place when Odysseus, like Telemachus later, had reached maturity on completing his nineteenth year. Whilst out hunting with his grandfather a wild boar burst out of the dense undergrowth and its curved white tusk ripped open Odysseus' thigh.[2] Metaphorically, the wild boar symbolises the winter solstice, and its curved white tusk the new crescent moon that heralds the beginning of a new cycle. There is a further pointer to the winter season in this event when Homer says the fields had been ploughed. References to Odysseus' kingship in Ithaca are scanty. In his younger years he had commanded nine expeditions against a foreign land (14.230) and acquired the epithet of 'sacker of cities' and had set up a council in Ithaca while he was ruler (2.25). His friend, Eumaeus, the pig-keeper, reports that he was respected and well liked by his court and sorely missed whilst away from Ithaca. At the end of the *Odyssey* and as his fourth 19-year cycle begins, Odysseus sets out again on his wanderings, leaving 19-year-old Telemachus as the effective ruler of Ithaca (1.359), just as Odysseus had been when, at the age of 19, he had assumed the kingship from Laertes. Odysseus was fated not to live out his life in peace with Penelope in Ithaca, for according to a prophesy by Teiresias (11.175 & 23.276) he

Odysseus & the 19-year Cycle

Odysseus is born; Autolycus decrees the boy should visit him when he is 'grown up'

(19 year interval)

Odysseus is scarred by a wild boar while hunting with Autolycus
Odysseus comes of age on his 19th birthday at a winter solstice;
Laertes abdicates

(19 year interval)

Odysseus leaves for Troy; he is 38 at that winter solstice

(19 year interval)

Odysseus returns home from Troy; the aging hero is 57 at the winter solstice

was doomed to travel far and wide, carrying an oar, until he came to a country where the people had never heard of the sea, and did not even mix salt with their food. When this unlikely aim was achieved he was promised a dignified death.

Telemachus Achieves Manhood

Twice Homer refers to Telemachus as a newborn child at Penelope's breast when Odysseus left home at a winter solstice, once in the words of Helen and secondly through the ghost of Agamemnon (4.145 & 11.446). When the *Odyssey* opens almost 19 years have passed since Odysseus left home and although Telemachus wants to be regarded as a fully grown man and dares to contradict his mother, the suitors view him with contempt. While setting an ambush to waylay Telemachus, one of the suitors, Antinous, expresses the hope that Zeus would intervene and kill him before he reaches manhood (4.669). The situation changes dramatically over the next five or so weeks and when Telemachus returns from Sparta his beard has appeared for the first time and this sign of manhood is confirmed by Eurynome, who tells Penelope: 'Your son is quite grown up now – it was always your special prayer … to see him with a beard' (18.17). On the day of the winter solstice, Telemachus asserts a new-found authority and orders the great bow to be given to Odysseus (21.344) before himself playing a major role in the slaughter of the suitors. So confident and brutal is the once-hesitant young man that he personally organises the hanging of 12 maidservants who had cavorted with the suitors. Amidst this mayhem, Eurycleia observes that Telemachus 'is only newly grown to manhood' (22.424 Murray). These dramatic changes to the status of Telemachus at the end of the 40 'real-time' days can be associated with his achieving maturity as he completed his nineteenth year, with the arrival of a new crescent moon at the beginning of a new 19-year cycle.

One oft-told tale of Odysseus and his son that might seem to contradict the view that Telemachus was born at the time of a winter solstice is that when Agamemnon and Menelaus visited Ithaca to persuade Odysseus to join their venture at Troy, he pretended to be mad. When the brothers called his bluff by laying the infant Telemachus in front of Odysseus' plough, he stopped before hurting the child and confessed that he was sane. Memorable as the story may be, it is not found in the *Odyssey* and it is important for calendrical purposes to consider only the incidents contained within the pages of Homer's epics.

In associating each of four generations of Odysseus' family with 19-year cycles, it is tantalising to ponder whether they, and the life of 76-year-old Laertes in particular, could have been linked, then or later, to the 76-year luni-solar cycle in which the renowned astronomer Callippus of Cyzicus (370–300 BC) further refined the 19-year cycle attributed to Meton.

Argus the Guard Dog

The touching tale of Odysseus' faithful hound, Argus, has long reflected the powerful bond between dog and master. During the absence of Odysseus, Argus is relegated to sleep on a dung heap but in recognition of his master's return the hound raises his tail and promptly dies. Odysseus says he trained Argus as a puppy (17.292) but left for Troy before the dog proved a useful hunter and so makes it difficult to be precise about the age of the animal. The importance of the episode is that Argus died 19 years after last seeing his master (17.327), making this sad little story another indication of the parameters of the 19-year cycle.

The chart 'Lives of Principal Characters: lunations and 19-year cycles' outlines the lives of Laertes, Odysseus, Penelope, Telemachus, Helen, the stag on Circe's island and the dog Argus within the framework of 19-year luni-solar cycles. The cycles of Laertes, Odysseus and Telemachus begin at winter solstices, while that of Helen begins at the summer solstice. From the birth of Laertes to the end of the *Odyssey* it is calculated there are four 19-year cycles (76 years) and in each cycle there are 235 lunations.

The fourth 19-year cycle encompasses the time span of the *Iliad* and the *Odyssey*; Telemachus is newly born when Odysseus sets off for war during the first lunation. At the summer solstice marked by the 106th lunation Hector is

Lives of principal characters: Lunations and 19-year cycles

19-year cycles	Lunation	Laertes	Odysseus	Penelope and Telemachus	Helen, the stag and Argus
1st begins	1	Laertes' 1st cycle begins			
	235	Laertes' 1st cycle ends			
2nd begins	1	Laertes' 2nd cycle, he is now King of Ithaca	Odysseus born at the winter solstice as his 1st 19-year cycle begins.		
	106				Helen born at summer solstice and 1st cycle begins.
	235	Laertes' 2nd cycle ends and he abdicates	Odysseus's 1st cycle ends. He visits Autolycus and is scarred by a wild boar.		
3rd begins	1	Laertes' 3rd cycle, he retires to farm.	Odysseus begins to rule in Ithaca as his 2nd 19-year cycle begins.		
	106		Assemblies are called and Odysseus makes nine expeditions.		Helen comes of age, and is abducted as 2nd cycle begins.
	235	Laertes' 3rd cycle ends	Odysseus performs feat with his bow *before* leaving for Troy.		
4th begins	1	Laertes' 4th cycle begins	Odysseus's 3rd cycle. He leaves for Troy. Telemachus born. No assemblies or tests of his great bow during his absence.	Telemachus is born and begins his 1st 19-year cycle. Penelope gives Odysseus warm clothing and a brooch at midwinter.	
	106		Hector dies at midsummer.	Royal marriage bed not used while Odysseus is away.	Helen's second cycle ends in her '20th year' at Troy and her 3rd cycle begins.
	112		Troy falls at dark of moon.		
	113		Odysseus leaves Troy.		
	118		Odysseus on Circe's island.		Odysseus kills a stag at midsummer.
Mid-point of 4th	135			Penelope weaves and unpicks Laertes' shroud.	
	230		Odysseus enters the Odyssey in 'real-time' days.		Helen & Menelaus return to Troy.
	234		At the solstice Odysseus fires an arrow through 12 axe-heads and kills the suitors as his 3rd cycle ends.	Maids expose Penelope's deception.	Helen, now 48 ½ years old meets Telemachus.
76-year cycle ends	235	Laertes on his farm as his 4th cycle ends		After 19 years Penelope is reunited with Odysseus. Telemachus comes of age.	19 years after last seeing Odysseus his dog, Argus, dies.

killed by Achilles, and Helen attains her 38th birthday (2 x 19-year cycles). Troy falls shortly after the winter solstice at the end of the 112th lunation. At the appearance of the new crescent of the 113th lunation, Odysseus and his fellow Greeks begin their homeward journey. At the summer solstice midway through the cycle at the 118th lunation Odysseus kills a stag on Circe's island. With the waning moon of the 234th lunation the *Odyssey* opens and at dark of moon Odysseus makes his first appearance. At the new crescent of the 235th lunation he builds a raft to begin the final leg of his journey and as the moon wanes to its dark period he reaches Ithaca. As the lunation ends and with the appearance of the new crescent, Telemachus comes of age and Odysseus takes up his bow, fires an arrow through 12 axe-heads and kills the suitors. That night he and Penelope are reunited and the next day is the first day of the next lunation and the beginning of a new 19-year cycle. On that day Odysseus meets his father, Laertes, before once more setting off on his wanderings, leaving Telemachus to rule the kingdom of Ithaca.

The House of Atreus & the Cycle of Kings

Just as the 19-year luni-solar cycles concerning Helen and the House of Laertes are entwined during the course of the *Odyssey*, so is the eight-year cycle (*octaëteris*) concerned with Agamemnon and his brother Menelaus of the House of Atreus. A cycle of eight solar years and 99 lunations is incorporated in the story of the dastardly murder of Agamemnon, who returned home from Troy only to be killed by his wife Clytemnestra and her lover Aegisthus. Curiously, as the *Odyssey* opens the gods discuss the fate of Aegisthus, who in turn was killed by Agamemnon's son, Orestes (1.30). Literary critics have remarked that it is strange the attention of the gods at this point should centre on Aegisthus and Orestes and not on Odysseus. There is literary justification in that the gods contrast the noble act

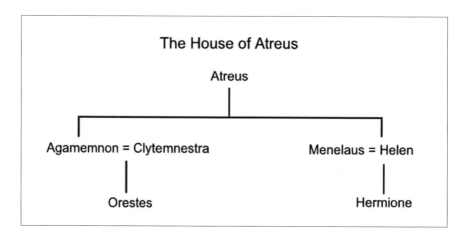

The House of Atreus

Atreus

Agamemnon = Clytemnestra   Menelaus = Helen

Orestes   Hermione

The House of Atreus and the 8-year cycle

Year BC	Menelaus	Agamemnon	Aegisthus	Orestes
2305 New crescent after winter solstice. Summer solstice: Odysseus kills a giant stag.	Menelaus leaves Troy (3.276) and reaches Sunium. His pilot is shot by Apollo & Menelaus is delayed, but not known for how long.	It is not recorded when Agamemnon leaves Troy. He is blown off course at Cape Malea.	Aegisthus murders a minstrel. Clytemnestra yields to him (3.270). A look-out is posted (4.528)....	
2304 As 99th lunation of the old cycle draws to a close. Summer solstice 1st **lunation of new cycle**	Storms at Cape Malea Five of Menelaus's ships are destroyed. Menelaus travels to many lands and eventually arrives in Egypt.	Agamenon arrives in his homeland and is murdered by Aegisthus and Clytemnestra. Odysseus meets Agamemnon's ghost in Hades (11.387).	... and after a year, spies the returning Agamemnon. As the 99th lunation draws to a close Agamemnon is murdered and Aegisthus begins his rule at beginning of new cycle.	Orestes flees to Athens.
2303 **2302** **2301** **2300** **2299** **2298** **2297**	1 Menelaus gathers a fortune 2 3 4 5 6 7		1 Aegisthus rules for 8 years. 2 3 4 5 6 7	1 In Athens 8 years. 2 3 4 5 6 7
2296 **99th lunation ends** Summer solstice 1st lunation, 230th in 18-year and 7 month cycle.	8 Menelaus departure from Egypt is delayed by the gods. Menelaus is marooned on the island of Pharos where he overcomes Proteus. He returns to the Nile and erects a burial mound to Agamemnon. Menelaus attends a banquet in honour of Agamemnon (3.311).		8 Aegisthus is killed by Orestes, son of Agamemnon.	8 Orestes returns and kills Aegisthus, Summer solstice. 1st lunation begins, funeral banquet as Orestes begins his reign.

of revenge of the grown man, Orestes, with the faltering actions of Telemachus, who has not yet reached manhood. From a calendrical point of view the god's condemnation of Aegisthus draws attention to the 8-year cycle from the outset of the *Odyssey*.

The 8-year cycles woven around the House of Atreus are drawn together from scattered accounts by Nestor, Menelaus, Proteus and briefly from Odysseus, as seen in the chart 'Principal players of the House of Atreus'. When Telemachus visits Nestor in search of news of his father, the old king declares it was 'seven years before Orestes took his revenge in the eighth' (3.305ff) and that Menelaus and Helen 'returned on the same day' that Orestes held a banquet to celebrate his killing of Clytemnestra and Aegisthus. Like Odysseus, the return home of Menelaus had been delayed by the gods but he was advised by Proteus, the Old Man of the Sea, to go back to the 'the heaven-fed waters of the Nile' and make sacrifices. The gods would then allow him to sail homeward (4.477). Since the Nile floods or fills with 'heaven-fed waters' at about the time of the summer solstice, the eight-year cycle can be linked to midsummer and both Menelaus and Orestes take up their roles of kingship at the first new crescent moon after the summer solstice.

As the 99th lunation of the previous eight-year cycle draws to a close with Agamemnon's death, so the first lunation of the following cycle begins with Aegisthus' rule. As the next 99th lunation draws to a close, Aegisthus' rule ends in his death and Orestes' kingship begins with the first lunation of the new cycle. Agamemnon's cycle and that of Odysseus momentarily touch at the point when Odysseus visits Hades and the ghost of the murdered king bitterly reflects that a wife is not to be trusted. The gory and unforgettable deeds surrounding Agamemnon and his family inspired the great dramatists of the Golden Age of Greece, Euripides and Aeschylus, whose works still bring a chill to the hearts of modern audiences.

During the era *c.*2300 BC, when the oldest origins of the astronomical learning of the *Odyssey* are found, the sun at midsummer rose with Regulus, α Leonis. Even then, as Homer probably well knew, the constellation of Leo had been associated with royalty and kingship and when the sun is in that constellation Odysseus symbolically kills a stag. In the *Iliad* at the same time of year Agamemnon is described in all his glory and Achilles kills Hector, the oldest son of Priam. In Chapter 10 it was recorded that Leo made its heliacal rising when Odysseus erected a funeral mound in memory of the young sailor, Elpenor. In similar fashion and with the heliacal rising of Leo, Menelaus erects a funeral mound to Agamemnon before leaving Egypt for home (4.584).

Menelaus' absence from home illustrates yet another cycle within a cycle. By the time he returns to Lacedaemon and resumes his kingship, he has been away from home for some 18 years and 7 months (18.6 years), and this possibly represents the lunar standstill which spans the same period. During a standstill the moon rises at its maximum northerly position and changes in its path from maximum high to minimum low on the horizon over a two-week period. The lunar standstill is a particularly spectacular event when seen from the standing stones of Callanish on the Isle of Lewis in the Outer Hebrides. There, at its lowest point, the moon skims along the tops of a range of hills on the southern horizon. The stone circle at Callanish is believed to have been constructed between 2900 and 2600 BC, several centuries before the oldest astronomical events recorded in the *Odyssey*. Stonehenge, too, has been said to be linked to the lunar standstill as well as the solar turning points.

Notes

1   From *Doctor Faustus*, by Christopher Marlowe (1564–93).
2   Bradford, E., *Ulysses Found* (London: Hodder & Stoughton, 1963), p. 7: '[Odysseus'] wounding in the thigh seems to equate him with a number of eastern gods, Tammuz, Adonis and Cretan Zeus, all of whom were wounded and killed by a boar. These stories stem from a Phoenicean legend of the 'year god' whose death occurred after harvest time … His wound in the thigh suggested his identification with the God of the Year.'

15

ANCIENT LEARNING & THE DAWN OF A NEW WORLD

A little more than a century after Homer's death, a philosopher who immensely influenced the way in which the Greeks looked at the world around them was in the forefront of an intellectual revolution. The polymath Thales of Miletus, *c.*624–547 BC, was one of the Seven Sages of Greece and acclaimed as the father of science and philosophy and 'the most senior in wisdom of all the astronomers' of his age.[1] None of his works have survived, but later sources affirm that he sought to explain the world in terms of reason and natural processes rather than as the realm of the gods and heroes of mythology. This fundamental shift in Greek ideas paved the way for the renowned natural philosophers who followed him and have echoed down the ages to our own times. The era of Thales may have been the time when an older supernatural cosmology about gods and the creation of the universe lost favour in the face of new ideas. A further event in Thales' lifetime would have reduced the importance of the oral poets, when *c.*560 BC the Homeric epics were preserved in writing on the orders of Peisistratus, the Tyrant of Athens, who thought them to be an heroic role model for the city's youth. Whether the epics might have been in written form before then is one of the mysteries of ancient Greece. It is, however, from study of the oldest known written sources that scholars in later centuries patiently pieced together the texts of the epics from which modern translations are derived.

There is a large amount of practical astronomy in the *Iliad* and the *Odyssey*, and it is unlikely that all of that learning, essential to everyday life in ancient Greece, would have vanished into thin air with the decline of the poet-astronomers. It is reasonable to suggest that Homeric knowledge of calendars, the mapping of stars and constellations and their use for navigation, was not lost but absorbed into the new culture that began with the first stirrings of Thales' ideas on the nature of the world. As time moved on, the popular appeal of the epics as a reflection of a glorious past in Greek history remained undiminished, but their purpose as a depository of ancient knowledge known only to an elite few almost faded from memory.

Contemporary sources relating to the Greece of *c.*700–500 BC are conspicuous only for their scarcity and what is known of astronomical knowledge in those times has largely been pieced together from the works of writers in later centuries. Specific recognition of Homer and Thales as astronomers is found in fragments from the work of Heraclitus, *c.*500 BC, and the epic poet's forgotten role could hardly be made more clear than when Heraclitus describes him as 'Homer the astronomer, considered wisest of all Greeks'. Chapter 2 recalls that centuries after his times Homer was regarded as an exceptional scholar whose talents extended far beyond those of being the ancient world's finest storyteller.

That Homer's influence in the study of astronomy lingered on, unrecognised, for many centuries after his death may be reflected in a technique used by Ptolemy in the *Almagest*, his famous astronomical treatise published *c.*AD 150. In *Homer's Secret Iliad* we drew attention to similarities between one way in which Homer defines the position of stars within a constellation and a comparable method used by Ptolemy. Both astronomers give physical attributes to constellations and in the *Iliad* a star can be identified as being in the arm of a constellation, or in the hip, foot, head etc.[2] For instance, by carefully studying text the Trojan warrior Echepolus, the first man to die in renewed fighting and killed by a wound to the head, was placed as the leading star in the 'head' of Ursa Major, the constellation allocated to the soldiers of Troy. Later examination of Ptolemy's *Almagest* revealed that he identified that same star as '*Praecedens earum quae in fronte sunt*', which in translation is 'the leading one of those that are in the forehead [of Ursa Major]'. Although Homer and Ptolemy also used other methods of placing stars in constellations, there are many examples of them both using bodily positions. While coincidence must be considered in the context of Ptolemy and Homer, it must also be seen within a wider picture in which other sources provide powerful indications of Homer's enduring reputation as an astronomer.

Work in Progress

Edna Leigh's challenging views of the Homeric epics were sustained throughout her studies and our contribution to her pioneering work has been carried on in the same spirit. Nevertheless, there are questions still to be resolved about data and narrative in the *Odyssey* and we believe there is more learning yet to be discovered there, as well as in the *Iliad*. We hope that publication of the *Homer's Secret Odyssey* will encourage fresh minds to begin these investigations and expand and improve our own conclusions.

In her surviving papers, Edna Leigh said she had 'devised calendars of five or six types to incorporate an *Iliad-Odyssey* combined time to equal the 6939–6940 days of the Metonic cycle or something similar'. Unfortunately, an unknown quantity of her work has been lost and what her extended list of calendars might consist of has yet to be resolved.

In Chapter 5, Telemachus' list of suitors and servants revealed information about the lunar month and full and hollow months, but it is presented in such a complex manner that we suspect there is still hidden treasure to be won from that and other numerical lists. There is also potential for further discoveries in numerical data embedded in the *Iliad*. We have already drawn attention to the 1186 Greek ships that sailed to Troy and a possible link with the planet Venus (see Chapter 5). Still intriguing is the full purpose of that listing, the colours attributed to the ships of the various contingents and the number of men carried to Troy. We have linked the adventures of Odysseus with constellations of the zodiac and the Phaeacians with Cygnus and the Milky Way, but it may not be all of the learning of constellations preserved in the *Odyssey*.

Homer knew much about the moon's synodic cycle of 29.5 days from new crescent to new crescent, but there is also a sidereal cycle of 27.3 days, the time it takes the moon to orbit the earth relative to a background of stars. Such were the observational skills of the Homeric Greeks that the sidereal cycle may also have attracted their attention. Homeric epic as astronomical treatise is still a large field to plough.

Inspiration in the Skies

Bringing *Homer's Secret Odyssey* and *Homer's Secret Iliad* to the point of publication has been a long and exhilarating project. After Edna Leigh's death in 1991 we catalogued her papers before unsuccessfully trying to interest experts in the field with a summary of her work. Although buoyed by an awareness of Edna's personal integrity and breadth of learning, there followed many frustrating months as we attempted to piece together a manuscript from scores of pages of her notes and diagrams. A breakthrough came in 1995 when we were introduced to a number of academics at the University of Texas at Austin who gave invaluable advice on lines of inquiry. A more complete story of those early years together with biographical details of Edna's life is told in *Homer's Secret Iliad*, which was published in 1999.

Our own growing interest and fascination with this work took us into the classroom for study of the classics and for several years we attended courses on astronomy at a small observatory high on the chilly – and often cloudy – Lancashire moorlands. We also made visits to classical Greece with an Open University study group. Computers and programmes such as 'TheSky' and 'Starry Night' were invaluable in projecting the skies and astronomical events of Homer's times and long before. Edna Leigh had to make her own calculations and draw her own charts, for the age of computers then lay in the future.

The finest schoolroom for an appreciation of Homer's astronomy is the wide outdoors on a clear, dark night. There can be seen a panorama of the heavens and astronomical events observed by Homer and other astronomers during thousands of years of antiquity. Away from the light pollution of our cities, the naked eye is adequate to see the stars and constellations in which the heroes and warring regiments of Greeks and Trojans play out the unforgettable astro-myths of the *Iliad* and *Odyssey*.[3] Homer's imagery comes alive with such events as the changing of the seasons, the spring and autumn equinoxes and the 'turning of the sun' at the solstices – observations of the heavens that are as important today as they were to the extraordinary calendar makers of 3000 years ago. Each month the moon's changing phases bring to mind the excitement of discovering how Homer uses the rhythm and moods of Odysseus' adventures to plot the passing of the days and months. There is still much to be learned from Homer's epics and we hope that others will be inspired to follow in the footsteps of Edna Leigh.

Florence and Kenneth Wood

2011

Notes

1   Attributed to Diogenes of Laertius, of the third century BC.

2   See *Homer's Secret Iliad*, 'Rule of Wounding', pp. 89–101.

3   See *Homer's Secret Iliad*, 'The changing heavens and the Fall of Troy', pp. 190–221.

Appendix 1

SHIP'S LOG OF ODYSSEUS' VOYAGE

For centuries ships' captains have kept logs or journals of their voyages across the oceans of the world in which they recorded the passing days, their position and events that befell their crews. When Odysseus held the Phaeacian court spellbound as he recounted his adventures the idea arose that it might be possible to create a hypothetical Ship's Log based on his lunar adventures across the wine-dark seas. This was done to test the idea that phases of the moon were linked to the rhythms of Odysseus' adventures and the journey of the sun along the ecliptic during the course of a solar year.

The Ship's Log draws together many of the metaphorical events linked to Homer's annual calendar system that can be found in the narrative of the *Odyssey*:

  Despair at the dark of moon
  The return of good fortune at the sighting of the new crescent
  Sailing days as phases of the moon
  Adventures taking place in the constellations of the zodiac
  The entwining of lunations with the passage of the sun along the ecliptic
  A model 19-year cycle, *c.*2300 BC, when Aquarius marked the winter solstice
  and Leo the summer solstice
  Fine tuning of the lunar calendar with the solar calendar
  The incidence of an intercalary month within the cycle
  Heliacal risings of constellations used to track the position of the sun

In Chapter 4, we explained how a 19-year cycle could be represented by the years 2314–2295 BC, which are listed in Panel 1. Odysseus' adventures take place during the tenth and eleventh years of the cycle. They begin as the tenth year commences with the sighting of the first new crescent after the winter solstice, the evening Odysseus sails away from his encounter with the Cicones. His adventures and the eleventh year of the cycle draw to a close the night Odysseus reaches Calypso's island of Ogygia.

Panel 1: The 19-year cycle of the *Iliad-Odyssey*

Year BC	
2314–13	Year 1 Odysseus leaves Ithaca with the appearance of a new crescent moon on the winter solstice which marks Day 1 of Year 1 of the 19-year luni-solar cycle.
2313–12	2
2312–11	3
2311–10	4
2310–09	5
2309–08	6
2308–07	7
2307–06	8
2306–05	9 During the ninth solar year, the *Iliad* takes place. Hector dies at the summer solstice and his funeral takes place a little later. Troy falls at the dark moon following the winter solstice.
2305–04	10 Odysseus sails for home at the appearance of the new crescent. The first part of his adventures end when Odysseus confronts Circe during the moon's dark period following the summer solstice.
2304–03	11 A year passes and Odysseus leaves Circe's island with the new crescent at the summer solstice. The second part of his adventures end when he reaches Calypso's island at the winter solstice.
2303–02	12 (1) Odysseus remains a captive on Calypso's island for almost eight years.
2302–01	13 (2)
2301–00	14 (3)
2300–99	15 (4)
2209–98	16 (5)
2298–97	17 (6)
2297–96	18 (7)
2296–95	19 (8) The *Odyssey* begins 39 days before the winter solstice. Odysseus leaves Calypso 12 days later and sails homeward. During his stay of two nights with the Phaeacians he recounts his homeward adventures after the fall of Troy. After leaving the Phaeacians, he arrives on Ithaca five days before a new crescent moon at the winter solstice. Odysseus' identity is revealed when the new crescent appears in the evening of the winter solstice. At this point one 19-year luni-solar cycle of 235 lunations is completed.
2295–	1 A new cycle begins.

The eleventh year of the 19-year cycle has important calendrical implications. After a year's break with Circe, Odysseus' homeward journey and the calendar recommence in the eleventh year, with the sighting of the new crescent at the summer solstice, and so momentarily adjusts the 354 days of the lunar calendar with the 365 days of the solar calendar. The eleventh year is also an example of an intercalary year when an extra month was inserted into the lunar calendar.

Design of the Ship's Log

The title above each monthly table names the constellation/s in which the sun lies during the adventure listed beneath.

The first of the table's four columns, 'Phase of the Moon & Day of the Month', gives the phase of the moon, the sequential number of the lunation (out of 235) since Odysseus left Ithaca for Troy and the day of that specific lunar month. The appearance of the new crescent moon is Day 1 and, depending on whether it is a full or hollow month, ends on either Day 29 or Day 30. It can be difficult to determine exactly when the new crescent appears but we used the guideline that the new crescent can be seen just before dusk when 5 per cent of the moon is illuminated. Similarly the 'dark' period of the moon is taken to be three days when this is not always the case. The moon may 'disappear' for only two days or may not be seen for four days.

The second column, 'Position of the Sun', marks the star in a constellation that is nearest the place of the sun on the ecliptic when an adventure begins. The sun's passing through the Milky Way and heliacal risings are also recorded.

The third column, 'Adventure', gives a summary of Odysseus' exploits during a lunation.

The fourth column, 'Date', gives the year, month and day in the Gregorian calendar of a particular event.

It will be noticed that the days of the year on which the equinoxes and solstices occur, change over long periods of time. Today the earth's axis is inclined at approximately 23° 26', but *c.*2300 BC, it was approximately 23° 57'. Today, the winter and summer solstices occur on or about 22 December and 21 June, while the spring and autumn equinoxes fall on or about 21 March and 22 September. At *c.*2300 BC, and reckoning by the Gregorian calendar, the winter solstice fell on or about 9 January, the summer solstice on or about 14 July, the spring equinox on or about 10 April and the autumn equinox on or about 11 October. These are the dates used in the Ship's Log to plot the path of the sun. The Gregorian calendar adjusted to compensate for precession of the equinoxes is used throughout *Homer's Secret Odyssey*.

Computer astronomy programmes can project the skies of ancient times with great accuracy, and the observational point on earth chosen for the Ship's Log is Chios (38° 22'N 26° 06'E), the frequently cited birthplace of Homer. Computer programmes were used to construct the log and data is derived from 'TheSky' by Software Bisque.

Embarking on the Ship's Log was a voyage into uncharted waters with a great sense of expectation. If navigated successfully it could provide support for the view that the stories of the *Iliad-Odyssey* cycle were the backbone of a calendrical model or template that could have been used when Regulus, α Leonis, was 'king' at the summer solstice and Polyphemus and the stars of Taurus reigned at the vernal equinox.

Ship's Log of Odysseus' Voyage

First month
Sun in Pisces
Cicones overwhelm Odysseus (9.39–9.67)
Zeus sends a hurricane (9.66–9.78)

Day of month, Phase of moon	Position of the sun	Adventure	Date 2305 BC
Last hours of dark moon. 1 New Crescent 113th Lun. ☽	γ Piscium Southern Fish	Cicone warriors arrive in the morning, beat back Odysseus and his men and kill six men from each of 12 ships. With the new crescent moon, Odysseus' fleet sets sail. The men taken represent the 72 days to the spring equinox.	29 Jan
2			30
3			31
4			1 Feb
5			2
6			3
7 1st Qtr			4
8			5
9			6
10			7
11			8
12			9
13			10
14			11
15 Full			12
16			13
17			14
18			15
19			16
20			17
21			18
22 3rd Qtr	δ Piscium	Hurricane strikes ships, land and sea hidden by cloud.	19
23		Fleet runs before the storm.	20
24			21
25			22
26		Sails torn to shreds.	23
27		Sails lowered and stowed for safety.	24
28 Dark ●	ε Piscium	Fleet forced to row towards land.	25

| 29 Dark ● | ε Piscium | On reaching land, the fleet takes shelter for two nights and two days. Day 1 Resting. | 26 |
| 30 Dark ● | | Day 2 Resting. | 27 |

Second month

Sun leaves Pisces and enters Aries and Cetus

Odysseus doubles Cape Malea (9.80 – 9.104)

Day of month, Phase of moon	Position of the sun	Adventure	Date 2305 BC
1 Crescent 114th Lun. ☽	ζ Piscium	On the third morning, the storm abates. Masts are raised, sails hoisted and the fleet sails safely on towards Cape Malea.	28 Feb
2			29*
3			1 Mar
4			2
5			3
6			4
7 1st Qtr			5
8			6
9			7
10			8
11			9
12	α Piscium		10
13			11
14 Full			12
15			13
16			14
17			15
18			16
19			17
20			18
21			19
22 3rd Qtr	Head of Cetus	Odysseus tries to sail round Cape Malea and head towards Cythera, but while doubling the Cape the winds and currents are hostile and drive his ships southwards. Day 1 Running before the wind.	20
23		Day 2 Running before the wind.	21
24		Day 3 Running before the wind.	22
25		Day 4 Running before the wind.	23
26		Day 5 Running before the wind.	24
27		Day 6 Running before the wind.	25

28 Dark ●		Day 7 Running before the wind.	26
29 Dark ●		Day 8 Running before the wind.	27
30 Dark ●		Day 9 Running before the wind.	28

★ Leap Year in Gregorian calendar

Third month
Sun in Taurus: Odysseus leaves the Lotus Eaters (9.83–104)
Goat Island and Polyphemus (9.105–9.565)

Day of month, Phase of moon	Position of the sun	Adventure	Date 2305 BC
Last hours of dark of moon 1 Crescent 115th Lun. ☽	Sun enters Taurus	Day 10 In the morning two men and a herald go ashore to explore in the land of the Lotus Eaters. The inhabitants do them no harm but feed them the flower of the Lotus which makes the trio reluctant to leave. The weeping men are brought back to the ships and tied beneath the benches before the fleet sets sail again towards the land of the Cyclopes.	29 Mar
2			30
3			31
4			1 Apr
5			2
6 1st Qtr			3
7			4
8			5
9			6
10			7
11			8
12			9
13	η Tauri	It is 72 days since 72 men were taken by the Cicones.	10
14 Full	Spring equinox		11
15			12
16			13
17			14
18			15
19			16
20			17
21 3rd Qtr			18
22			19
23	α Tauri	Land of the lawless Cyclopes appears.	20

24	Auriga	Neither near nor far away from the island of Polyphemus lies an uninhabited island overrun with goats.	21
25	ι Auriga	A god guides the fleet through a dark misty night to a harbour where the crews go ashore and fall asleep.	22
26		Seeing many wild goats Odysseus organises a hunt to replenish stores. The men are divided into three parties and kill 9 goats for each of 12 ships (9 x 12 = 108). Odysseus takes 10 more for himself (108 + 10 + 118). The men then feast throughout the day and at sunset sleep on the seashore. In the distance can be seen the land of the Cyclopes and the sailors can hear the noise of men and beasts.	23
27 Dark ●		Odysseus takes one ship and 12 crewmen to the land of the Cyclopes where they find a cave with baskets of cheeses and pens of sheep and kids. Odysseus ignores pleas to leave, and they are all trapped when Polyphemus returns and seals the cave's entrance with a massive stone. The stone is so huge that 22 four-wheeled wagons would not be enough to move it (4 x 22 = 88). After Polyphemus devours two seamen and falls asleep, Odysseus is about kill Polyphemus with his sword when he realises it would leave them all trapped in the cave.	24
28 Dark ●		In the morning Polyphemus devours two more men before leaving the cave. Odysseus sees a large stake of green olive wood which is sharpened and hardened in the fire. Four men are chosen by lot to help Odysseus overcome the Cyclops. After Polyphemus returns he devours two more men before Odysseus plies him with wine and makes him drunk. While Polyphemus sleeps, Odysseus and his four companions take a hardened olive stick and drill out the monster's single eye. Polyphemus calls for help and his fellow countrymen come running and cry out to him: 'Who has harmed you?' 'Noman,' replies Polyphemus, at which the Cyclopes go on their way.	25

| 29 Dark ● | Heliacal rising of Aries | To let his sheep out of the cave, blinded Polyphemus must move the stone blocking the entrance. To escape without being caught, Odysseus fastens rams together in threes and ties a man underneath each middle one; selecting the finest ram for himself they leave the cave. When safely out Odysseus and his men steal sheep and drive them to their ship before rowing away. Safely at sea, Odysseus mocks Polyphemus who throws such a large stone at them that it causes a tidal wave that drives them to Goat Island where the rest of the fleet waits. There they sacrifice the ram and feast until sunset. | 26 |

Fourth month
Sun in Milky Way and Gemini
Odysseus stays with Aeolus (10.1–10.28)

Day of month, Phase of moon	Position of the sun	Adventure	Date 2305 BC
1 Crescent 116th Lun. ☽		At dawn the ships' cables are cut and the fleet rows sorrowfully from Goat Island towards Aeolia, island home of Aeolus, King of the Winds.	27 Apr
2		88 wagon wheels represent the 88 days from the 1st new crescent after the spring equinox to the 1st crescent after the summer solstice.	28
3			29
4	Milky Way	Surrounding Aeolia is a wall of bronze and a sheer cliff. Odysseus and his men make their way to the palace where Aeolus, his wife and children feast continually. Aeolus' six daughters are the wives of his six sons.	30
5	β Tauri	Aeolus welcomes Odysseus and his men and questions them about Troy, their ships and the return of the heroes from that city. They enjoy Aeolus' hospitality for one month.	1 May
6			2
7 1st Qtr			3
8			4
9			5
10			6
11	ζ Tauri		7
12			8
13			9

Day of month, Phase of moon	Position of the sun		Date
14 Full			10
15			11
16			12
17	1 Gem.		13
18			14
19			15
20			16
21 3rd Qtr			17
22	ε Gem.		18
23			19
24			20
25			21
26			22
27			23
28 Dark ●	δ Gem.		24
29 Dark ●	γ Gem.		25
30 Dark ●			26

Fifth month

Sun in Gemini and Cancer
Odysseus leaves Aeolus (10.55–10.80)
Eleven ships lost to the Laestrygonians (10.80–10.103)

Day of month, Phase of moon	Position of the sun		Date 2305 BC
1 Crescent 117th Lun ☽			27
2			28
3			29
4			30
5			31
6 1st Qtr	Milky Way ends		1 Jun
7			2
8			3
9			4
10			5
11			6
12			7
13			8

14 Full	Enters Cancer; Full moon rises in Capricornus		9
15			10
16			11
17			12
18			13
19			14
20 3rd Qtr			15
21			16
22			17
23			18
24	Helical rising of α Geminorum (Castor) and β Geminorum (Pollux)	Day 10 They land once more on Aeolus' island where the men eat and drink. Odysseus takes a member of the crew and a messenger who sit at the door posts of the palace. Aeolus is far from welcoming and orders them to leave immediately. With no wind to help they row for six days towards the land of the Laestrygonians. Day 1 Rowing	19
25		Day 2 Rowing	20
26		Day 3 Rowing	21
27 Dark ●	δ Cancri	Day 4 Rowing	22
28 Dark ●		Day 5 Rowing	23
29 Dark ●		Day 6 Rowing	24

Sixth month
Sun in Leo
Odysseus kills a stag (10.156–10.184)
Odysseus and Circe (10.183–10.465)

Phase of moon Day of month	Position of the sun	Adventure	Date 2305 BC
Last hours of dark of moon 1 Crescent 118th Lun ☽	α Cancri	Day 7. The fleet of 12 ships arrives in the land of the Laestrygonian giants. Eleven of Odysseus' ships moor in a narrow but calm harbour surrounded by steep cliffs. Odysseus anchors someway off and ties his ship's cables to a rock. Two men plus a messenger are sent to explore and meet the daughter of Antiphates, King of the Laestrygonians. She leads them to the palace where Antiphates' huge wife calls to her husband, who eats one of Odysseus' men as the other two flee to the ships. Antiphates raises the alarm and other Laestrygonian giants throw big boulders and destroy all of Odysseus' ships except his own, and spear men like fishes and take them home for their meal. Odysseus cuts his ship loose and tells the men to row for their lives. He sails on happy to have escaped but sad to have lost men and ships.	25 Jun
2			26
3			27
4			28
5			29
6			30
7 1st Qtr			1 Jul
8			2
9			3
10			4
11			5
12			6
13			7
14 Full			8
15			9
16			10
17			11
18			12
19	Summer Solstice	Mid-point of the 19-year solar cycle which began on 2314 BC and ends 2295 BC.	13
20	α Leonis		14

21 3rd Qtr			15
22			16
23			17
24			18
25			19
26			20
27	ρ Leonis	Odysseus' ship arrives at Aeaea, the island home of the witch Circe. A god guides them into the harbour where they go ashore in silence and rest for two nights and two days. Night 1.	21
28 Dark ●		Night 2.	22
29 Dark ●		On the third day Odysseus is returning to his ship after surveying the land when a great stag crosses his path and he kills it by striking it in the middle of its back. His men welcome the food and they feast all the rest of the day and go to bed as the sun sets.	23
30 Dark ● New crescent imminent		In the morning no one can tell in which direction the sun rises or sets, but the island according to Odysseus appears round and low with smoke coming from a chimney. Odysseus divides his men into two groups of 22 plus himself and Eurylochus as their leaders. Eurylochus' men go to the home of Circe and he later tells Odysseus that in her yard were drugged wolves and lions and Circe was sweetly singing as she wove a great web. With the exception of himself, all of Eurylochus' men go into her house where they are drugged and turned into swine. On his way to challenge Circe, Odysseus meets Hermes who gives him the black-rooted, white-flowered plant 'Moly', to ward off her magic. When Circe drugs his wine and casts a spell they have no effect. Odysseus draws his sword from his side but does not kill Circe when she tells him that no one had ever withstood the drug before and that he must be Odysseus on his way home from Troy. They then go to bed together.	24

Last hours of dark of moon. 1 Crescent 119th Lun. ☽	δ Leonis	Annoyed at Eurylochus' words of caution Odysseus contemplates cutting off his head with his sharp sword. Odysseus is bathed and given new clothes by Circe and at his request she turns the swine back into men. Odysseus and his men begin a year's luxurious stay with Circe. Note: 88 days have passed from the 1st new crescent after the spring equinox to the 1st crescent after the summer solstice.	Jul 25
2			26
4			27

With the appearance of a new crescent moon on 25 July 2305 BC, some 11 days after the summer solstice, Odysseus begins his one-year stay on Circe's island. At the solstice on July 14 the sun was at Regulus, α Leonis, but with the arrival of the new crescent it has now reached a position between the 'rear legs' of Leo.

Eleven months then pass and as the twelfth month reaches its dark period Homer recommences both his annual calendar and his account of Odysseus' adventures. At this point the narrative reflects the discord and gloom associated with the dark period: Odysseus' homesick men press him to leave, Circe tells of the horrors he has yet to face, he takes Circe to bed and the sailor Elpenor is killed falling off a roof.

The new crescent moon appears on the following day, 14 July 2304 BC, the same day as the summer solstice but 11 days earlier than the previous year. Odysseus sets sail for an uneventful month's voyage to Hades. The year's break has not only continued the progress of the 19-year cycle but also brought the annual lunar and solar calendars into line with the new crescent moon making its appearance at the summer solstice.

The Annual Calendar is suspended for a year. Odysseus' adventures resume at the end of the seventh month of the following year.

Seventh month (Intercalary)

Sun in Leo

Odysseus' year with Circe comes to an end (10.470)

Day of month, Phase of moon	Position of the sun	Adventure	Date 2304 BC
Last hours of the dark of moon 1 Crescent 131st Lun. ☽	Regulus, α Leonis. Summer Solstice	An intercalary month is inserted as the sun passes through Leo.	14 July
2			15
3			16
4			17
5			18
6			19
7 1st Qtr			20
8	ρ Leonis		21
9			22
10			23
11			24
12			25
13			26
14 Full			27
15			28
16			29
17			30
18			31
19			1 Aug
20			2
21 3rd Qtr			3
22			4
23			5
24			6
25	β Leonis		7
26	Leaves Leo		8
27			9
28 Dark ●			10
29 Dark ●	β Virginis	After a year, Odysseus' men urge him to continue their homeward journey. That night he sleeps with Circe and asks if they can leave. Circe warns he has to make a fearful journey to the home of Hades and Persephone.	11
30 Dark ●		The drunken Elpenor is killed falling from a ladder.	12

Eighth month

Sun in Virgo

Odysseus' voyage to Hades. Meets the ghosts in Hades (Book 11)

Day of month, Phase of moon	Position of the sun	Adventure	Date 2304 BC
Last hours of dark moon 1 Crescent 132nd Lun ☽	β Virginis	At dawn, Odysseus is given a 'new tunic' by Circe and the ship's mast and sails are raised as they sail towards Hades. Now begins a story within a story: The ship is beached in the land of the Cimmerians who live in perpetual darkness and Odysseus walks along Oceanus to Hades. Anticleia tells Odysseus of the state of affair in Ithaca. Odysseus draws his sword from his side and digs a trench and waits for the souls of the dead to appear. Elpenor comes first and asks him to give him a good funeral. Next Odysseus briefly sees his mother, Anticleia. Teiresias then appears and Odysseus sheaths his sword. The seer forecasts that once Odysseus has regained Ithaca and his wife, he must immediately set off on his travels again.	13 Aug
2		Odysseus draws his sharp sword from his side and Persephone sends up the ghosts of the dead. In the following days, Odysseus sees … Tyro whom Poseidon deceived,	14
3		… Antiope who believed Zeus had been her lover,	15
4		… Alcmene who Zeus made love to; she gave birth to Hercules,	16
5		… Megare who married Heracles,	17
6		… Epicaste, mother of Oedipus but who married her own son and hanged herself,	18
7 1st Qtr		… Chloris who married Neleus, King of Pylos,	19
8		… Leda who was mother of Castor and Pollux,	20
9		… Iphimedeia who slept with Poseidon,	21
10		… Phaedra,	22
11		… Procris,	23
12		… Ariadne, who was the daughter of Minos,	24
13 Full	γ Virginis	… Maera,	25
14		… Clymene,	26
15		… Eriphyle who killed her husband. After a short interval back in the 'real-time' of Alcinous' court, Odysseus …	27
16		… then met Agamemnon,	28
17		… and Achilles,	29

18		… saw Patroclus,	30 Aug
19		… Antilochus,	31
20		… Aias who stands aloof,	1 Sep
21		… Minos who was the King of Crete and son of Zeus,	2
22 3rd Qtr		… Orion who wanders with his club of bronze,	3
23		… Tityus who has two vultures picking at his liver,	4
24		… Tantalus, son of Zeus who suffers from everlasting thirst,	5
25	α Virginis Spica	… Sisyphus who forever pushes a boulder uphill,	6
26		… Heracles who carries his bow and arrows.	7
27		Odysseus wished he could have met with Theseus	8
28 Dark ●		and Peirithous …	9
29 Dark ●		… but was afraid Persephone would send up the dreadful Gorgon.★ He then left Hades … (his return journey)	10
30 Dark ●	Helical rising of Leo	… and sailed until early dawn. Elpenor is cremated with honour with an oar placed on his mound. During the night Od. tells Circe of his experiences in Hades, and she tells him of the perils to come: the Sirens, Wandering Rocks, Scylla, Charybdis, and the temptations of Helios' cattle.	11

★ Perseus and Algol are in the east at sunset

Ninth month
Sun in Libra – α and β Librae
Odysseus sails safely past the Sirens (12.182–12.200)

Day of month, Phase of moon	Position of the sun	Adventure	Date 2304 BC
Last hours of dark moon 1 Crescent 133rd Lun. ☽		Circe departs inland and Odysseus' crew row away from her island in fair and gentle winds. While at sea Odysseus repeats some of Circe's warnings of the perils his men have yet to face.	12 Sep
2			13
3			14
4			15
5			16
6 1st Qtr			17
7			18

8			19 Sep
9			20
10			21
11			22
12			23
13 Full			24
14			25
15			26
16			27
17	α Librae	Wind ceases and the sea is deadly calm, stilled by a god.	28
18			29
19			30
20		Crew stow the sails and row speedily onwards. The sea is churned white with their rowing.	1 Oct
21 3rd Qtr		Odysseus cuts a cake of beeswax into 88 pieces and kneads it in his hands before plugging his men's ears with wax and being tied to the mast. There are now 88 days to the destruction by Zeus of Odysseus' last ship.	2
22		Odysseus' ship approaches the island of the Sirens who burst into wonderful song. To lure Odysseus to their island and his doom they seek to flatter him by recalling the bold deeds of Troy.	3
23	β Librae	As the two Sirens continue singing, Odysseus signals to his crew to untie him, but they ignore him …	4
24		… and continue rowing.	5
25		Despite his pleas, Perimedes and Eurylochus tie him tighter to the mast.	6
26		When past the Sirens the men unplug their ears and free Odysseus, who had been able to both hear the Sirens and escape a lingering death on their island.	7
27 Dark ●			8
28 Dark ●			9
29 Dark ●			10

Tenth month
Sun in Scorpius and Ophiuchus
Wandering Rocks, Charybdis, Scylla (12.207–12.260)
Arrival on Thrinacia (12.261–12. 402)

Day of month, Phase of moon	Position of the sun	Adventure	Date 2304 BC
Last hours of dark moon 1 Crescent 134th Lun. ☽		As their ship passes the Wandering Rocks the crew see smoke and a violent sea. The men are too terrified to row and the ship comes to a standstill until Odysseus encourages them to continue their journey. Odysseus puts on his armour and grasps two spears while looking for the six-headed monster Scylla. They sail up a narrow strait towards the swirling whirlpool Charybdis on one side and the fearsome Scylla on the other who reaches out from her cave and snatches one man for each of her six heads. Looking like small helpless fishes writhing on a fisherman's line, she carries the screaming seamen to her lair. Odysseus continues his voyage.	11 Oct
2	Autumn equinox	The plugs of wax which blocked the ears of Odysseus' crew represent 88 days from the autumn equinox to the 1st new crescent after the winter solstice.	12
3			13
4	β/δ Scorpii	(Convenient markers for the autumn equinox)	14
5	Milky Way begins		15
6			16
7 1st Qtr			17
8			18
9			19
10	α Scorpii		20
11			21
12			22
13			23
14 Full			24
15			25
16			26
17			27
18			28
19			29

20	η Ophiuchi	While at sea the crew can hear the lowing of cattle and bleating of sheep on Thrinacia, island of the sun god Helios. Odysseus recalls the dire warnings of both Circe and Teiresias and orders his men to row on past the island. Eurylochus challenges him: 'You might be a man of iron but the crew are not.' Reluctantly, he agrees they can tie up for the night. After supper they drift off to sleep and weep for the loss of their six comrades.	30
21 3rd Qtr		During the third watch of the night Zeus sends a hurricane so fierce that neither land nor sea could be seen.	31 Oct
22		Helios' island: In the morning the ship is dragged to a hollow cave. Although they have ample grain and wine on board the crew do not know how long it will last. Odysseus warns his men not to harm Helios' cattle. An offshore wind next blows for a month and they are marooned on the island. On Thrinacia they eat provisions from the ship's stores. Day 1 Ship's stores	1 Nov
23		Day 2 Ship's stores	2
24	θ Ophiuchi	Day 3 Ship's stores	3
25		Day 4 Ship's stores	4
26		Day 5 Ship's stores	4
27		Day 6 Ship's stores	6
28 Dark ●		Day 7 Ship's stores	7
29 Dark ●	51 Ophiuchi	Day 8 Ship's stores	8
30 Dark ●	Pool of dark sky	Day 9 Grain and wine run out	9

Eleventh month
Sun in Sagittarius
Odysseus marooned on Thrinacia (12.312–400)

Day of month, Phase of moon	Position of the sun	Adventure	Date 2304 BC
Crescent 135th Lun. ☽		Day 10 Men search for prey game, fish or fowl	10 Nov
2		Day 11 Search for prey	11
3		Day 12 Search for prey	12
4		Day 13 Search for prey	13

5	Dark sky ends	Day 14 Search for prey	14
6 1st Qtr	Milky Way	Day 15 Search for prey	15
7	λ Sagittarii	Day 16 Search for prey	16
8		Day 17 Search for prey	17
9		Day 18 Search for prey	18
10		Day 19 Search for prey	19
11		Day 20 Search for prey	20
12		Day 21 Search for prey	21
13		Day 22 Odysseus goes across the island to offer up his prayers. He learns later that Eurylochus has aroused the men's anger. 'It is better to lose one's life by drowning, than to die of lingering hunger.' In defiance of Odysseus the men foolishly collect and kill Helios' best cattle and prepare them for sacrifice.	22
14 Full	σ Sagittarii	Day 23 Odysseus awakes and makes his way to the ship where he can smell the cooking of meat. All is evil: the cattle hides crawl, the animals both cooked and raw bellow. Although they have done a terrible thing the men feast for six days. Feast Day 1	23
15		Day 24 Feast Day 2	24
16		Day 25 Feast Day 3	25
17		Day 26 Feast Day 4	26
18		Day 27 Feast Day 5	27
19		Day 28 Feast Day 6	28
20 3rd Qtr	Milky Way ends	Day 29 On the 7th day the wind drops and they sail away from Thrinacia.	29
21		When they leave land behind there is only sky and water to be seen. The sun now passes along the ecliptic for 30 days where there are no significant 'stations of the sun'.	30
22			Dec 1
23			2
24			3
25			4
26			5
27			6
28 ●			7
29 ●			8
30 ●			9

Twelfth month

Sun in Capricornus,
Odysseus' ship destroyed by Charybdis (12.404 – 12.450)

Day of month, Phase of moon	Position of the sun	Adventure	Date 2304 BC
1 Crescent 136th Lun. ☽			10 Dec
2			11
3			12
4			13
5	β Capricorni		14
6			15
7 1st Qtr			16
8			17
9			18
10			19
11		.	20
12			21
13			22
14 Full			23
15	θ Capricornii		24
16			25
17			26
18			27
19			28
20 3rd Qtr		Zeus sends a hurricane that destroys the ship: the forestays break … the mast falls and crushes the pilot's skull … a bolt of lightning tosses men overboard … and sides are torn from the keel. The only survivor, Odysseus, binds the mast and keel together with a backstay and climbs astride a makeshift raft.	29
21	Heliacal rising of Scorpius	In the morning Odysseus is blown back to Charybdis and Scylla's rock On the rock he finds a fig tree and clings onto it like a bat … until … the ship's timbers resurface. He drops into the water, climbs onto the wreckage and sitting astride it, paddles with his hands. Night 1 Drifting	30
22		Night 2 Drifting	31
23	δ Capricornii	Night 3 Drifting	1 Jan 2303
24		Night 4 Drifting	2

25		Night 5 Drifting	3
26		Night 6 Drifting	4
27		Night 7 Drifting	5
28 Dark ●		Night 8 Drifting	6
29 Dark ●		Night 9 Drifting	7

Thirteenth month
Sun in Aquarius
Odysseus arrives at Calypso's Island 12.450

Day of month, Phase of moon	Position of the sun	Adventure	Date 2303 BC
Last hours of dark moon 1 Crescent 137th Lun. ☽	β/α Aquarii winter solstice	Night 10 Odysseus arrives on Calypso's island and with the appearance of the new crescent begins almost eight years of captivity. Although a captive, Odysseus is made welcome and looked after well by the fair-tressed goddess.	8 Jan
2			9
3			10
4			11
5			12
6			13

Annual calendar ends on Odysseus' arrival on Calypso's island.

Annual calendar on hold for almost eight years.

Appendix 2

LUNATIONS OF THE 19-YEAR CYCLE

The moon's phase at the beginning of the cycle will be repeated after 19 years on the same calendar date to an accuracy of some two hours. In the case of the *Odyssey* the cycle begins and ends with the sighting of a new crescent moon at a winter solstice.

The 19-year cycle is also of use in a shorter term of four to five recurrences as an eclipse cycle and to an accuracy of less than a day is equal to 255 draconic months (see Appendix 3).

The Gregorian calendar, adjusted for precession of the equinoxes, is used for the following tables

Solar Year 1   2314–13 BC

Lunation	Month of Year	Crescent
1	1	09 Jan
2	2	07 Feb
3	3	09 Mar
4	4	08 Apr
5	5	07 May
6	6	06 Jun
7	7	05 Jul
8	8	04 Aug
9	9	03 Sep
10	10	03 Oct
11	11	01 Nov
12	12	30 Nov
13	13	30 Dec

Solar Year 2   2313–12 BC

Lunation	Month of Year	Crescent
14	1	28 Jan
15	2	27 Feb
16	3	27 Mar
17	4	25 Apr
18	5	25 May
19	6	23 Jun
20	7	23 Jul
21	8	21 Aug
22	9	20 Sep
23	10	20 Oct
24	11	19 Nov
25	12	19 Dec

Solar Year 3   2312–11 BC

Lunation	Month of Year	Crescent
26	1	16 Jan
27	2	15 Feb
28	3	17 Mar
29	4	14 Apr
30	5	14 May
31	6	13 Jun
32	7	12 Jul
33	8	11 Aug
34	9	09 Sep
35	10	10 Oct
36	11	08 Nov
37	12	08 Dec
38	13	07 Jan

Solar Year 4   2311–10 BC

Lunation	Month of Year	Crescent
39	1	04 Feb
40	2	06 Mar
41	3	05 Apr
42	4	04 May
43	5	02 Jun
44	6	01 Jul
45	7	31 Jul
46	8	29 Aug
47	9	28 Sep
48	10	28 Oct
49	11	27 Nov
50	12	26 Dec

Solar Year 5   2310–09 BC

Lunation	Month of Year	Crescent
51	1	25 Jan
52	2	24 Feb
53	3	25 Mar
54	4	24 Apr
55	5	23 May
56	6	21 Jun
57	7	21 Jul
58	8	19 Aug
59	9	17 Sep
60	10	17 Oct
61	11	16 Nov
62	12	15 Dec

Solar Year 6 2309–08 BC Leap Year

Lunation	Month of Year	Crescent
63	1	15 Jan
64	2	13 Feb
65	3	14 Mar
66	4	12 Apr
67	5	12 May
68	6	10 Jun
69	7	09 Jul
70	8	08 Aug
71	9	06 Sep
72	10	05 Oct
73	11	04 Nov
74	12	03 Dec
75	13	03 Jan

Solar Year 7   2308–07 BC

Lunation	Month of Year	Crescent
76	1	02 Feb
77	2	03 Mar
78	3	01 Apr
79	4	01 May
80	5	31 May
81	6	29 Jun
82	7	28 Jul
83	8	27 Aug
84	9	25 Sep
85	10	24 Oct
86	11	23 Nov
87	12	23 Dec

Solar Year 8   2307–08 BC

Lunation	Month of Year	Crescent
88	1	21 Jan
89	2	20 Feb
90	3	22 Mar
91	4	20 Apr
92	5	20 May
93	6	19 Jun
94	7	18 Jul
95	8	16 Aug
96	9	15 Sep
97	10	14 Oct
98	11	13 Nov
99	12	12 Dec

Solar Year 9   2306–05 BC

Lunation	Month of Year	Crescent
100	1	11 Jan
101	2	09 Feb
102	3	11 Mar
103	4	09 Apr
104	5	09 May
105	6	08 Jun
106	7	07 Jul
107	8	06 Aug
108	9	04 Sep
109	10	04 Oct
110	11	02 Nov
111	12	02 Dec
112	13	31 Dec

Solar Year 10 2305–04 BC Leap Year

Lunation	Month of Year	Crescent
113	1	29 Jan
114	2	28 Feb
115	3	29 Mar
116	4	27 Apr
117	5	27 May
118	6	25 Jun
119	7	25 Jul
120	8	23 Aug
121	9	22 Sep
122	10	21 Oct
123	11	20 Nov
124	12	19 Dec

Solar Year 11   2304–03 BC

In this year the new crescent appears
on the winter solstice but is not in
the same position in the sky as at the
beginning of the cycle.

Solar Year 12   2303–02 BC

Lunation	Month of Year	Crescent
125	1	18 Jan
126	2	17 Feb
127	3	18 Mar
128	4	16 Apr
129	5	16 May
130	6	14 Jun
131	7	14 Jul
132	8	13 Aug
133	9	12 Sep
134	10	11 Oct
135	11	10 Nov
136	12	10 Dec
137	13	08 Jan

Lunation	Month of Year	Crescent
138	1	06 Feb
139	2	08 Mar
140	3	06 Apr
141	4	05 May
142	5	03 Jun
143	6	04 Jul
144	7	02 Aug
145	8	31 Aug
146	9	30 Sep
147	10	30 Oct
148	11	29 Nov
149	12	29 Dec

Solar Year 13   2302–01 BC

Lunation	Month of Year	Crescent
150	1	27 Jan
151	2	25 Feb
152	3	27 Mar
153	4	25 Apr
154	5	24 May
155	6	23 Jun
156	7	22 Jul
157	8	20 Aug
158	9	19 Sep
159	10	19 Oct
160	11	18 Nov
161	12	17 Dec

Solar year 14 2301–00 BC Leap Year

Lunation	Month of Year	Crescent
162	1	16 Jan
163	2	15 Feb
164	3	15 Mar
165	4	14 Apr
166	5	13 May
167	6	11 Jun
168	7	10 Jul
169	8	09 Aug
170	9	07 Sep
171	10	07 Oct
172	11	06 Nov
173	12	06 Dec
174	13	05 Jan

Solar Year 15   2300–99 BC

Lunation	Month of Year	Crescent
175	1	03 Feb
176	2	04 Mar
177	3	03 Apr
178	4	03 May
179	5	31 May
180	6	01 Jun
181	7	30 Jul
182	8	28 Aug
183	9	26 Sep
184	10	26 Oct
185	11	24 Nov
186	12	24 Dec

Solar Year 16   2299–98 BC

Lunation	Month of Year	Crescent
187	1	23 Jan
188	2	22 Feb
189	3	24 Mar
190	4	22 Apr
191	5	22 May
192	6	20 Jun
193	7	19 Jul
194	8	18 Aug
195	9	16 Sep
196	10	15 Oct
197	11	14 Nov
198	12	13 Dec

Solar Year 17   2298–97 BC

Lunation	Month of Year	Crescent
199	1	12 Jan
200	2	11 Feb
201	3	13 Mar
202	4	11 Apr
203	5	11 May
204	6	09 Jun
205	7	09 Jul
206	8	07 Aug
207	9	06 Sep
208	10	05 Oct
209	11	03 Nov
210	12	03 Dec
211	13	01 Jan

Solar Year 18   2297–96 BC Leap Year

Lunation	Month of Year	Crescent
212	1	31 Jan
213	2	01 Mar
214	3	30 Mar
215	4	28 Apr
216	5	28 May
217	6	27 Jun
218	7	26 Jul
219	8	25 Aug
220	9	23 Sep
221	10	23 Oct
222	11	21 Nov
223	12	20 Dec

New cycle

Solar Year 19   2296–95 BC

Lunation	Month of Year	Crescent
224	1	19 Jan
225	2	18 Feb
226	3	19 Mar
227	4	18 Apr
228	5	18 May
229	6	16 Jun
230	7	16 Jul
231	8	15 Aug
232	9	13 Sep
233	10	13 Oct
234	11	11 Nov
235	12	11 Dec

Solar Year 1   2295–94 BC ...

Lunation	Month of Year	Crescent
1	1	09 Jan
2	2	

Appendix 3

19-YEAR CYCLE & DRACONIC MONTH

The 19-year cycle of 235 synodic months was not the only cycle over that period of time with which Homer may have been familiar. The second concerns the draconic month of 27.21 days, which is 'the interval between two successive passages of the moon through the same node of its orbit'. The orbit of the moon is tilted to the plane of the ecliptic and the two points at which the orbit intersects the ecliptic are called nodes. When the moon is at one of the nodes the sun, moon, and earth are in line and when this occurs a solar or lunar eclipse is possible. It is a cycle of draconic months that offers a solution to one of the puzzles of the *Odyssey*.

Some hours before the sighting of the new crescent moon at the climax of the epic, the seer Theoclymenus addresses the suitors in terms that set the mood for the imminent scene of bloodshed and slaughter and describes a total eclipse when 'the Sun is blotted out from heaven, and a foul mist has crept upon the world' (20.357).

Here Homer may have been drawing attention to a coincidence concerning the 19-year cycle and a cycle of 20 eclipse years or 255 draconic months of 27.21 days.

19-year luni-solar cycle	=	6939.6 days
255 draconic months 27.21 days	=	6938.55 days

In observational terms this means that it is possible for a short series of four or five eclipses to occur on the same dates 19 years apart.[1] Homer may have used Theoclymenus not only for dramatic literary reasons, but also to state that a 19-year period could also predict a limited cycle of eclipses, the most spectacular of all astronomical events.

Much more information on eclipse cycles can be found on Robert Harry Van Gent's website at http://www.phys.uu.nl/~vgent/eclipse/eclipsecycles.htm.

Notes

1   Royal Greenwich Observatory publication, http://www.oarval.org/metonic.htm

Appendix 4

SUMMARY OF METHODOLOGY

The creation of a 'reverse' calendar that plotted the daily phases of the moon during the last 40 days of the *Odyssey* was the key to the discovery of calendrical data and narrative. On Day 39 the suitors are killed and one full lunation comes to an end. With the sighting of a new crescent moon at the winter solstice a new one begins. By working backwards it is possible to determine the daily phases of the moon during the full lunation (30 days) and the preceding nine days (1 to 9) of the epic.

This observation made it possible to advance on three fronts:

1. By again working backwards, a chart was constructed of each of the 235 lunations of the entire 19-year luni-solar cycle. This made it possible to create a timeframe of events in the *Iliad-Odyssey*, such as the death of Hector, the fall of Troy and the time Odysseus spends with Circe and Calypso, and to link them with specific months and years in the cycle. An analysis of data embedded throughout the *Odyssey* provided remarkable results concerning lunar and solar years, the precise definition of lunations during lunar-solar and eclipse cycles, cycles of the planet Venus, and the roles of important characters in time keeping.

2. Examination of narrative of the final 40 days suggested a link between phases of the moon and Odysseus' activities. For instance, as the waning moon moves into its dark period matters do not go well for Odysseus but with the arrival of the new crescent his fortunes change. This rhythm connected to phases of the moon occurs twice in the final days of the epic.

Next began the task of comparing the rhythm of all Odysseus' adventures after leaving Troy with those of the final days of the epic. We enquired whether, in general, Odysseus sails along without harm until the lunation approaches its close when he runs into trouble. The answer was encouraging and it became possible to create a hypothetical annual calendar of the sun and moon.

3. At the same time as our research into the matters above, the role of the sun in the annual calendar had also to be established. Bearing in mind a study by Edna Leigh on extended metaphor and Odysseus' adventures 'in the wine-dark

seas' of the night skies, we began an extension of her work into how narrative might be considered as memorable images of the stars and constellations through which the sun passes on its annual journey along the ecliptic.

When combined and applied to the *Iliad–Odyssey* cycle, these three lines of inquiry have, we believe, produced a stimulating and interesting study.

BIBLIOGRAPHY

Homer's Odyssey *and commentaries*

de Jong, Irene, *Odyssey, A Narratological Commentary* (Cambridge University Press, 2001)

Fowler, Robert (ed.), *The Cambridge Companion to Homer* (Cambridge University Press, 2004)

Hesiod and Theognis, trans. Dorothea Wender (Penguin, 1973)

Heubeck, Alfred, Stephanie West & J.B. Hainsworth, *A commentary on Homer's Odyssey, vol. 1, introduction and Books 1–8* (Clarendon Paperbacks, 2008 reprint)

Heubeck, Alfred & Arie Hoekstra, *A commentary on Homer's Odyssey, vol. 2, Books 9–16* (Clarendon Paperbacks, 2006 reprint)

Hexter, Ralph, *A Guide to the Odyssey*, commentary on the trans. of Robert Fitzgerald (Vintage Books, New York, 1993)

Jones, Peter, *Homer's Odyssey*, commentary on the trans. of Richmond Lattimore (Bristol Classical Press, 2007)

Murray, Gilbert, *The Rise of the Greek Epic* (Oxford, 1967, first published 1907)

Russo, Joseph, Manuel Fernandez-Galliano & Alfred Heubeck, *A commentary on Homer's Odyssey, vol. 3, Books 17–24* (Clarendon Paperbacks, 2002 reprint)

Stanford, W.B., *The Odyssey of Homer*, commentary (Books 1–12 & 13–24, Macmillan, 1947)

The Odyssey, trans. Robert Fitzgerald (Collins Harvill, London, 1988)

The Odyssey, trans. E.V. Rieu (Penguin Classics, 1961, Harmondsworth)

The Odyssey, trans. E.V. Rieu (Penguin Classics, revised 1991, London)

The Odyssey, trans. Robert Fagles (Penguin Classics, London, 2004)

The Odyssey, trans. A.T. Murray, Books 1–24 (Loeb Classical Library, Harvard University Press, 2003)

The Odyssey of Homer, trans. Richmond Lattimore (Harper Perennial, 1991)

The Odyssey of Homer, trans. S.H. Butcher & Andrew Lang (Globe edition, Macmillan, London, 1963)

The Odyssey of Homer, trans. Samuel Butler (http://classics.mit.edu/Homer/odyssey.html)

The Odyssey of Homer, trans. Alexander Pope, 1725 (Grant Richards, London, 1903)

Mythology & Reference

Campbell, Joseph, with Bill Moyers, edited by Betty Sue Flowers, *The Power of Myth* (Anchor Books, Doubleday, New York, 1991)

Trail, David, *Schliemann of Troy* (John Murray, London, 1995)

Willetts, R.F., *The Civilisation of Ancient Crete* (Phoenix Press, London, 2004)

Willetts, R.F., *Cretan Cults and Festivals* (Routledge & Kegan Paul, London, 1962)

Wood, Michael, *In Search of the Trojan War* (BBC Books, London, 1987)

Astronomy & Calendars

Aveni, Anthony, *Empires of Time* (Tauris Park Paperbacks, London/New York, 2000)

Aveni, Anthony, *Stairways to the Stars* (Cassell, London, 1997)

Hannah, Robert, *Greek and Roman Calendars* (Duckworth, London, 2005)

Hinckley Allen, Richard, *Star Names, their Lore and Meaning* (Dover, New York, reprint of 1899 edition)

Lippincott, Kristen, *The Story of Time* (Merrell Holberton and National Maritime Museum, London, 2000)

North, John, *History of Astronomy and Cosmology* (Fontana, London, 1994)

O'Neill, W.M., *Early Astronomy from Babylonia to Copernicus* (Sydney University Press, 1986)

Pannekoek, A., *A History of Astronomy* (Dover, New York, 1989)

Philip's Night Sky, astronomy map and guide (Reed international books, London, 1991)

Ridpath, Ian (ed.), *Norton's 2000 star atlas* (Addison, Wesley, Longman, Harlow, 1996)

Toomer, G.J. (trans.), *Ptolemy's Almagest* (Duckworth, London, 1984)

Computer Software

'TheSky' (Software Bisque)

INDEX

References entered under the various headings in the index are arranged alphabetically – except for Adventures in Zodiacal Constellations, which are in the order in which the sun travels along the zodiac.